Jack Costello

D0829554

The Sky is Red

The Sky is Red

Discerning the Signs of the Times

KENNETH LEECH

In the evening you say, 'It will be fine, there's a red sky', and in the morning, 'Stormy weather today; the sky is red and overcast'. You know how to read the face of the sky, but you cannot read the signs of the times.
MATTHEW 16:3

DARTON·LONGMAN + TODD

First published in 1997 by
Darton, Longman and Todd Ltd
1 Spencer Court
140–142 Wandsworth High Street
London SW18 4JJ

Reprinted 1998

© 1997 Kenneth Leech

ISBN 0–232–52167–0

The right of Kenneth Leech to be identified as the
Author of this work has been asserted in accordance with the
Copyright, Designs and Patents Act 1988.

A catalogue record for this book is available from the British Library.

Scripture quotations, unless otherwise stated, are taken from the
New Jerusalem Bible, published and copyright © 1985
by Darton, Longman and Todd and Doubleday & Co Inc.

Phototypeset by Intype London Ltd
Printed and bound in Great Britain by
Page Bros, Norwich, Norfolk

Contents

Introduction

This is a very personal book, a reflection on the current and future state of religion, politics and human society, as well as on the life of worship, prayer and what is often termed 'spirituality'. It is written from the perspective of an urban priest, pastor and thinker working within the Christian tradition. It is less systematic than some of my earlier writing, more reflective, perhaps more reticent – a kind of extended meditation. There are many areas where I am unclear and would welcome the critique, development and extension, maybe the refutation, of my ideas by others who can take the arguments further. It has therefore the character of an epistle – and indeed a warning – to the Christian movement and to anyone else in the wider world who will listen.

The life of faith, and a person's own spiritual and political commitment, develops and changes over the years. History is of crucial importance, and, as Marx said, it is out of our old history that our new history must be made. We grow and discover our true ends and goals through conflict, sometimes only through conflict. While I am deeply unhappy with, and wary of, people whose positions seem not to have changed at all over many years, I also believe that our early formative years are extremely significant in shaping our values and positions, and in providing a framework of thought and practice. For me, the 1950s and the early 1960s were the key periods. It was in those years that I came to the Christian faith, began to pray, became a socialist, and was inspired by a number of movements and individuals. I hope that I have learned, and am still learning, from movements of thought and from people who have called many of my earlier assumptions into question.

I wrote this book in 1996, but its origins lie 40 years back. I was 17 years old. The year 1956 represented a turning-point in the history of socialism, and of radical movements across

1

Europe and elsewhere. It was a critical year for anyone with a social conscience. The Civil Rights movement was well under way in the USA. Trevor Huddleston had returned from South Africa and was addressing massive audiences around Britain. The resistance to nuclear weapons was building up. The Russian invasion of Hungary, and the Twentieth Congress of the Communist Party of the Soviet Union, had thrown the Stalinist left into confusion and led to mass exoduses from all the Communist Parties, and to the growth of what is, curiously, still termed the 'New Left'. At the end of the year came the Suez crisis. The year 1956 saw the publication of such important books as Marcuse's *Eros and Civilisation*, and Colin Wilson's *The Outsider*, as well as the first performance of John Osborne's *Look Back in Anger*. In the East End of London Arthur Downes was elected to the council where he still remains as a comrade and friend.

In 1956 I had only been a Christian for a short time, and in January of that year I read in the *Socialist Christian* an article by Gresham Kirkby entitled, 'The earth shall rise on new foundations'. I had no idea who this man was, but it was the first piece of writing to alert me to the existence of a revolutionary social and political tradition within Anglo-Catholicism – a term I shall use for the moment, though I shall have reason to raise some questions about it. This article was about the good news of the Kingdom of God as a hope for the transformation of this world, and it argued that if Christian hope was to respond to the challenge of Marxism it must include and move beyond, not diminish, the hope that 'the earth shall rise on new foundations'. The article was a turning-point in my life as a socialist Christian. I came to the East End two years later as an undergraduate. I fell in love with the place and stayed. I also met Gresham Kirkby, who was parish priest of St Paul's Church, Bow Common, for over 40 years, and who was a major influence on my thought.

Throughout this book I shall refer to the East End of London, which is my home and the context of my life and work. I locate myself within this context, historically and spiritually; and I shall try to reflect on the East End as a site of continuity and upheaval which is a kind of microcosm of change in British, European and global society today. In some respects London, and the East End in particular, are *sui generis*, unique, distinct – not only in relation to other British cities, but also on a world scale. Yet they do reflect and embody trends, struggles, forces, which are at work over a wider area. I will therefore use this small, turbulent, boisterous, exciting, depressing, hopeless, resilient area as a paradigm of where we are in our world and in ourselves.

In the Whitechapel district of East London, where I live and work, the Christian community exists as a minority faith-tradition in the midst of a large Muslim population, surrounded by an even larger population of the uncommitted and unattached. In this context of plurality, diversity and confusion, the Church seeks to live and testify with integrity, without either failing to respect diversity of belief and lifestyle, or compromising its own authentic witness. This Church is faced now, as always, with the false polarities of ghetto or surrender, of the heroic sect surrounded by impenetrable walls or the shapeless pseudo-community of the unclear and the vague.

This book arises in part out of my attempt to be a community-based theologian in the Whitechapel district. In this context I have tried both to reflect within, and in co-operation with, the small faith community called church, and to struggle towards a public discourse which is nourished by, but not restricted to, the Christian tradition. So this book is in part my attempt to grapple with my own future, with what it means to do theology in this part of London, where the quest for some kind of common language becomes more urgent by the hour. That 'dream of a common language' of which Adrienne Rich wrote is not only a dream but a struggle, always incomplete and ambiguous, filled with setbacks and misunderstandings, but never to be abandoned as long as human beings recognise and affirm common bonds of humanity and yearnings for a better future.

The result is a personal, and certainly partial as well as partisan, reflection on the current state of reality as I see it from Whitechapel Road. It is therefore a 'This is how it looks to me' kind of book, but, I hope, none the worse for that – all theological work has an element of autobiography and of personal quest. At the same time I have tried to be faithful to the orthodox Christian tradition in which I stand, out of which I am nourished, from which I am challenged, and to which I wish to remain faithful in the future.

The book is also in part a critical reflection on my own

experience and thinking over the past 40 years, in part an encounter with a future which is still unclear. While there is inevitably some overlap with my other writings, I hope that I have avoided simply repeating the themes of earlier books. Readers who seek more detailed accounts of my earlier ministry should read *Care and Conflict* (1990), while those who want a more sustained reflection on the current state of Christian spirituality are referred to *The Eye of the Storm* (1992). The present book differs from them both in two ways: first, I have looked back, sometimes to reaffirm, sometimes to modify, my earlier responses and thoughts; secondly, I have tried to identify, and to engage, trends, dangers, options, and opportunities which I perceive to characterise the coming century.

I begin in Chapter 1 with the claim that the central question facing the world is: how can persons live in communion? I argue that the understanding of, and response to, human personality cannot be attained by some 'objective' study, but only by a principled and passionate commitment. Such a commitment needs to draw on the insights of psychological, sociological and scientific enquiry, but I suggest that there are also crucial insights from Christian theological and spiritual reflection and practice, specifically from desert spirituality and from the tradition of Catholicity and communion – insights which need to be recovered and reaffirmed.

I continue my argument in Chapter 2 by claiming that Christian theology, at its best, is a discipline of commitment both to the reality of God and to the future of humankind, and that it is both mystical and social. The paths of theological inquiry in the twenty-first century need to be nurtured and cultivated by an openness to the beauty, mystery and transcendent potential of the human person in community. In Chapter 3, I argue that if these paths, rooted in reverence for human dignity and solidarity, are not followed, dangerous mutants of religion – fundamentalism, fascism and other forms of bigotry and fanaticism – are likely to assume the ascendancy. Their unimpeded growth would certainly assure an anti-human future, perhaps a future culminating in universal destruction.

While many may be drawn to movements rooted in false certainties and destructive visions, I suggest, in Chapter 4, that despair, hopelessness and the experience of exclusion are likely to be the fate of an increasing proportion of people in the West, particularly in our cities. Without a strong and passionate movement of humanism, a real ethic of care and justice, the future for excluded communities is extremely bleak – and this means a bleak future for all of us, if solidarity means anything.

In Chapter 5 I return to a theme which has been central to my writing since the early 1970s, that of the resurgence of 'spirituality'. Here I argue that, while we need to welcome, respect and learn from, much in recent spiritual movements, it is essential to recognise that spirituality can be a form of self-indulgence, a reinforcement of escapism and irresponsibility, or even a diversion from the demands of justice and mercy. 'Spirituality' needs to be set free from its privatisation and restored to its rightful – and only defensible – place within a social vision. In such a vision, justice will be aligned with sanctity, and this is the theme of Chapter 6.

Chapter 7 is concerned with the place of worship and liturgy in the present and future Church. No religion can survive on thought and moral rhetoric without a rich imaginative life in which beauty, art, music, poetry and vision are released in the adoration of God. In Chapter 8, I raise the questions of eschatology, apocalypse and prophecy, and I suggest that the recovery of a visionary sense – a sense of hope linked to struggle, and of yearning aligned with vigilance – is vital if religion is not to become, as it so often has in the past, a mere adjunct to social and cultural conformity. But such a visionary stance, a future-focused stance, needs to be rooted in a tradition. Tradition is the theme of Chapter 9, where I try to distinguish a living, dynamic tradition from fearful and fossilised convention. Finally, in Chapter 10 I examine some of the consequences of what I have written for pastoral ministry in the future.

Throughout this book I have tried to make a number of arguments. I argue that various paradigms in religion and theology are becoming, or have become, obsolete and harmful, and that, unless a major imaginative and conceptual shift occurs, the harm done will be considerable, and the possible benefits to the progress of humankind will be seriously reduced. There is therefore a strong element of warning running throughout this book. I do see the sky as red and threatening. As the current state of the economy and of political life worsens – as it seems bound to do – the likelihood of various mutants of Fascism increases, and support from religious people can be safely predicted. Religion itself is likely

to increase, but much, perhaps most, of it will be of a fundamentalist kind or of an unhealthy esoteric type. Many of the
achievements of the last century may well be undermined and
undone. None of this needs to happen, so this book is also a
call to alertness and mobilisation.

I argue that religion and theology need to take serious
account of changes in modern thought, including post-Dar-
winian developments in evolutionary theory, the revolutions in
physics, biochemistry and pharmacology, and critical Marxism.
There are insights and conceptual shifts which can help to
transform religion and theology in ways which can only inade-
quately be called a 'new reformation'. Yet I see these major
changes in the context of Christian tradition. In arguing for
the importance of tradition, I am not advocating a return to a
mythical golden age (though there are important insights from
past history which need to be reclaimed). Rather, I am arguing
for a dialectical relationship between tradition and that
stretching towards the future which is the essence of prophetic
insight.

In a sense, the twin themes of evolution and revolution run
through the book. The development of evolutionary consciousness since Darwin and of revolutionary consciousness since
Marx and his successors have transformed our view of the
world. There are greater transformations to come. Evolutionary
and revolutionary positions are often contrasted, but evolution
both includes revolution and is its necessary condition, just as
revolution is an integral part of the evolutionary process. My
theological position can be described as one of 'revolutionary
traditionalism'.[1]

I want therefore to claim that, as we enter the twenty-first
century, we are being challenged to extend and expand our
understanding of evolution to encompass our religious and
theological consciousness, and that those religious movements
which fail to do this will either become extinct or will survive
in a harsh, rigid and dangerous form. I will have a good deal
to say in Chapter 3 about the movements lumped together
under the umbrella term 'fundamentalism'. Fundamentalism,
in its historic Christian formation, developed as a movement
of opposition to Darwinian theory, and it remains a significant
and growing movement against the culture of late modernity.

My thesis is that we are on the verge of a major shift in
Christian consciousness at a wide range of levels. In this

process, many individuals and groups will be left behind like dinosaurs, and the traditions they reflect may be heading for extinction, along with elements which could be transfigured. The phase of survival on the road to extinction is perhaps one of the most dangerous phases, and serious damage can occur during this final phase.

I am grateful to those who, through their friendship, debate and criticism of my thinking, have helped me to clarify the ideas in this book, or who, by their writings, have influenced and challenged my thought. I have been helped greatly in my thinking and practice by a number of people who are now dead – through long personal contact with Alan Ecclestone, Stanley Evans, Ruth Glass, David Nicholls and David Randall, and through the writings of Thomas Merton and William Stringfellow. Among the living, I am especially grateful for ongoing help, support and inspiration (including, in some cases, their writings) to Janet Batsleer, Andy Delmege, Terry Drummond, Bill Fishman, Alan Green, Savi Hensman, Gresham Kirkby, Alasdair MacIntyre, Sara Maitland, Paul Oestreicher, Robert Schreiter, A. Sivanandan, and Cornel West; to Kaushika Amin, who helped me to think about the 'underclass' concept; to Liz Ellis, from whom I have learnt much about the relationship between art and society; to Elizabeth Frazer, and to Greg Smith and members of the East London Community Group, for help in understanding 'community'; to the late Peter Hebblethwaite, who, more than anyone, helped me to understand the thought of Pope John Paul II; to Margaret Ronchetti for her support, not least for lending me her flat in Bournemouth where I was able to write much of this book without the interruptions of London; to Pat Wright, for her regular prayers that this book might be finished; and to Julie Wood who has consistently challenged me, undermining some of my rootedness in the past and forcing me to face uncomfortable and unfamiliar areas.

1

Solitude and Solidarity

Our duty to preserve the human person in his integrity, his freedom and his individuality, and to arm him spiritually against the evil of totalitarianism, is not just something it would be nice for us to discuss and perhaps to study. It is an urgent task which demands insistently to be acted out . . . It is the most important task of the Catholic intellectual.

THOMAS MERTON

All over the world at this *fin de siècle* time, the integrity and freedom of the human person, indeed the very survival of the human community, is under strain and serious threat. While the scale of the threat can be exaggerated, as has been the case at other historical moments, it would be unwise to ignore the signs which indicate serious trouble ahead.

The threat to persons is inseparably linked to a crisis in the approach and response to the very nature and significance of personality itself. What is personality? Of what value is the human person? What is it to be human? – an ancient question, still asked liturgically in Jewish and Christian worship (Ps. 8:4). How can human integrity be affirmed and valued in the face of the disintegration wrought by famine, war, and global inequality, the growing refugee crisis, or the more recent destruction wrought by AIDS on so many thousands of young, as well as not so young, people? How can we preserve and affirm human dignity in a climate where homelessness and 'unemployability' are increasingly accepted as normal features of life in 'advanced' societies? Historically it has been assumed that human dignity is tied up with the existence of fulfilling work. But today, according to the International Labour Office, 30 per cent of the global workforce are out of work or under-employed. So what happens when, not only does mass unemployment afflict entire communities, but when the whole future of work and even the concept of a 'job' is in question? What then happens to human dignity?

Again, what becomes of human dignity and human equality in a world, where, according to the economist Amartya Sen, 100 million women are now dead because they were given unequal nutrition and health-care? Or where many thousands of people exist as refugees and asylum-seekers, in struggle with increasingly repressive and cruel bureaucracies? More and more, the fate of the human person is one of exile and displacement. Human dignity is under attack all over the world.

I believe that our predicament goes even deeper, to the very notion of 'self'. The idea of self is in turmoil and confusion at this time which some call 'late modernity' and others call 'postmodernity'. We know that the self does not float freely, but only exists in relationship, and that many of the structures of relationship in our epoch have been eroded, leading to a sense of lostness, of fragmentation, of exile.

Threats to persons

While my mind has changed over many issues since the 1950s, there is one where it remains, depressingly, unchanged. I believe that the commitment to nuclear-weapons policies involves a threat not only to the future of humankind but also to the sanctity of human persons and of the world – that it throws most other problems into the shade. The threat of nuclear war and nuclear accident remains at the centre of our problems. I joined the Campaign for Nuclear Disarmament when it was formed in 1958. In those days we were ridiculed for saying what today every reputable atomic scientist knows. The danger of nuclear accident, documented in the early 1960s in the Mershon Report, has been shown to be even more of a threat than was the case then. The possibility of the extinction of human life and the destruction of the earth remains a distinct possibility. Atomic scientists predict that a major nuclear exchange would involve the greatest biological and physical disruption of the planet in 65 million years. Any dis-cussion of the future of the human person therefore needs to face squarely the question: will there be human persons and a habitable human environment?

Thomas Merton and Karl Barth died on the same day, 10 December 1968. Both of them saw the nuclear threat as posing a theological and spiritual crisis for the Christian community. Merton linked nuclear madness and the rhetoric of 'nuclear-speak' with the collapse of Christian values, and in one famous passage associated the growth of nuclear ideology with the entry into a 'post-Christian' phase of human culture. Barth believed that the most important spiritual and ethical dilemma facing the Church was its inability to stand firmly on theological ground against the evil of nuclear weapons.[1] The history of the last 50 years has vindicated their testimony. The future will be one in which the witness against nuclear ideology will be a real diagnostic test of Christian fidelity. For nuclear commitment exposes, in its most extreme form, that contempt for human-kind and for the material world which is the essence of the threat confronting us all.

So the threat to human persons cannot be located at a single point. It is multifaceted and includes the human environment, the areas of work and leisure, and the state of the economy, as

11

well as personal neglect, discrimination and abuse. One possible way of estimating the value attached to human persons and communities is to look at the environment in which they live – and die. Here it becomes clear that some human persons are seen as more valuable than others. Let me refer to my own area of East London: while it has many distinctive features which make the district unique in the life of Britain, there are many others which make the East End a microcosm of Britain as a whole.

The East End of London was one of the earliest urban areas in Britain. Parts of it were being built up by the late sixteenth century. Today it is an environment characterised by pollution, congestion, and numerous threats to physical and mental health. Monitoring of air-quality has shown that Mile End Road in the East End is one of London's areas most seriously polluted by road traffic. The levels of asthma have massively increased since the 'development' of Docklands, so that today one in ten children is asthmatic, and prescriptions for anti-asthmatic drugs have more than doubled in the last 15 years. There has been an increase in chest diseases as thousands of people in the areas of Poplar, Limehouse and the Isle of Dogs have found themselves living on the biggest building-site in Europe. The story of Docklands shows up in high profile the lack of respect for human beings when they happen to be working-class and poor. They are in the way of the developers, and profits always come before people. They are in fact dispensable – the latest layer of dust, as one government minister called the inhabitants of these districts.

I will have more to say about the problems of health in the East End, but the central point to emphasise here is that the East End experience of inequality is repeated in other British and world cities. In parts of Liverpool, deaths from coronary heart disease and lung problems are twice the national average. In Glasgow poor people are more likely to die before the age of 70 than in the rest of Britain. If we look to the USA, the infant mortality rate is higher in Washington than in Nepal, and higher in Harlem than in Bangladesh. The state of a local environment is a fairly reliable indicator of whether we think that people matter or not.

Since the 1970s large numbers of people, particularly among the younger generation – many of whom, unlike today's politicians, will still be alive to suffer the worst results of pollution

12

and contamination – have come to see the importance of the environment. The fate of non-sustainable ecological systems has become a matter of life and death on a world scale. Ecological systems are inseparable from the fate of personality, and it is now apparent that, if human beings are to survive, some models of progress will have to be repudiated. The Indian physicist Vandana Shiva has shown that progress in knowledge is not linear: the development of certain forms of 'knowledge' of itself creates seas of ignorance and neglect of other ways of looking at, and reacting to, the world. Forms of knowledge of their nature shape human beings – nourish, inspire, damage and distort them.

The nature of the attack on the person needs to be understood. It is not a freak default within a largely humanitarian system. As we move towards the end of this millennium, we do so within a world which has been shaped by anti-human forces and structures. The traffic in human souls of which the author of the Book of Revelation speaks (Rev. 18:13) has now become a cosmic traffic. The boundaries and range of Babylon are now enormous, and the resistance is often marked by weakness, gentility and ambivalence. As I share thoughts with comrades in different countries who are working at the desperate end of the scale, I find a recurring theme: that there is no great hope in conventional politics or in conventional Church approaches (which for the most part follow, rather than inspire or refute, the politics). The fundamental question which Christians and other humanists (for Christians are humanists first and Christians second) must always ask of political and social systems is: what are they doing to the human person?

As I write these words, I have just returned from spending some time in Moscow where the gulf between wealth and poverty, power and displacement, was as manifest as in the West. The terrible state of the rouble, the shortage of food and the relative availability of vodka, stand in contrast to the McDonaldisation of Russian society, along with Marlboro cigarettes, 'Carol's Burgers' and other features of Western capitalism.

My life has been shaped by a concern for persons, for persons in communion, persons in their alienation, persons in their own unique and often unsharable distress and affliction. Like all those who, with fear and trembling, call themselves pastors, I have been involved with persons at deep and troubling levels

13

over many years. What happens to persons is central to my being, for I am a person too. This concern is at the same time personal and political. It has never seemed to me possible to minister to deeply troubled people without addressing the social, economic and political forces which contribute to and shape the depths of that trouble. So I look with increasing horror at what is happening to human personality in contemporary Britain. Like the author of the Book of Revelation, I see a city which traffics in human souls.

Individualism versus persons in relationship

The experience of Britain as a site of human life in recent years is horrifying – not least because this is a nation in which ideas of democracy, equality, justice and liberty have made more significant progress than in many other places. The question is often posed: how can we judge Britain when there are far worse injustices elsewhere? But this is the wrong question. It is more helpful and more disturbing to ask: if such injustices can happen here, what hope is there for humankind in places where these values are not respected, even at the level of lip-service? There is a legitimate pride in British achievements, but it must be a pride which recognises that most of these achievements have been made through prolonged and painful conflict with the establishment (who then claim the credit for them). But this pride can degenerate into complacency and arrogance when it refuses to face the horror of injustice and oppression within its own life.

Central to this discussion is the issue of democracy. In 1974, when a group of friends and I formed the Jubilee Group (a network of socialist Christians), our first discussion paper was entitled, 'Crisis of democracy: which way for the churches?' The question remains, but the urgency has increased. Over the years since 1974, many Christians have come to accept the basic framework of capitalist society, often throwing their support uncritically behind the Labour Party which has done precisely the same. A mood of resignation, the pragmatism which abandons vision and is satisfied with what can be salvaged, seems to be the dominant mood of mainstream politics.

In my own struggles over many years to engage with the needs and fate of the person in society, I have concluded that neither individualism (in which persons are seen merely as consumers, as customers, as disconnected, privatised units) nor statism (in which personhood is dissolved into the omnicompetent state machine) are able to sustain a genuine community of persons in relationship. In fact a statist society, of whatever political complexion, depends for its effectiveness on an individualistic view of the person. Persons are merely isolated individuals who support the political process, a process which is operated by an elite on behalf of the people. They are there to be 'done good to'. 'We are all here on earth to do good to others', W. H. Auden once observed with cynical perception. 'What the others are here for, I don't know.' Such a posture represents the end both of authentic politics and of human dignity.

I write as a Christian – a Christian who has emerged from an entirely irreligious background, and who has spent most of his life in non-Christian communities. Today 80 per cent of the population of the ward in which I live are Muslims. I hope that I am both a convinced and a humble Christian. At the end of the day, I believe that the Christian tradition, which sees the person in relationship, provides a stronger basis for a viable human future than any alternative approach. Yet I need to take serious notice of, and learn from, the insights, wisdom and experience of people of other traditions and other experiences. We all need to learn from recent work on human personality, particularly in the fields of psychology and sociology, as well as in that of scientific research into the nature of the brain and of consciousness. We need to learn too from such areas as recent feminist ethical thought, which has reinforced the relational and social realities of what it is to be a person.

Psychology: insights and dangers

The psychological insights since Freud have been more acceptable to Christians than the political insights since Marx, mainly because the former seem to address the 'inner' world and offer no apparent threat to the structures. The last century has been a century marked by a series of revolutions in psychology, psychiatry and psychotherapy, terms previously unknown. Of course, these insights have been helpful: how could anyone deny their value? Through psychological work we have come to a better understanding of human need – the need for food, security, for a sense of belonging, the need to be respected and valued, the need for 'self-actualisation', and so on. Freud, and his successors in the psychoanalytic disciplines, have helped us to see how fundamental is the struggle between the forces of death and those of life, how important are the unconscious forces. Freud's insights were as profound at the personal level as they were naïve and undeveloped at the structural. Jung greatly illuminated the religious crisis of the West, though his influence on Christianity and on social insights has been a mixed blessing. Many Christians found in Jung a link with their religious life, and there have been many connections made between Jungian therapy and spiritual direction, particularly in the USA. More recently the disciplines of transpersonal psychology have helped us to understand the human person as an unfinished animal, yearning for fulfilment. Some traditions within psychology have moved more and more towards an approach resembling, and increasingly drawing upon, classical spiritual disciplines. There has been an enormous mass of literature on the relevance of psychology to the practice of Christian ministry, while some psychoanalysts have seen the yearning for eternity as part of the human genetic make-up.[2]

The interest in personal growth and insight is part of a broader struggle, which has been going on for the last 30 years, around the question of personal and political liberation. This struggle involves a wide range of movements, including the changing face of psychotherapy and psychoanalysis, the revival of Jung, Melanie Klein and Bion, and the growth of a political therapeutic tradition. It is evident in Britain in Free Association books, in the USA in the work of Joel Kovel, and in the whole area of 'psycho-politics'. The intensely political work of Frantz Fanon on mental health, the insights of R. D. Laing, Sheldon Kopp, and others, the movement of liberation psychology – all these are elements in a process of trying to bring together the inner and outer worlds, and it is essential that Christian and other religious traditions try to understand the relevance of all this to theology and spirituality.

Among Christians, much pastoral activity in the last two decades has focused on personal work with deeply troubled persons, and the movement of pastoral counselling, which grew up originally in the United States, has provided a growth area for clergy and others in Britain. The emphasis on 'wholeness', and the 'clinical pastoral care' model, have much to commend them – but, as usual, many people have accepted uncritically and simplistically some of the often dated and questionable assumptions of the movement.

So let me look at some dangerous paths. There is a recurring temptation for Christian people to adopt naïvely some half-digested parts of the therapeutic disciplines, and to misuse them in pastoral care. This is most clearly seen in the USA where the 'triumph of the therapeutic' has been most dramatic. I believe that the spread of psychotherapy in the USA has aided the developmental triumphalism which was already part of American culture. In Britain the growth of psychology has been ambiguous. Developmental psychology began with an evolutionary concern with the purity of stock, a concern reflected most clearly among the disciples of Francis Galton.[3] So Christians who pick up this language need to be very careful. Of course, the idea of 'development' is applicable to human beings as it is to human societies, but it is one of many models which need to be scrutinised.

For example, to rely on 'stages of development' or 'personality type' is to fall into an old trap of theoretical primitivism. This is not to deny the value of some of the techniques and methods which have been produced, but they need constantly to be subjected to critical examination, and not accepted as *de fide*. Let me give an example which is part of the conventional wisdom of the present day in certain areas – the Church and personnel departments, in the main. The way in which religious communities, Church bureaucracies and some selection committees have adopted the Myers-Briggs Type Indicator (MBTI) is not only alarming and depressing, but has a terrible sense of *déjà vu*. Rooted in a nineteenth-century understanding of personality, with little sense of the social relational dimensions of personhood, the MBTI is in danger of becoming a kind of astrology for the bourgeosie. Helpful as it undoubtedly can be at certain levels of understanding, its use as a guide to marital compatibility or in providing grounds for creating redundancies or for selecting candidates for jobs is potentially, and

17

actually, highly dangerous – while some of the literature relating ways of prayer to personality type are little short of absurd.[4]

More serious even than the uncritical acceptance of fashionable methodologies is the all-pervasive spread of psychological jargon among Christian pastors. Over 20 years ago the American sociologist Andrew Greeley pointed out that the rhetoric of the personal growth movement, and of self-fulfilment, life satisfaction, and interpersonal encounter, was so pervasive that many clergy and laity in the Church could not use any other rhetoric. The new psycho-jargon had replaced theology.[5] I fear that Greeley was right, and that many Christians have fallen for this rhetoric at the very point at which they were beginning to become more critical of the rhetoric of the Church itself.

Linked with this is the danger of elitism, and there are enough signs and to spare that the Church in England is becoming more elitist, and more remote from ordinary people. Of course, the Church's grass-roots involvement with poor and working-class people is in stark contrast to the class location of therapists, which has been, in Paul Hoggett's words, 'expressed in an exaggerated spatial form through that locality lying within a two-mile radius of London's Swiss Cottage underground station'.[6] Yes, it is bad, but we must not let the Church off the hook, and I will come back to it.

Not surprisingly, the therapeutic story has been marked by the isolating of persons from their socio-economic context. Therapy as a historical phenomenon is a socially disengaged movement. The very method which has proved so valuable in unveiling the struggles between life and death within the psyche has been unable to connect this with the struggles within society. Yet we know that personhood is distorted by economic and class position, and that the creation of social bonds is vital to corporate and personal health. It is not surprising, therefore, that research has suggested that mentally ill people do better in Third World countries than they do in the 'developed' world. Thirty-seven per cent of people identified as 'schizophrenic' recover in 'underdeveloped' countries, compared with 15 per cent in the West. Recovery rates are as low as 14 per cent in Dublin, 7.9 per cent in Moscow, and 5.7 per cent in Nagasaki – compared with 51 per cent in Ibadan and 54 per cent in Agra in North India.

Another factor to remember is the apparently considerable

evidence that many people, including Christian pastors, retreat into the world of 'psychopolitics' as a result of exhaustion and disillusionment with the possibilities of political struggle. It is therefore encouraging to see the appearance of more socially aware groups, such as 'Antidote' and 'Psychotherapists and Counsellors for Social Responsibility', within the therapeutic disciplines.[7]

What seems to me to be necessary in this field is to encourage a humble and critical dialogue between Christian theology and the work of therapy, and this is impeded by the tendency for Churches to latch on to some area of psychological work at the precise moment at which psychologists themselves are becoming critical of it. For example, many Christians in the late twentieth century have just started to take Freud seriously, at the point where he is being seriously questioned. I think we need to take Freud with great reservations. Yet this is, and must be, a post-Freudian observation, and the problem is that many people in the Churches are pre-Freudian and have not yet caught up with the major insights of the Freudian tradition. The critique of Freud cannot begin until we have moved beyond that point, moved beyond a recognition of the import-ance of the Freudian revolution. After Freud, we are bound to ask deep questions. His suppression of his female patients' accounts of sexual abuse are deeply worrying – as are his low scientific and ethical standards, the excessive value he placed on free association (a technique which may well reveal the present state of mind but does not treat symptoms at source), and his total lack of social awareness. In contrast to Darwin, there has never been a 'social Freudianism', yet this is a mixed blessing. Freud saw the person as a total singular entity in a way which must raise major questions among Christians and others. Most importantly, we need to see that Freud was a figure of the Enlightenment, and subject to all the cultural assumptions of that era – assumptions which are increasingly being examined as the Enlightenment project comes under heavy scrutiny.

I owe a considerable debt to the insights of depth psychology, but I see much of it both as a collusion with the values of capitalism and as an evasion of the structural crisis of our society by focusing ideologically on the inner crises of indi-viduals. So much psychological work is determined by ideological assumptions derived from the dominant culture.

The profound insights shown by psychotherapists into the conflicts of the mind stand in stark contrast to their lack of perception into their own social and class position.

However, there is one facet of the changing face of therapy which is of importance to religious people. Since the 1960s there has been a striking shift among some psychotherapeutic traditions toward a transpersonal, and even transcendental, approach. No longer concerned exclusively with the excavation of neuroses and the unveiling of deeply hidden areas of the unconscious, many therapists have come to see their role in what we can only call spiritual terms. Figures such as R. D. Laing, Victor Frankl, Gerald May, and Sheldon Kopp are among many who come to mind. So today, much therapeutic work is now concerned with transformation and the exploration of potential, rather than simply with corrective emotional work. Thus we see increasing numbers of therapists who speak of crises of personal transformation or of 'spiritual emergency' rather than of 'illness'.[8]

Laing is of particular importance to Christians. His work with schizophrenics has been heavily criticised, yet I believe we need to take many of his insights with great seriousness. He believed that in the encounter with 'madness', physicians and priests were encountering common problems. Among physicians and priests, he claimed, there should be at least some who would help to educt people from the surface world and induct them into the deeper world of transcendental experience. Laing believed that there was a state of profound spiritual undernourishment among Western people which, in a famous passage, he compared to the prophecy in Amos that there would be a famine of hearing the word of the Lord. The desperate quest for what he called 'meta-egoic' experiences would often lead people to take routes which conventional psychiatry, and conventional religion, identified as 'madness'. Yet, Laing suggested, perhaps the mad see more clearly and more precisely what the 'sane' cannot see. Perhaps what we call sanity is in fact a state of deprivation.

I am not uncritical of Laing. I think his belief that psychosis is a higher form of sanity, while it does witness to some important truths, treats the terrifying affliction of psychotic breakdown less than seriously. Nevertheless we need to build on Laing, and I believe that his perception of the thirst for transcendence is of critical importance for the twenty-first century. Like many prophetic figures, he was quite deranged – and yet I am convinced that no movement of religious renewal in future years can ignore the impact of *The Politics of Experience and The Bird of Paradise*.[9] I will say more about Laing's role in Chapter 5.

A less well-known work, Theodore Roszak's *Unfinished Animal*, was also for me an important turning-point in linking psychotherapy and spiritual perception. Our future image of the human person, Roszak argued, would be a paradoxical blending of the optimistic and the tragic. It would assume not a fundamentally fallen human condition, but an original splendour aspiring to transcendence, a godlike image of humankind. The psychotherapy of the future will be concerned with the tension between potentiality and actuality, with enabling people to become what they most truly are, and with the knowledge of our potential godlikeness. Roszak argues for the need to rediscover the spiritual wisdom of the past, and sees psychic tension as the potential energy of the spirit. While Christians may rightly wish to emphasise human fallenness and the harsh dimensions of evil, many will agree with Roszak's emphasis on the potential for glory. Indeed, his approach to psychotherapy has much in common with the Eastern Orthodox tradition from the Cappadocian Fathers to the present day.[10]

Years ago Rieff wrote of 'the triumph of the therapeutic'.[11] So much of our cultural life in the West is dominated by therapeutic models, to the neglect of other ways of looking at human life. Not surprisingly, much of the psychological approach to spirituality and to pastoral care which has become fashionable (as well as extremely lucrative) in church circles tends to have a weak base in Christian theology. It often identifies the unconscious with God, and spiritual progress with psychological maturity. On this basis, of course, much of what is termed pastoral theology is not theology in the classic sense at all – an issue to which I will return in Chapter 2. Yet theology and self-awareness are intimately connected. There can be no theology which does not involve what the spiritual tradition terms 'the warfare of the heart'. God is the searcher of minds and hearts (Rev. 1:23), and theology is an ascetical discipline concerned with human transformation, with personal holiness and with the transfiguration of the self.

The Christian tradition stresses the place of self-knowledge.

21

But its view of the self differs crucially from that of the Enlightenment, in which the self is seen as an autonomous entity, existing freely within a zone of objective rationality. The Church of the twenty-first century will need to grapple with the fact that notions of 'self', 'soul' and 'person', which have been central to its life, but which arose from Enlightenment thinking, are in fact obsolete. Much recent work in psychological development has called earlier notions into question. The work of Carol Gilligan, for example, has queried the male-centred, individualistic psychology of thinkers such as Lawrence Kohlberg. For Gilligan, and for most feminist thinkers, the self is defined by connectedness, relationality and context. Indeed, 'connectedness' has been a central theme in recent feminist writing, and in this it has rediscovered and reinforced a central emphasis of the Christian social tradition.[12]

Sociology: a means of theological insight

We have also experienced during the last century the rise of the social sciences. The emergence of university social science departments took place in the first 20 years of the twentieth century – ten were established, for example, between 1904 and 1919. But these were primarily focused on social work and social reform. To this day, many clergy still confuse sociology with social work, and refer to both with contemptuous and dismissive ignorance. Sociology – the study of human interactions and interrelations, their conditions and consequences – took a long time to become accepted as an academic discipline. It was not in the Cambridge University syllabus until 1961, or in that of Oxford until 1962. As late as 1965 one writer was complaining that in Britain, alone among advanced industrial nations, there was not one single structural study of our society.[13]

I have benefited greatly since the early 1960s from co-operative work with urban sociologists, not least through working with the late Ruth Glass at the Centre for Urban Studies at University College, London. The Christian tradition has much to learn from the social sciences, and it is sad that much of the conventional Christian critique of sociology is based on a flimsy knowledge, or often on total ignorance, of that

22

discipline. Even where sociology is studied in the Church, it is often only the 'sociology of religion', to the neglect of other crucial areas which throw enormous light on theological and pastoral activity and the society within which it occurs.[14]

Sociological research is helpful to clergy and pastoral workers at a whole range of levels. It is so easy to accept conventional assumptions, for example, about the collapse of 'community', or the 'withering away of class' – assumptions which have been exposed as false or simplistic by careful social research. The recognition of the persistence of class divisions and the way in which class inequality affects health and education, or the scrutiny of government statistics on unemployment or crime or ethnicity, have come from the painstaking work of sociologists. Much sociological work has been concerned with policy-orientated research, and it has been empirically grounded and rigorous in its analysis.

Sociology has been affected by and has itself affected, other disciplines such as town planning, environmental studies and social geography. It has been influenced since the 1960s by revisionist Marxism (especially in France) and critical theory (especially in Germany). It has been from sociologists and political theorists that we have gained an increased awareness of the social, political and cultural factors which shape and influence our lives and thoughts, while economists have shown us how important is the material base of our lives. We must stop thinking about theological ideas as if they appeared from nowhere. Many theologians speak airily of 'non-theological factors' as a kind of afterthought. The work of David Nicholls, whose sudden death in 1996 deprived us of one of the most astute political thinkers in the Church of England, showed how political structures have major effects on theological patterns of thought and worship.[15] More recently, the work of social geographers has been of immense value in the approach to such areas as housing, health and the uses of space.

Scientific advances: challenges and implications

While increasing numbers of Christians have been willing to learn from the work of psychotherapists and sociologists, there

23

is still a widespread resistance to the work of the 'hard sciences'. There has been a kind of semi-gnostic stream in much Christian thinking which has been suspicious of work in the 'hard sciences', and of giving serious attention to the material basis of human personality. In this neglect, so much of the wonder of the creation has been bypassed. Of course, religion and the physical sciences have had an uneasy relationship for centuries, but not all of it has been hostile. (It is to be hoped that the deterioration in the level of argument about theology among some Oxford scientists is a temporary aberration.) The theologian-scientist is not a twentieth-century phenomenon, though it looks as if the scientist-theologian may be increasingly a phenomenon of the twenty-first century. Christians on the edge of that century need to take recent work in the hard sciences seriously, and learn from it.

Many Christians assume that scientists have no time for faith, and believe that all problems have a scientific solution. And, among the wider population, the idea that science has solved every problem is still with us. There are actually two historical problems here, one affecting members of the scientific community, and one affecting sections of the Church – though this is not to imply that the two communities are mutually exclusive. Many scientists have assumed that scientific knowledge is the only reputable type of knowledge, while many non-scientists (including some theologians) have swallowed a simplistic version of this view, and believe that science can in principle solve all problems, including the mysteries of theology.

In fact, in recent years there has been a crisis in the whole enterprise of knowledge. The canon of certitude which ran from Bacon and Descartes has been exposed by contemporary philosophers as an exercise in control and domination. Distinguished scientists have pointed out that the scientific researcher is not personally uninvolved in the process, and that the dimensions of mystery, of awe and wonder, are not alien to the scientific enterprise. The work of Michael Polanyi, in particular, showed that scientific language, like other forms of discourse, is rooted in a tradition of research and enquiry. Polanyi's work has undermined the simple division between subject and object, showing that human beings are participants in the process of knowing, and pointing to the need to develop a participatory consciousness.[16] We have seen the demise of the non-participatory scientific method. Of course, many individuals and organisations, not least within the Churches, cling to a crude myth of 'objectivity'. But we need to move 'beyond objectivism and relativism' to a more holistic model of knowing, and in this task the 'hard sciences' can help us.[17]

Again, the idea of the person as a separate entity – an idea much beloved by evangelical Christians in particular – was derived from classical Newtonian physics. Isaac Newton saw matter in terms of separate atoms, and his view can be seen in Freud who held a mechanistic model of the self. But both Newtonian physics and Freudian individualism are now obsolete.

In a memorable essay of 1917, Freud wrote of three moments at which the human self had received severe blows: the Copernican revolution in the understanding of the earth, the Darwinian insights about how humans related to animals, and Freud's own discoveries about the place of the unconscious. There is now a fourth area of disturbance – the blurring of the division between humans and machines. Computers have created a virtual community which has called into question earlier concepts of relationship.[18]

Recent work on the brain has shown that one human brain has more potential states than the universe has physical particles. The nature of consciousness has, in the last few years, become a major issue among academics, not least among those within the 'hard sciences'. It is focused on the relationship between brain and mind. Francis Crick, whose work in identifying the molecular structure of DNA led to the age of molecular biology, is still working on the nature of consciousness. The debate about consciousness has involved not only neuroscientists, physicists and molecular biologists but also philosophers and theologians. The revolution in the neurosciences leaves us still with conflict about how the human brain works, and about what we mean by consciousness and personality, and it seems clear to me that these debates will gather momentum in the twenty-first century. It is a revolution which raises vast questions for Christian people and all who are concerned with 'the spirit'.

For instance, how should people of faith engage with such issues as the relative importance of genetics, and social, cultural and psychological forces? There has been major work in recent years on the relevance of Chromosome 6 to schizophrenia, and of Chromosome 18 to manic depression. Or what do we make of work in psychopharmacology which looks at the effect

25

of drugs on personality? The last few decades have seen major advances in the use of antidepressant, mood stabilising and antipsychotic drugs. What are the real moral and spiritual issues at stake in these debates? In recent years too there have been genetic 'explanations' of schizophrenia, homosexuality, racial differences, and even (in the case of Mickey Kraus) income inequality. We have even seen archaeologists looking at the prehistory of the mind.[19] Theologians need to take these debates with the greatest seriousness, for they affect the whole issue of the soul and the nature of human personality, as well as the relationship between brain and mind.

The whole area of chaos theory has undermined earlier mechanistic and determinist ideas, and we have come to see reality not as an accumulation of objects so much as a web of structured energies in tension. Chaos theory has shown how minute changes can have gigantic effects. The changing face of science has undermined much earlier thinking, and much of this should be received by religious people with great joy and relief. The so-called 'new physics' has made it clear that reality is elusive, and many people have found in this field of research a new zone of freedom for religious belief.[20]

Of course, conflicts between scientific and theological work will remain. Certain positions are, it seems to me, plainly incompatible with a Christian ethic. Rigid forms of biological determinism and social Darwinism fall into this category. Many deterministic notions, sometimes moving to so-called scientific racism, are rooted in particular interpretations of genetics. It is equally difficult to see how dualist interpretations of consciousness can co-exist happily with an incarnational faith. Scientific work in the field of the neurosciences is moving strongly away from the dualism of Descartes and Galileo to a more holistic understanding of the world and of human personality.

There has certainly been, in much post-Enlightenment thinking, a mechanistic strain which has tended to reduce human beings to the sum of their physical components. As a result, some have seen science as a whole as reductionist and mechanistic. On the other hand, the reluctance of many Christians to accept the breakthroughs in our knowledge which have come from genetics, biochemistry and neurophysiology shows a continuity of the dualistic mode of thought. Over 20 years ago Robert Lambourne observed:

Sometimes one feels that the particular fleshy historical body of Jesus Christ is an embarrassment to Rudolph Bultmann, and that the particular abnormal cell structured brain is a defilement to which R. D. Laing cannot admit. Both psychotherapy and theology seem tempted to seek a docetic saviour.[21]

To reject such crude positions as 'it's all in our genes', or 'better living through chemistry', should not lead to the illogical and unwarranted conclusion that there are no physical origins of, or solutions to, human problems, and that change of attitude is the only important response.

The deaths in 1996 of Thomas Kuhn and Abdus Salam brought home to me the centrality, in both theological and scientific work, of turbulence and reconciliation. Kuhn, in his seminal work *The Structure of Scientific Revolutions*,[22] showed that the course of scientific knowledge is marked by peaceful interludes punctuated by intellectually violent revolutions. Scientists identify with a particular structural framework (paradigm) within which research continues, often cautiously and peacefully. But at certain points the structure of the framework is destroyed, and a new paradigm, appropriate to a new order, is created. The emergence of new paradigms is not a painless process, and turbulence and disruption are vital to its progress and movement.

Salam, a theoretical physicist and director of the International Centre for Theoretical Physics in Trieste, received his Nobel Prize for physics in 1979 for his work on elementary particles, electromagnetism and weak nuclear force. His central concern was the reconciliation of the world of particle physics, and the visible world of material reality. The human search for unity in the physical universe and in the understanding of the nature of matter was to him a task of immense poetic beauty. In the same way, it seems to me, theological enquiry proceeds by a process of peaceful enquiry interrupted by violent revolutions. Turbulence is at its heart, but its aim is a unity of purpose issuing in wonder and worship.

The work of researchers such as Kuhn and Salam bring to the surface something which is of great importance to Christians: the fact that much apparently useless thought and research may suddenly become 'relevant'. Most of the major scientific discoveries of the past – such as electricity, X-rays, radium, and atomic energy – were the results of years of pure research, most of which was hidden from public view. Here too is a link with the religious tradition of solitude. The moment of breakthrough cannot easily be predicted. Obscure and apparently useless aspects of pure mathematics have suddenly become relevant to work in physics. In the same way I believe, with the late Eric Mascall, that a prior condition for a sound Christian social consciousness is the existence of a tradition of serious theological thought.[23]

Human sexuality: the need for repentance and rethinking

All reflection on human beings in relationship raises the key issues of sexuality and gender. Here the Christian record is ambivalent and ambiguous: at moments rich with wisdom, sensitivity and realism; much of the time positively unhelpful and destructive to human flourishing. It seems to me that, if we are to move into the twenty-first century in a theologically creative way, and in a way which is faithful to the Christian tradition, two shifts need to occur. The first is a shift towards greater honesty and greater engagement with the reality of human sexual relations. The second is a shift towards serious re-evaluation of some key areas of our approach to sexuality. Of course, some of those who term themselves 'traditionalist' will dismiss such a proposal as 'woolly liberalism', but it is essential to be undeterred by slogans and cliché mentalities when serious issues are at stake. Traditions either change and develop or they become extinct. The low level of argument of many of those who rejoice in the traditionalist label suggests that they wish to move to extinction fairly quickly.

Since my time as a priest in Soho, just before and after the passing of the 1967 Sexual Law Reform Act (which decriminalised male homosexual activity), I have been involved, pastorally and personally, with issues of sexual orientation and identity. I have been aware of two opposing dangers within Christian practice. There is the danger of an aggressive, crusading approach to sexual morality which is almost always damaging both to its victims and to its perpetrators. But there is also the privatising of sexual behaviour, associated with the tradition of liberalism – a tradition which, by failing to see the social and political dimensions of sex, erodes the potential for a social ethic in this area.

We need to recognise, and express penitence for, the damage done by the Christian tradition, and I am not at all sure that the Church is prepared for such a stance. Yet I see little hope for change until there is a realistic response to the Church's record. Grace Jantzen is one among many recent writers who have pointed out that the reason that spirituality was held to require sexual control was that bodiliness, and particularly sexuality, was seen as being opposed to the life of the spirit.[24] It is not a new point, but it still needs to be made. The general impression left on most people by the teaching of the Church is that physical relationships are unworthy, if not shameless and obscene. This impression has left an almost indelible mark on the record of Christian thought and practice about sexuality. I am not clear whether we can ever recover from it.

It may be that our problems relate more to the lack of change in sexual behaviour than to the pace of change. Numerous studies since the 1960s have shown that, in spite of the persistent warnings of sexual anarchy and of the collapse of 'family values', the overall pattern of change in behaviour (in contrast sometimes to attitude) has been very slight. The 'sexual revolution' has been quite restricted in its effects, the increase in cohabitation without, or prior to, marriage being the most significant shift. While the conservative character of these changes may be reassuring to some, I am disappointed that we have made so little progress.

I have suggested that a gnostic contempt for the flesh has been a major factor in Christian attitudes to sexuality. But equally problematic has been a romanticising of sexual experience, linked to a kind of 'deadly innocence' which pays little attention to the power of sex to enslave and destroy. It is very likely that, for all his faults, Augustine had a better grasp on human reality than the proponents of what Angela West has called the 'Californian ethnic' view of sexuality.[25]

During the last few decades we have seen a far healthier approach to sexuality and to the body, most of it coming from outside the Christian tradition. James Baldwin is one writer who has stressed the inexorable link between sensuality and the materiality of eucharistic solidarity.

> To be sensual ... is to respect and rejoice in the force of life, of life itself, and to be present in all that one does, from the effort of loving to the breaking of bread.[26]

In recent years too there has been a heated debate in various cultures and faith traditions about homosexuality. Although this is a question on which Jesus Christ seems to have said nothing whatever, it threatens to divide the Christian community in various places. In one sense this is not surprising, for it raises fundamental issues about the nature of human personality, identity and behaviour – issues which affect people at a level beneath and beyond that of conventional rationality. So important are these issues that they need to be handled in a spirit free from panic, over-heated rhetoric, and the crusading mind. Yet even distinguished theologians write articles which are crude and unsophisticated to a disturbing degree, though they pale into insignificance when compared with the gutter-level polemic associated with groups like the evangelical Reform or individuals like the Archdeacon of York.[27] Evangelicals have always found this area particularly difficult, and there is certainly more repression here than in other sections of the Church. But we are faced with much deeper dilemmas, and I see a real danger of regression and of the triumph of fear.

It looks as if the Church of England, and perhaps other Churches, will polarise over homosexuality. Indeed, by the time these words are published, more events in this area may already have occurred. My sense is that the crisis is not about homosexuality, but about honesty, and about the inability of many Christians to be open and honest. There is often an inverse relationship between the ferocity of attack and the degree of sexual confusion. After the gay organisation Outrage had made their attempt to 'out' David Hope, the present Archbishop of York, the *Church Times*, in congratulating the bishop on his handling of the incident, argued that he had transformed 'a damaging episode into a helpful and positive one', and that the incident might be 'a significant period in the progress towards a more enlightened view of sexuality'.[28] I hope that this may be true, but my experience is that the movement towards enlightenment, truth and justice is always a movement marked by struggle, pain and resistance. Any harm done to the image of the higher clerics is a mere symptom. Our experience at St Botolph's has been a joyful and liberating one, as well as being marked by the experience of hatred and violence, and by a striking lack of support from the hierarchy. The work here has had something of a prophetic character about it. For thousands of gay and lesbian Christians, this church has been a lifeline.[29] It is essential that we build on what has been achieved and do not allow the resurgence of bigotry and prejudice to throw us off-course.

In the future I see the need for some major rethinking and revision of our approach to sexuality.

1. We need to reconsider the commitment to heterosexual monogamy. The former Archbishop of Canterbury, Michael Ramsey, addressing the Jubilee Group in 1977, suggested that the re-examination of the commitment to monogamous marriage was one of the major issues facing Christian social thinkers.[30] But no serious attention seems to have been paid to it, and most statements from the Church simply assume that sex only properly occurs within heterosexual marriage, without giving any good theological reason why this is so.

2. We need to look again at the areas of passion, lust, pleasure and 'inordinate affection'. The Western Christian tradition has been hard on passion and pleasure, strong on control and abstinence. Sexuality has been seen largely in terms of its problems, not its potential. Yet love-making and justice-making are closely connected, and those who cannot love, and have no experience of love, are likely to be weak in their commitment to justice. There has been a suspicion of pleasure and delight, yet, as Aristotle saw, we only do something well if it gives us pleasure. The one area of Christianity in which there has been a freedom to express wildness and ecstasy has been the mystical tradition, and I suspect that the separation of mysticism from ethics, and the marginalisation of the mystical, has been disastrous in terms of the approach to sexuality.

3. We need to give more attention to friendship.[31] The obsession with anatomy and genitalia has made many Christians timid about deep, passionate and committed friendships, and this has had detrimental effects on the whole area of solidarity and communion. As in so many areas, Christians have allowed their theology and practice to be determined

by convention, respectability and the ideology of the secular establishments.

4.   We need to reaffirm and revalue the erotic, and, in my opinion, to repudiate the theology of Anders Nygren on which many generations of theological students were reared. Nygren held that *agape* and *eros* were quite different: that *agape* was largely an act of the will, as opposed to *eros* which was to do with passion and the lower nature. He even saw the separation of *agape* from *eros* as 'the meaning of the Reformation'.[32] On the other hand, Eastern Christian thought has always related erotic love to the love of God. Most recent work on the erotic has come from non-Christian writers such as Herbert Marcuse, who saw the erotic as the bridge between spirituality and politics, or Audre Lorde who saw the erotic as the nurturer of all our deepest knowledge.[33] In contrast, much recent Christian writing on sex is pessimistic, and has a too exalted view of the 'rational'. Thus the document from the House of Bishops of the Church of England, *Issues in Human Sexuality*, claims that there is nothing in us which is not to some degree marred, disordered or out of tune (3.17), and that the raw energies of feelings and physical vitality must be harnessed and guided by the 'rational, ethical and spiritual self' (3.24). This seems to imply a dualist and Platonist view rather than one derived from an incarnational Christian faith.[34] I believe that a central task of twenty-first century Christians will be the revaluation of the 'carnality of grace',[35] and a commitment to the belief that human beings are made in God's image in the whole of their nature, not simply in their minds.

5.   Most importantly, we need to undermine the notion that sexuality belongs to the private realm. I see the future at its most hopeful as a time of renewal of social consciousness after decades of dry atomisation and privatisation. We can be fairly sure that there will continue to be an increased social and spiritual awareness within psychotherapy, that urban sociology and geography will continue to be committed to a human environment, and that there will be new directions in the understanding of human sexuality. We cannot be sure that the Churches will keep pace with these developments, but some parts of them will do so. However, I believe that, while the insights of psychology, sociology and the hard sciences can

help us enormously, they are no substitute for the renewal of a God-centred spiritual theology and a social vision focused on the City of God.

Communion and solidarity

In the recent past, thinkers such as William Morris, John Macmurray, and R. H. Tawney influenced Christians in their understanding of what Tawney called 'fellowship' and Macmurray 'persons in relation'.[36] In recent years, much of the relational approach to personhood has been rediscovered and reaffirmed in feminist social thinking. Feminist writers have stressed that a person is a historical being whose history is one of relationship to others, and that the self is foundationally social. Mutuality is basic to the whole understanding of personhood.[37] In this emphasis, feminist thought converges with developments in other fields in a way which Sara Maitland has powerfully expressed.

> A central intellectual claim of the women's movement is that things do not have to be as things always have been; that femininity, for example, is not 'natural' in the sense of immutable or transcendent, but is socially constructed. More, feminism has argued consistently that the social construction of gender changes both in time and in place; and that it can be deconstructed (a process most popularly known as revolution, but within Christianity more comfortably called transformation). This reflects so limpidly the claims of post-Einsteinian physics (that the position of the observer affects the phenomenon observed), of evolutionary theory (that things are not now as they always were), and of theories of class (that the social and economic circumstances affect personhood) that it would be preposterous not at least to note the coincidence.[38]

I shall emphasise in later chapters that the Christian gospel is social at its very heart. It is embodied in a community, and it is the life of this community which is the central concern of the New Testament. In the coming years we will need to take more seriously the character of the Church as a communion

33

of persons, a way of being together which enables human personhood to flourish. The members of the Church are not simply units of labour for the maintenance and promotion of the institution, but limbs and organs of a living body. The Church should be a model of a people at peace with one another. The Church should be the primary social structure through which Christians seek to effect transformation – revolution – elsewhere in society.

The idea of the Church as communion, solidarity, is at the heart of the notion of catholicity. Catholicism, as Henri de Lubac showed, is social at the very heart of its mystery and dogma.[39] The central theological position of the book is that an authentic tradition for the future must lay equal emphasis on solitude and on solidarity, mysticism and community. Only a renewed Christian tradition can do justice equally to the solitary and the social dimensions of what it is to be human, to the complexity as well as the God-directedness of human life, and to the need for a strong sense of common life, rooted in God and in human solidarity. We need both the spirituality of the desert and the tradition of Christian social thought and action. The rediscovery of the important concept of solidarity is a major task for Christians in the new millennium. Over 50 years ago V. A. Demant stressed that the re-creation of solidarity is part of the work of redemption. It is not, he argued, a question of creating union out of the materials of discord, but rather of combating those forces which disrupt solidarity through a return to the source of solidarity, that is, to God.[40]

The theme of solidarity connects with one of the key concepts of Christian life, that of catholicity. One of the most widespread and most consistently promoted falsehoods in the Church is the idea that 'catholic' means 'universal'. In fact, in its root meaning, *kat'holou* means wholeness, completion, fullness of life – in fact, solidarity. It has nothing to do with geography or statistics, but is an intrinsic feature of the Church's being. I believe that the recovery of catholicity is crucial to Christian understanding and life. It is over 60 years since Michael Ramsey, in his seminal work *The Gospel and the Catholic Church*,[41] stressed that the structure of catholicism is an utterance of the gospel. Catholicism, he argued, is about internal wholeness. The life of the Church and the life of the soul are identical. Eastern Orthodox thinkers, such as the late George Florovsky, have consistently argued that the meaning of catholicity is linked with the unity and communion of the human race.[42]

I hope that the twenty-first century Church will be a Church committed to that quest for unity and communion – but I believe that there are some paths which Churches are taking at present which are dangerous and which call for extremely serious scrutiny.

1. I see many clergy and ministers moving uncritically into the secular, professional and therapeutic or quasi-therapeutic schools as a result of a loss of confidence in their own role within the Christian theological tradition. Of course, this has been going on for several decades, but it does seem to have accelerated in recent years, and I will have more to say on it in Chapter 10 in terms of its effect on the shape of pastoral care.

2. The Western Churches have been heavily deformed since the Reformation by individualism and privatised approaches to religion. Since the 1980s this process of deformation has become much worse under the malign influence of the Reagan –Thatcher species of capitalism. If the Churches continue to adopt the ethos and jargon of consumerism, we are likely to see the worst features of privatisation without the best features of individualism in its concern for the lives and rights of persons. The religion of the mega-church or of the gathered community of like-minded people is likely to be superficial – one which gives people what they want, but does not respond to human needs at any deep level.

3. It is important to look at the question of abortion. The unhealthy obsession with abortion, evident both in the speeches of Pope John Paul II and in the 'pro-life' movement in Britain and the USA, should not obscure the fact that widespread abortion does raise crucial issues about human personality, issues which many 'pro-choice' individuals and groups have ignored in their commitment to an ideology of individual rights. However, it does seem to me that the issues have been wrongly formulated for some considerable time.

I have rarely, if ever, met anyone who regards abortion as desirable, and we all need to struggle to make it unnecessary. But to focus on abortion as an evil to be combated seems

35

to me to start at the wrong place. The questions of sexual exploitation, rape, inadequate education about sex, and contraception, must surely take precedence. Nor does the identification of abortion with murder seem to me morally helpful or correct. Where it is illegal, abortion flourishes in crude and dangerous forms.

However, while the 'pro-life' groups are usually inconsistent, and often seem to show more concern about human life in the womb than they do about human life as a whole, they are making some important points which liberals have neglected. I believe that the most hopeful response to the present polarisation is for those Christians who are committed to the dignity and human rights of women to take the initiative and make it plain that they are committed to a struggle to make abortion obsolete. But to do this involves attacking the whole culture which treats human beings as dispensable. Abortion cannot be isolated and treated as an evil which is unconnected from the culture of inhumanity.

Solitude, selfhood and others

I want to stress, in concluding this chapter, the crucial place of solitude in the emergence of selfhood. The Christian tradition – and not least the Eastern Christian tradition – has always stressed the role of solitude within the corporate life of Christians. I want to argue that no approach to human personality will do justice to our contemporary and emerging insights, to our political struggles, or to the profound wisdom of the Christian tradition, unless it takes full account both of the human person's inalienable solitude and also of the essentially social character of personhood. Solitude is necessary to authentic communion. Communion is the prerequisite, the root, the life, of the solitary. True solitude is in every way different from the individualism of the consumer culture. Solitude itself grows out of, and contributes to, the sense of communion and interdependence. Human beings in Christian thought are unique individuals, but can only be understood, and only reach fulfilment, in solidarity. Yet solidarity depends on a high degree of personal awareness and discipline. Undisciplined, immature and dependent people are of little use in, or to, organised movements, and can both damage, and be damaged by, them. Solitude plays a vital part in helping us to be disentangled, focused and committed. It is not surprising that today more and more committed people are being attracted by the image of the desert and solitude.

It is equally no cause for surprise that we have witnessed in the last few decades the revival of the vocation to solitude and to the hermit life. One of the people who influenced me greatly as a young priest was Mother Mary Clare, for many years the Superior of the Sisters of the Love of God. It was Mary Clare who, more than any other single figure, revived the solitary and hermit life within British Christianity. She in her turn was influenced by the Trappist monk Thomas Merton. It has been said that the people of the twenty-fifth and fiftieth centuries will judge the spirituality of our age by Merton, and he has been widely seen as the most significant Christian figure of the twentieth century.[43] Yet much of Merton's importance lies in his concern with solitude and the contribution of the solitary to the life of society. The Church in the twenty-first century will need to help men and women to live with their own solitude, and, through that encounter, to realise, and respond to, their communion with all humanity.

2

Theology and the Future

We have written then in this volume not as 'guessers at
truth', but as servants of the Catholic creed and church,
aiming only at interpreting the faith we have received. On
the other hand, we have written with the conviction that
the epoch in which we live is one of profound transformation, intellectual and social, abounding in new needs,
new points of view, new questions... That is to say,
theology must take a new development.

CHARLES GORE

For many years I have been troubled by the compartmentalising of much human activity, and by the false polarities which
such compartmentalising has produced. Nowhere is this more
dramatically and depressingly seen than in the Christian theological tradition where, for example, systematic theologians
and biblical critics often seem to inhabit different worlds,
where historians and moral philosophers seem poles apart,
and where academia and the back streets, theologians and
pastors, study and prayer, all experience the brokenness and
fragmentation which is so prevalent. I guess this is also true in
non-Christian areas. Fragmentation and incoherence are often
seen as among the central features of our time. Increasingly
there seems to be a loss of confidence – the collapse of the
centre – in our corporate life, in these final years of the twentieth century, an era seen by many commentators as one of
decomposition and crisis.

This decomposition and crisis is not simply a feature of the
dominant society, but affects religious and political traditions
which once seemed confident, secure and even aggressive in
their evangelising style. But today in the Christian movement
(by which I mean the organised Church and its satellite
groups), we seem more and more to be drawing on an impoverished and inadequate tradition. In spite of this, the Church
(or part of it) holds on to the vision of, and often manifests as
a reality, the Kingdom of God, the life of the coming world.
In every generation that hope arises persistently to trouble the
waters, to disturb, challenge and inspire human beings, and to
recall the community to its original hope.

Yet the fragmentation of which I write has never quite corres-
ponded to my own life experience, where prayer and politics,
theology, psychology, sociology and history – not to mention
the interplay of local struggles and global shifts in economic
power – jostle each other and cannot be viewed or engaged in
separately. There is, in my own life and reflection, a sense
of the holistic, the interdependence and connectedness, the
relational character of all life – a sense which has not been
simply an ideal but a vivid awareness of what is in fact the case.

My worries are specifically linked to the nature of theology.
Since I began to study 'theology' in the 1950s, I have been
concerned at the decayed state of the theological world, at
the severance of academic theology from pastoral ministry, of
theological study from prayer and the pursuit of holiness, and

of academia from social and political struggles. Of course, there are striking exceptions, and I am greatly encouraged by an increased integration in some areas; but it is still widely assumed that theology has nothing to say to the wider issues of society or to the practical problems which confront human beings and their social lives. Yet there is a way of trying to make theology 'relevant' which in fact evacuates it of all significance. Something like this occurred during the 1960s, though we need to be careful how we interpret it. Nevertheless, the early 1960s, the time of the publication of John Robinson's *Honest to God* (1963), are a good moment at which to begin evaluating the current state of Christian theology and the prospects for its future.

The 1960s and the 'theological revolution'

'The history of recent theology', wrote Alasdair MacIntyre in 1965, 'is one more reason for not believing in it'.[1] MacIntyre, who by that year had ceased to be a Christian, was expressing one form of reaction to some of the theological reductionism of the 1960s. His comment is interesting, for, nine years earlier, he had written:

> What is this theological revolution? It is the recognition that God is not a super object behind phenomena, and that if he were, the atheists would be right.[2]

It seems to me that the revolution to which MacIntyre referred continues to this day. The fate of theology is inextricably bound up with our understanding of, and response to, transcendence, to ultimate mystery, to what we call 'God'. By the early 1960s MacIntyre himself had become an atheist, and his subsequent career, to which I will return, is a commentary on the intellectual and cultural developments of these years.

I was ordained in the early 1960s, though, for good or ill, my theological and spiritual formation began in the mid-1950s. But my first five years of priesthood covered the period of the controversies over John Robinson, the 'death of God', and the so-called 'South Bank theology'. The more I look back at these years, the more ambiguous, paradoxical and complex

41

they appear, and the less adequate are the simple catch-phrases – 'South Bank religion', 'Sixties' theology', or even the umbrella term 'the Sixties'. We are speaking of a decade of enormous complexity, in which no unifying theme can be discerned but, rather, a range of diverse and conflicting trends. It is important therefore to warn of the danger of trivialisation of this decade. Much of today's trivialising comes from politicians aged roughly 45–55, who, on the whole, played no part in the creative movements of those years, and who still do not understand them. In their minds and rhetoric, the Sixties has become demonised, a period of horror, an age of 'permissive claptrap' (as Margaret Thatcher once called it), of naïve Utopian optimism, and so on.[3]

One interesting example of trivialisation, though it is seductive because of its wonderful satirical rhetoric, occurs in Richard Holloway's book *Let God Arise* (1972), itself an attempt to restate the Christian message positively after years of confusion and uncertainty.

> The whole decade flashes across my mind like some lunatic kaleidoscope: the Rector of Woolwich pushing a beauty queen through the streets in a wheelbarrow; Malcom Boyd going on TV to announce with passionate solemnity that Jesus Christ, like all men, had a penis; Canon Montefiore of Cambridge electrifying the world press by saying that Jesus Christ could have been a homosexual; an up-to-date harvest festival in the South of England, in which the liturgy had been written by the vicar, ending with the following responsory: 'Are we happy? You bet your life we're happy!' Appropriately the 60s ended with another awe-struck pronouncement from John Robinson. In the pages of the *Sunday Times* he breathlessly intoned: 'The August issue of *Playboy* . . . contains some marvellous cinephotographic stills of Paula Kelly dancing completely in the nude, pubic hair and all. Nothing could have been more beautiful and entrancing.' Ah, the 60s![4]

It sounds good, but it trivialises an important, serious and creative period.

The much-ridiculed John Robinson, Bishop of Woolwich in the early 1960s, was actually an extremely important figure in the theological world. He was in some ways a microcosm of the Church of England: middle class, academic, aloof, remote, awkward, cut off from working-class people, doing his earnest best. As Valerie Pitt once commented, sweetly but candidly, 'It's nice to know he wants to be with us'. Yet Robinson's achievement was to bring theology into the public arena, to make matters of fundamental belief, of what, following Tillich, he called 'ultimate concern', talking-points, at least for a time, beyond the confines of church and academy.

Of course, the notion of theology as a public discourse was not new. There had been times when theology was a *lingua franca* in the public squares, bars and streets. One theologian wrote:

> In this city, if you ask anyone for change, he will discuss with you whether the Son is begotten or unbegotten. If you ask about the quality of the bread, you will receive the answer that the Father is greater, the Son less. If you suggest that a bath is desirable, you will be told that there was nothing before the Son was created.

But this was Gregory of Nazianzus in the fourth century, and by 1963 things were a little different. Robinson's book achieved a major breakthrough. After *Honest to God* people were beginning to talk theology outside the confines of churches, seminaries and universities – just as, in a form unrecognised by the intellectual elites, they always had.

In the thought of some people – including the then Archbishop of Canterbury, Michael Ramsey (though he later apologised) – Robinson's offence lay not so much in what he said as in his method, in the fact that, by writing a popular work with extracts in *The Observer*, he had broken the chain of normal discourse, ignored the proper channels by which ideas were meant to filter through to the laity, and had spoken directly not only to men and women in the pews, but to the general public. He had engaged in 'abnormal discourse'. It was this mode of address which was seen as subversive, harmful to the beliefs of the 'simple faithful', disloyal to the teaching office of the bishop and the theologians. *Honest to God* was a landmark in paperback theology and signalled the beginning of the end of trickle-down theology as a respected method. It can be argued that, by helping to democratise and popularise theology, Robinson aided that process in other disciplines too. Certainly the paperback book industry has never been the same since.

But theology is not only about thought and speculation: it is about the pilgrimage of a community. The sense of theology as movement was brought out in the thinking of that very influential but neglected figure, Stanley Evans, who was Robinson's close colleague on the Southwark Ordination Course. Evans was a brilliant sailor and his concern with navigation and movement forward comes out strongly in the last paper he ever wrote, read by Father Percy Coleman to the Federation of Catholic Priests in South London after Evans' death in 1965. Here he contrasts earlier dogmatic theology with that spate of religious writing in the early 1960s which was initiated by the volume *Soundings*, and which provoked a minor epidemic of books whose titles were all derived from Paul's navigational escapades in Acts 27. (In addition to *Soundings*, there was *Four Anchors from the Stern* and *Praying for Daylight*, while the inimitable Eric Mascall added his own *Up and Down in Adria*.) Evans, commenting on the period, stressed the importance of movement and struggle, and his last published words sum up his entire world view.

The two theologies, old and new, both seek for an impossible stability. Both think in terms of rest; the one will sound and the other will lie at anchor. But the only purpose of taking soundings is to aid navigation, and they have, in practice, to be taken from a vessel under way. The Pauline vessel in the Sea of Adria dropped its anchors because its navigation had failed, and it was on the verge of wrecking. Navigation is really learned only by those who sail, and this is a fundamental principle of the Church. 'He that doeth the will shall know of the doctrine'. We are concerned to discuss faith as a handmaid to the living of the Christian life, as a navigational aid to those who would be in the way that leads to God's kingdom, not as an academic exercise for members of a hydrographical department who have lost their taste for putting to sea, or as a reflective study for those who would spend their days lying quietly at anchor.[5]

Evans was impatient with much of the radical theology of the early 1960s, and felt that it had lost its historical roots in the Christian tradition.

Clearly these years were years marked by what Langdon Gilkey called 'dissolution and reconstruction in theology'. Like

Evans, Gilkey used the imagery of water, but in a rather diferent way.

> No more than five years ago, the 'younger theologians' seemed to have a comfortable basis for their task, fashioned by the great theologians of the 20s, 30s and 40s ... We saw ourselves as a generation of 'scholastics' whose function would be to work out in greater detail the firm theological principles already forged for us. We knew from our teachers what theology was, what its principles and starting points were, how to go about it, and above all we were confident about its universal value and truth.
>
> The most significant recent theological development has been the steady dissolution of all these certainties, the washing away of the firm ground on which our generation believed we were safely standing. What we thought was solid earth has turned out to be shifting ice – and in recent years, as the weather has grown steadily warmer, some of us have in horror found ourselves staring down into rushing depths of dark water.[6]

So as the 1960s moved to their close, things once thought solid were melting, and people spoke of the theological mood as one of ferment, revolution and turbulence.

Of course, all this is easily exaggerated. As Laurie Taylor wrote of the 1960s' counterculture, life in Burslem, Tadcaster and Crewe was not noticeably affected.[7] The theological ferment can also be overstated. Debates among academics do not necessarily reflect the views or feelings of the wider population. Sociologists such as Andrew Greeley were swift to point out that, for most people, the controversies among theologians had made no significant difference to their religious needs. These, Greeley argued in 1973, had not changed significantly since the late Ice Age.[8] And if degrees of religious piety and secularisation continued to be matters of controversy, there seemed little controversy, as far as some academics were concerned, about the fate of theology. In his 'Reflections on Leaving the Chair' in 1982, Ronald Preston, for many years a professor of theology at the University of Manchester, lamented the widespread lack of interest in theology within the Church.

These were years of dissolution, but also of reconstruction. But this was not all we were experiencing. There had been a shift in the very nature of theology, and this was certainly not a result of the 1960s – though it came to a head in that decade. E. L. Mascall, writing in 1982 (the same year as Preston's lecture), quoted N. P. Williams, who in 1933, 30 years before *Honest to God*, had noted that theology had come to mean the historical and genetic study of the ideas of Christianity, and how they had developed. It seemed no longer concerned with the truth of these ideas or with how that truth might be grasped in a living encounter with God. Mascall argued that what was often termed theology in the 1980s was not theology at all in the classical sense. Indeed, he believed that theology, in the sense of reflection on God and on God's work in the world, was in danger of becoming an extinct discipline.[9]

I believe that Mascall was mistaken in his pessimistic prediction, and in fact recent years have seen considerable renewal and growth in theological thought. While areas of great perplexity remain, and will remain, we are in the time of reconstruction, and we need to return to first principles, looking again at what theology is, and what its contribution is to the Church and to human society. This will call for the recovery of humble confidence – confidence in the conviction that we are rooted and grounded in God. It will call for the renewal of the tradition of social thought, for the rediscovery of the mystical character of all theology, and for the recognition of plurality and diversity in theological work.

The changing face of theology

All genuine, living theology is rooted in a profound, and, at the end of the day, ineffable experience of the mystery which enfolds and transcends all being, the mystery which, in fear and trembling, we call God. If my general thesis so far is correct – that human beings can only attain true fulfilment in communion with God – then a concern with God must be central both to an understanding of human personality and to the social and political structures which form the context for the human predicament. A concern with God, with discerning the activity of God, and with seeking communion with God, is the meaning of *theologia*, theology. Literally the word means the study of God, reflection on God, a word of God or about God – or simply 'God talk'.

Over many centuries, the understanding and practice of theology has undergone major changes, and while it is important to move into the future, we need to learn from the collective wisdom of the past. Early Christian thinkers related theology closely to holiness and prayer. In the writings of the Cappadocians of the fourth century, for example, *theologia* was more specific than it is in much current usage, in that it was expressly and only concerned with God. Yet it was also a broader and deeper concept than it is today, when reason and concept have been emphasised to the exclusion of other dimensions of life. In early usage, prayer, a holy life and the existential encounter with God were more important than study. So the Venerable Bede virtually equated *theologia* with *contemplatio*, while later St John of the Cross identified contemplation with mystical theology. Central to much early Christian thought was the theme of love as itself a kind of knowledge, a theme which was first stated explicitly by Gregory the Great. Too much definition in theology was dangerous, according to Ephrem the Syrian, and was maybe even blasphemous.[10]

A great deal has happened to theology since these formative years. Early medieval theology still laid a stress on the poetic and imaginative aspects, as well as on the role of the theologian in the spiritual life of the community. Medieval thinkers distinguished *ratio* (discourse, logical, abstract thought) from *intellectus* (understanding, vision, a broader idea involving the imagination). The disintegration of the unity of theology and what later came to be known as spirituality, often described as the division between heart and head, began quite early. By around 1300 Western Catholicism had exhausted the resources at its disposal to express that ecstasy and mystery from which all genuine theology must begin.

The impact of the Enlightenment led to a further narrowing of theological horizons. For example, in North America, until the nineteenth century, the primary focus in theological education was on such areas as knowledge of the Bible, liturgical practice, and the technique of preaching. Only towards the end of the nineteenth century was there any concern with relating theological issues to the needs of an urban industrial society. Even within the Catholic tradition, in which there was formally a tradition of social thought, the lives of ordinary

Christians were hardly, if at all, affected by it. Moreover, theology increasingly came to be seen as a matter which only concerned the clergy, and even for them it was a preparation for doing something else – the practice of ministry – better.

So increasingly, theology came to be seen as irrelevant theory which most practical people could do without – indeed, which was perhaps a hindrance to practical issues – and this view is linked with a tradition of anti-intellectualism in public life as a whole. One of the most prevalent features of recent political life has been the repeated attacks on intellectuals, and indeed the contempt for serious, systematic thought. Thinkers – as opposed to 'experts', the organic intellectuals who service the system – are seen as subversive, as threats to the moral order, as sources of confusion, even of contamination. How much better life would be without the intellectuals, who have muddied the waters, stirred up discord, corrupted the minds of the young. I want to argue, first, that this is a wildly incorrect analysis – that, on the whole, intellectuals offer no threat whatever to the social order, but are all too comfortably integrated into it; and, secondly, that the labels of troublemaker, dissident, disturber of the peace, subversive, do accurately describe what intellectual life, and theology in particular, should be. But this is to anticipate the argument.

While traditional Christians – by which I mean those Christians who are rooted in, and are familiar with, the Christian tradition, not conservatives who are ignorant of the tradition but resistant to change – have held, from early times, the position that theology is closely related to social, economic and political issues, this is not the view of governments. Moreover, recent governments in Britain are so distant from the Christian tradition that such a traditional theme is very strange to them. Their understanding of the role of theologians and of the Church as a whole is quite different from that held by informed Christians themselves. What was emerging, or re-emerging, in the 1980s was a clear conflict between two views of the role of the Church and of religion. For Margaret Thatcher, Douglas Hurd and later John Major, the Church was one of the pillars of society which upheld, reinforced, and where necessary helped to restore 'traditional values', the necessary structures of civic order. But was this how the Church, and theologians, saw themselves? It seems fairly clear from such an event as the publication of *Faith in the City* (1985), and the responses to it, that there were two vastly different understandings of the place of religion, and of theology in its contribution to religion, in social criticism.

I need to add a word of caution here. I am not arguing that the government has been correct to portray bishops, Church leaders, theological thinkers, or other representatives of what Henry Clark calls the 'social action curias',[11] as serious dissidents. They are in fact well within the cultural conformities of established religious life as it has manifested itself at least since the 1880s. The kind of social critique offered, for example, by *Faith in the City* is of an essentially conformist type, easily containable within dominant social structures. The point is that even this level of critique is seen as threatening by those for whom religion serves only the purpose of reinforcing the established order.

The attack on, and contempt for, theology is part of a more widespread mistrust of theory, and a mistrust of intellectuals, evident in the speeches at recent Tory Party conferences. But something strange was taking place between the 1960s and the 1990s. The 1960s were marked by claims about the 'end of ideology'. Daniel Bell's book called *The End of Ideology* was in fact published three years before *Honest to God*.[12] According to this perspective, ideological positions were obsolete. The future lay with pragmatism, with technical decisions based on short-term needs. But by the mid-1970s ideology was in again with a vengeance. It was the free-market ideology – or theology if you like – of the Institute of Economic Affairs which brought Margaret Thatcher to power in 1979, even though her future direction was to be shaped more by the ideologues of social authoritarianism than by those of free-market liberalism. Yet it was part of the success of Thatcherism to disguise its ideological rigidity under the label of 'common sense'. It was the left – socialists, even Church leaders – who were the slaves of ideology; while the government stood only for the traditional values, the basic decencies, which everyone in their hearts knew to be true.

The beginnings of the modern political attack on theology can be dated fairly precisely to Hugh Gaitskell's leadership of the Labour Party in the early 1960s. In his opposition to Clause Four (on common ownership), Gaitskell dismissed the opponents as being guilty of 'mere theology'. The identification of theology with irrelevant, out-dated, abstract theory was to remain, and it flourishes to this day. Theology is seen as something unrelated to real life and practical issues.[13]

The theology of the future

I want to look now at three kinds of development which, I believe, are necessary to the theology of the future: the expansion of the theology of liberation; the recovery of the mystical, poetic and liturgical dimensions of theology; and the construction of 'local theologies'.

1. The theology of liberation

The only theology to which I am committed is one which is part of a current of liberation, also known as redemption. If theology does not help to liberate human beings and the created order, it helps to oppress them. There is no neutral theological position. Indeed, the belief that there is such a position is itself part of the ideological captivity of theology.

Theology may be seen as irrelevant in Britain and North America. But there are parts of the world where theology is seen as not merely relevant but as subversive and dangerous. The most obvious example is the liberation theology which has grown up in Latin America and elsewhere. It is common today to say that liberation theology is dead, and certainly Cardinal Ratzinger has done his best to kill it. But, while there have been major developments and changes, as there are in all living and creative movements of thought, liberation theology has not only survived but has spread its influence far wider than Latin America. It is a genuine movement of God's Spirit, and the dictats of the Vatican will be impotent to stop its growth. The twenty-first century will be a critical time for theologies of liberation in many countries, as the forces of reaction gather and seek to destroy these movements. By its very nature, liberation theology is a theology shaped by poor and relatively powerless people. To the extent that official Christianity continues to side with the powerful, the two theologies will continue to be in conflict. Yet, while there will continue to be debates within liberation theology, it does seem to me that much of traditional Christianity will survive within the liberation theology tradition or not at all.

2. Mystical theology

All true theology is mystical. It involves the whole person and the whole community in its relation to God. It is not simply a movement of thought and conceptual reason. The place of the imagination has been seriously neglected in Western theology, though it is emphasised in the writing of Samuel Taylor Coleridge and, more recently, of Nathan Scott. In the Eastern Christian tradition, all theology has been seen as mystical. Much of the writing of those identified as 'theologians' in the Eastern tradition is in fact poetry. Vladimir Lossky, in his formative study, *The Mystical Theology of the Eastern Church* (1957), stressed that in Eastern Orthodox perception, mystical theology was not a department of theology but a way of describing theology's essential character and its very core.[14]

Mystical theology is prayerful, open, reticent, humble. It is a theology which is reduced to silence by the awesome mystery of the divine. It stands in dramatic contrast to the arrogance of fundamentalisms which seek to name and to control both 'their' god and 'their' people. At the heart of the mystical theological tradition is the insistence that God cannot be controlled, conceived, imprisoned or even named. God is the hidden God (Isa. 45:15). Anyone who thinks that God can be named, according to Justin Martyr, is 'hopelessly insane'.[15] There is a strong biblical stress on keeping silence before God (Hab. 2:20). I believe that, both for the sake of truth and for the sanity and integrity of humankind, it is vital to recover this mystical heart of all theological reflection, work and testimony.

3. Localised theology

Theology must be localised, concretised, rooted in particular communities and sites of significance. So here I want to describe the attempt to construct a local theology from St Botolph's Church, Aldgate.

St Botolph's Church stands at the point where the City of

London meets (or collides with) the East End. Within minutes, one moves from the financial centre of London into the most overcrowded ward in the United Kingdom. For many years the church has been a centre for crisis ministries of various kinds, as well as for pastoral and social care of people in many different communities. There has been a long history of Jewish-Christian dialogue and co-operation, while today many of the children in the church school are of Muslim background. There is a well-established work with homeless people, and with people with HIV/AIDS, as well as the 'normal' activity of a parish church in the city.

In 1990 we decided that it was important to employ a theologian, a member of the team whose primary activity was to pray, reflect and think – not on behalf of others or instead of them, but in co-operation with them – and to contribute to the work of theological reflection within the Christian community in this area. We believe that it is very easy for local churches to avoid serious thinking, and simply to carry on doing what they have always done. It is particularly dangerous for us to operate a crisis ministry, binding up the wounded and responding to one urgent need after another, but never to make the time to reflect on what it is all about, what it has to do with the gospel, what the wider social and political issues are, and what God is up to in the struggles and upheavals which confront us. It was because of this need that I was employed as a community theologian based here. So what does it mean to be a theologian in the East End of London? Is there an 'East End theology'?

The question raises issues which are relevant way beyond this area. Is there any locally characterised theology, or merely theology as such? Are people in the East End, or in other local communities, interested in theology anyway? I need to explain in what sense I use the term theology, and why I prefer to call myself a theologian instead of, as a friendly, local atheistic doctor suggested recently, a 'community thinker'.

I use theology in two senses: first, a general sense of a continued questioning of fundamental issues of life and death, a search for truth and for insights into the meaning of human living; and secondly, a more specific sense of such a process of enquiry which (in my case and that of others) goes on within the tradition which looks back to the faith of Israel and to the community which gathered around Jesus of Nazareth. I use 'theological' in both senses, to refer to movements of thought within other faith-traditions (such as Islam), and outside all specific faith-traditions (such as most questioning which goes on locally, as well as the specific theological tradition within Christianity).

In the first sense, clearly theology goes on in the East End as it does in other places. People here have experiences of life and death, of joy and tragedy, of insight and of terrible suffering. People here think deeply about the meaning of life and search for answers, for approaches which 'make sense'. These experiences are shaped by the unique, concrete context of the East End – a context marked historically by the dominance of the river and the docks, and by waves of immigration, and currently by unemployment, racism, redevelopment, further migration, and so on. Some people, a minority, try to make sense of their experience within the framework of the Christian tradition. Many more, while not claiming any definite commitment to the Church, owe much to its tradition and look to it at important points in their lives. Others, perhaps a majority in Spitalfields, do so within the tradition of Islam, though Islam itself is changing as it encounters Western consumerism, the culture of modernity and urban existence.

What then are the characteristics of theology as observed and practised in the East End of London?

1. **East End theology is oral theology.** The theology which goes on in the East End is not, for the most part, written down. Most of it goes on in pubs, at street corners, in laundrettes, etc. Most of it is not directly related to the Church as institution, though that institution figures at certain key moments. There are major questions about how this informal theology is linked to a concrete tradition of thought and reflection, but there seems to me no doubt that it is a kind of theology, albeit lacking in system and precision. John Reader, writing from the background of rural Shropshire, makes a similar point.[16] It should not be despised for being an oral tradition – indeed, it may be to its advantage. If this is so, the theologian who seeks to articulate in written form – as I am doing at this moment – something of the reality of East End theology must realise that s/he is, by this very act, distorting and minimising that reality. The core of theology is at the point of acute reflection, not at the 'joined-up writing' juncture.

2. **East End theology is theology in a hurry**. Whether we think of theology in general or of Christian theology in particular, East End theology is a street theology, theology under stress. In such a theology it is important to seize on critical moments, moments of disclosure, of revelation, of vision. Of course, this is not unique to this area, but the pressure of life in the East End does, in my view, affect the character of theological reflection which is done here. It is not tidy, comfortable, secure or 'systematic' theology. It is theology in a hurry, and, if it is not rooted and grounded in a disciplined tradition, it can become theology in a panic.

3. **East End theology is historical theology**. The East End presents a very rich and diverse history. It is important to enter into this history, most of which has taken place in a state of distance from Christian theologians. Yet the Christian Church has played an important role in this history, and this needs to be examined and critiqued. However, the history of the East End is greater than that of the Church within it, and this history helps to convey something of the struggles, hopes and aspirations of the people over many years.

4. **East End theology is political theology**. This is true in two senses. Historically much theology is linked with the *status quo* and with the reinforcement of dominant political values and structures. The term 'political theology' has a dubious pedigree, owing the origin of its modern usage to the work of Carl Schmitt who helped prepare the way for the Nazi state. In Britain most of what is called theology is deeply entangled with the established order in Church and state. The history of the Church in the East End is in part a history of social control and of the attempt to impose a theology on the local people. Yet there is, not least in the East End, an alternative tradition in which theology has been the impetus for resistance, and for the creation of a different approach to politics. Both Jewish and Christian traditions have provided resources for radical movements which have enriched this area.

5. **East End theology is plural theology**. There are many different faiths here. Islam is particularly strong. But there are also many very different Christian streams, each with roots in East London history. An East End theology needs to work

54

within this framework, and to work across divisions in practical and theoretical ways. In the coming years, the practical encounters between Muslim and Christian streams of thought and action will be of great importance. A current plan, initiated by a Servite priest, to establish an inter-faith ashram on the Ocean Estate could be a most important development.

6. **East End theology is community theology.** The word 'community' is used loosely and vaguely, and this usage has increased recently as a result of the resurgence of interest in the writings of Amitai Etzioni among 'communitarians' in the USA and in Britain, including his followers in the Labour Party. I am very critical of much of this community politics, and it is important to be aware of the current debates around the concept. I will have more to say about this in Chapter 7. As far as the East End is concerned, there are many communities, many local allegiances and local histories of common identity and commitment. When I am called a community theologian, which community is being referred to? Initially the gathered community around St Botolph's, a 'community of choice' and of commitment, not one arising from residential settlement. Yet I am also related to other communities characterised both by residence and by interest.

7. **East End theology is pastoral theology.** The whole issue of pastoral ministry is complex. Are theologians necessarily pastors? Certainly I find myself doing considerable amounts of pastoral work with individuals, partly as a by-product of other work, and partly because of my accessibility. This raises issues about my priorities, and I need to be a little more personal here as this aspect of the work particularly involves personal work. One issue is that the contemplative, reflective and thoughtful side of me is always in danger of being swamped beneath urgent and immediate demands. The trouble is – though it is not really trouble and it does not actually trouble me most of the time – I am good at dealing with urgent demands. I am an activist, and I am, sadly, aware that many pastoral people are pretty useless in a crisis. So when I need to act, I act quickly. I am not sorry about this but I wish it was not necessary. I am accessible: people in this area know how to get hold of me at all hours.

Yes, theology is pastoral, it is about people. Yet there is a problem here about the relationship of theology to pastoral care. I don't think I could be a good theologian without a certain amount of personal pastoral involvement. But how much? Or how central should this be? I am aware of it as a difficulty, but at present am not clear what to do, except to be prayerful, sensitive, responsive, and to rely on others to tell me if I am taking on too much. I suspect that theologians in other places may be in the same position. If they are concerned about God and God's people, it is difficult to see how this could not be so. Indeed, can there be authentic theology which is unconnected with a commitment to the welfare and future life of actual people?

8. **East End theology is liberation theology** – or rather, it should be. What is called liberation theology is normally associated with Latin America – although it should be remembered that one of the first texts in English to use the term, that by Rosemary Ruether, addresses the North American situation.[17] However, it is the 'Third World' and the context of revolutionary upheaval which has shaped such theologies. Can liberation theology have relevance for the advanced urban society of Britain? This is a question to which I will return.

Current positions in Roman Catholic theology

I want to conclude by looking at some dangers for theology within the Catholic world, and at whether Anglicanism, as a mutant of Western Catholicism, can make a useful contribution to the theology of the future.

There is one exponent of theology as a critical discourse who has no doubts whatever as to its role. Pope John Paul II, in his Instruction on *The Ecclesial Vocation of the Theologian*, of June 1990, and, more recently, in the encyclical *Veritatis Splendor* of October 1993, presents a view of theology which seems to be entirely at loggerheads with mine. I say 'seems' because in much of his theology – his emphasis on the dangers of relativism, on the centrality of truth and justice, on solidarity, liberation, and the sanctity of human life – I find the pope challenging, and certainly not the simple reactionary that he has been painted in much of the media. There is a sense of theological wholeness about much of his teaching and thought.

But in John Paul's vision, there can be no theological dissent or debate. He is utterly clear what 'truth' is – the word appears 40 times in the encyclical. In contrast to his predecessor Paul VI, who saw, and said, that Christian social thought must arise from concrete contexts which were necessarily diverse, and who recognised the pluralism within theology, John Paul seeks to return to a pre-modern understanding.[18] The word 'dissent' appears early on in *Veritatis Splendor*, in paragraph 4, and it is obvious that the disciplining of dissenting views is central to its concern. The faithful, he says in paragraph 116, need to be protected from theological error. 'Dissent', says paragraph 113 with emphasis, is opposed to the hierarchical constitution of the people of God, and bishops are urged to take 'appropriate measures' to deal with it. The language is ominous, and the practice accords with it. The papacy of John Paul II has been marked by the increased disciplinary activity of the magisterium.

The new Catechism of the Catholic Church was produced with the express purpose of bringing back people who had been led astray by 'theological ferment' and it would seem that the encyclical has a similar purpose. While the pope does stress justice, solidarity, honesty and openness (paragraph 98), the general thrust of this and other documents is towards a more closed, authoritarian system with discipline as a central focus. Indeed Cardinal Ratzinger, the central figure in this operation, explicitly sees part of the present task to be the creation of a new balance after years of exaggeration and indiscriminate openness to the world. Pope John Paul certainly seems to see dialogue with modern culture as vain (paragraph 88). There is no dialogue, only proclamation. *Roma locuta est, causa finita est.*

We are assured, in paragraph 29, that there is no intention 'to impose upon the faithful any particular theological system, still less a philosophical one' – but in fact this is precisely what the encyclical does, with its reversal to the timeless, immutable Thomism of the 1940s. The close link between Thomism and Catholic theology is, of course, an old one, and I would be the last person to deny the immense value of the Thomist tradition. But we cannot simply resurrect St Thomas, or one particular phase of Thomist interpretation, and apply it to the needs of the twenty-first century. Pope John Paul seems unaware that theological thinking within orthodoxy has moved on. The official association between Roman Catholic thought and one philosophical tradition dates from Leo XIII's *Aeterni Patris* of 1879. John Paul himself belongs to a small school of Thomist thinkers associated with the Catholic University of Lublin, and particularly with the theology of Andrzej Szostek.

What Pope John Paul is offering, at the dawn of the twenty-first century, is a model of theology as a total and unchanging substance which can be injected into any and every historical situation. He has recently produced his *Agenda for the Third Millennium*,[19] but this too is depressing and disappointing. It abounds with clichés and unexamined assumptions. He sees the year 2000 as an 'epochal turning-point' – but, if this is to occur, there needs to be a real renewal of theological perception and vision, and of this there is no sign in the pope's thought. It would seem that the Roman communion is moving increasingly and rapidly backwards, backwards to a monolithic view of theology, a view dominated not only by the West but by a very small section of Western thought. While there is always the encouraging fact that diversity of theological work in the Roman Church seems to continue in spite of particular popes, the future for creative theological thought within the Roman Church at the official level seems bleak.

Anglican theology, past, present – and future?

What then of Anglicanism? Does this tradition have a future as a form of Christian presence and consciousness? I must confess that my relationship to Anglicanism has always been a marginal, and, in the strict sense, an eccentric one. Yet here I remain – troubled, irritated, often profoundly uneasy with this strange Church, this *église ridiculeuse* (as the late Hugh Maycock used to call it), yet not knowing where else I could go and be more at home. I find my relationship with the Church increasingly complex and ambiguous.

Yet the history of Anglicanism is itself complex and filled with ambiguity. The close links with monarchy, aristocracy and establishment, with national identity and state, are inextricable elements of dominant Anglican history, and I see them as serious obstacles to the future of Anglicanism as a coherent Christian tradition in the modern world. On the other hand, I look around at other parts of the Christian world, and am often relieved that I am an Anglican! Part of the relief is due to the fact that within Anglicanism there are deviant, dissident, minority traditions, some of them products of the Oxford Movement and its fusions with other forms and developments. One Orthodox writer used to say that the genius of Anglicanism was its ability to preserve for the Christian future the vision of unity in diversity, while others have seen Anglicanism as a form of 'Western orthodoxy' – an orthodoxy which takes account of the insights of modern (and postmodern) thought.[20]

To be an Anglican intelligently is to enter into a particular way of doing theology which brings together pastoral and academic approaches as well as socio-political struggle. This is true in spite of the immense differences in the way such a theology is interpreted. Thus, at their best, and clothed in their right mind, evangelicals, liberals, Anglo-Catholics, and all the people who do not fit these increasingly problematic labels, do tend to have in common a broad view of pastoral care, a respect for the intellect and for freedom of thought, and a commitment to some kind of involvement in the issues of the wider society. Such a posture cannot be taken for granted in the same way in other Churches or traditions, and it is a major strength of the Anglican way.

It seems to me beyond doubt that there is a long and rich tradition of Anglican theological thought which goes back, at least, to the seventeenth century. At this time, for example, a school of Anglican moral theology grew up which was much closer to Thomas Aquinas than was much contemporary Roman Catholic thought. It was a tradition which integrated moral and ascetical theology, discipleship, and a theological vision of the final end of humanity in glory. Much nineteenth-century Anglican theology – F. D. Maurice is a clear example – shaped the thinking of Christians in many communions, while much of the thought of the Second Vatican Council was anticipated in Michael Ramsey's *The Gospel and the Catholic Church* (1936). This small Church has pioneered many areas of thought which have later become normative in the Christian world.

There has been debate for many years about whether there is a distinctively Anglican theology at all. Michael Ramsey, in a famous passage, stressed incompleteness, clumsiness, mess, and lack of neatness as central features and strengths of Anglicanism. Its strength, he claimed, lay in its very brokenness. In an article of 1945, Ramsey discussed the question of whether there was an Anglican theology, answering his own question positively. Anglican theology, he argued strongly in the post-war years, was sorely needed. It was not a confessional system so much as a method, a use, a direction – and only provable by its fruits. Ramsey stressed the need to prevent Latin scholastics dominating the Church's theology (a view which he re-empha-sised in my presence during the papacy of John Paul II), but he was also highly critical of the neo-orthodoxy of Barth. For him, the Anglican sacramental and incarnational thrust was of crucial importance to the Christianity of the future.[21]

Certainly the Anglican Church is one of the most pluralistic Churches in the world, and the idea of a *via media* seems often to have a disintegrative rather than a unifying effect.[22] Halevy, writing of the nineteenth century, commented that England was the only country in Christendom which did not require any theological knowledge from candidates for ordination.[23] But the concept of the *via media* is usually misunderstood. It is not a broad path of vagueness, rather a precarious way of holding together paradoxical truths in an uncomfortable but creative dialectic.

I certainly do not believe that the civic tradition within Anglicanism, with its lack of any clear dogmatic belief or serious spiritual life, can make any creative contribution to the Christian future. I see the de-Englishing of Anglicanism as a major breakthrough, and it is certainly the case now that the most vigorous areas of growth of the Anglican form of Christianity are in Africa, Asia and Latin America. But I do believe strongly that there are elements in Anglican history – its rich sacramental life, its respect for scholarship and free enquiry, its commitment to biblical reflection and preaching, its liturgical discipline, and its emphasis on pastoral theology – which have enormous, and at times unique, contributions to make to world Christianity. Many people have come to Anglicanism as a result of their felt need for a deeper and richer liturgical and sacramental life; or as refugees from the Roman communion with its often slipshod and mechanical approach to worship, or its harsh and uncomprehending approach to sexuality; or because they find their intellects are respected here. There are all kinds of reasons why people become Anglicans. But in order for them to come at all, the Church has to stand for something.

The belief that the Anglican Church does not stand for anything has in recent years provoked a number of documents which have sought to recover 'Anglican essentials', or to restate the fundamentals of the faith. Some of these are very narrow, others are a needed corrective to much sloppy 'liberal' thinking.[24] Some have lamented that today, orthodoxy is only one option among many; while others have suggested that the future of Anglicanism involves an increasingly orthodox theological profile.[25]

The strength of Anglican Catholicism lies, first, in its ability to offer a form of Catholic faith and life which is compatible with intellectual freedom and with a creative engagement with contemporary thought. Secondly, its strength is in the fact that, at its very heart, it is deeply mystical, social, sacramental and thoughtful, offering synthesis and integration. Thirdly, its strength lies in its ability to offer a way forward for apostolic Christianity which avoids the ethnic captivity and pre-Enlightenment perspectives of Eastern Orthodoxy, and the narrow authoritarianism of the Vatican, while learning from, and absorbing, the best in these streams. Finally, its strength is in its ability to offer a place of nourishment for Christians who are escaping from bigotry but who do not wish to abandon the positive and valuable aspects of the tradition.

At the heart of classical Anglican theology is a view of pastoral care which extends way beyond the confines of the congregation. In a moving essay on being Anglican in South Africa, Mamphela Ramphele speaks of her experience as one of pain and privilege. She lays particular emphasis on the opposition to rigidity and the openness both to people and to new ideas. For Ramphele, it was loving pastoral care which brought her into the Anglican Church, and this is a really important pointer for the future.[26] The future of Anglican Catholicism is still unclear, and some of the pastoral dimensions of this – including the ordination of women to the priesthood, and the prospects for disestablishment – will be discussed in Chapter 10.

A final struggle in Anglicanism concerns the question of purity. Problems around purity have been central to religion since ancient times, and one of the radical contributions made by Jesus was to redefine the approach to notions of pure and impure. Anglicanism has to a large extent avoided sectarianism and its tendency to make sharp divisions between pure and impure, recognising the need to deal with impure and ambiguous realities. John Kevern has argued that the future of Anglican theology depends on its ability to take seriously the doctrine of analogy, to do for the twenty-first century what Aquinas did for the thirteenth.[27] Whether Anglicans take the opportunities seriously probably depends on factors about which I have no knowledge and over which I certainly have no control.

3

Fear and Fascism

A spectre is haunting Europe – the spectre of Fascism.

MICHAEL BINYON

The last chapter ended with a reflection on the phenomenon of Anglicanism, the particular form of Christian identity which is inevitably associated in people's minds with England. But England is part of Europe, and, however critical we may be of the movement which, since 1945, has led to the present European Union, no adequate reflection on the future of England can ignore the wider European context. Equally, religions which are inextricably bound up with nationalities and ethnic identities are almost certain to be at best irrelevant and at worst extremely dangerous in the future, as they have been in the past.

Many Christians seem to think that, because there have been no major wars between the countries of Europe since 1945, the threat of war has receded – a belief which is often linked with the theory of the nuclear deterrent. Yet such a belief, while it contains some truth, owes more to establishment propaganda than to reality. There have been hundreds of wars since 1945. There have been nuclear accidents, many of which have been covered up and have only recently come to light. The possibility of nuclear war by accident remains a serious one. The arms trade remains a major threat to human life: between 1989 and 1993 the USA alone sold 116 billion dollars worth of arms to 160 nations.

So Christians need to take very seriously their responsibility as disciples of the Prince of Peace in a world increasingly violent and erratic. There needs to be what the Nobel Peace Prize-winner Joseph Rotblat has termed a war on war. The engagement in such a war against war is, I believe, the only form which the classical doctrine of *justum bellum*, the just struggle, can take for Christians in the twenty-first century. I therefore believe that Christian work for peace and against the arms trade, the nuclear threat, and the mentality of aggression will be a critical test of our discipleship in the coming century. At the same time, as European Christians, we need to face very seriously our responsibilities in and for this continent as it takes new forms and attracts both new possibilities and new dangers. This chapter therefore, while it will look at developments elsewhere (particularly in the USA), is primarily about the future of Europe and of Christians within Europe.

The concept of a Christian Europe

In 1964 the Conservative Central Office issued a leaflet which included these words:

> The Common Market was set up by the Treaty of Rome. This has nothing to do with the Pope or the Vatican. The treaty just happened to be signed in Rome. The Common Market has nothing to do with religion.

It is significant that, as late as 1964, it was still felt necessary to placate the residual anti-papal side of the British psyche, and to reassure any doubters that the move towards a united Europe 'has nothing to do with religion'. In fact, in its historical origin, the idea of European unity was deeply religious and Christian, associated with Charlemagne and Charles V, with Aquinas and Erasmus. It could be argued that the first combined action of the European community was the first Crusade of 1095.

Early discussions on the modern European Community, which grew out of discussions about iron and steel, were phrased in mainly economic terms – yet there has been, since the 1930s, a consistent impulse, emanating from very diverse sources, towards political unity. Walter Funk, Hitler's Minister of Economic Affairs, spoke of the need for 'a profitable and permanent European community'. The notion of a 'United States of Europe', a phrase which goes back to Victor Hugo in 1849, has been used by a variety of people from Winston Churchill, in his speech at Zurich in 1946, to Helmut Kohl in 1991. In somewhat different form, it was used by the Comintern in the 1920s. 'Europe a nation' was a favourite theme of Oswald Mosley. Indeed, Mosley saw himself as the pioneer of European union and of European white identity. In a speech in 1945 he said:

> The union of Europe becomes not merely a dream or desire but a necessity. The union of Europe is no new conception: the only novelty is its present necessity.[1]

The modern idea of European unity is one which runs across the political spectrum, and its supporters and opponents can be found in very strange alliances.

However, during the last few years, a number of people have

been stressing the need for a moral and spiritual vision at the heart of the European idea. This too goes back to an earlier period. Jean Monnet, in the 1940s, referred to the need for 'a new brand of humanism' and for a 'moral basis' for Europe – indeed for spiritual foundations for the community.[2] Both Konrad Adenauer and Maurice Schumann were deeply influenced by the ideas of Christian Democracy and by the need for spiritual foundations. (It is not without significance that one of Schumann's assistants was the philosopher and mystic Simone Weil.)

In more recent times, discussion in this area has flowed thick and fast. In a sermon in Leeds in September 1991, Cardinal Basil Hume spoke strongly of the inner emptiness at the heart of Europe. 'Europe', he claimed, 'is a continent in search of identity, meaning and purpose'. He warned of an 'immense danger', and expressed the fear that pluralism might slide into confusion and incoherence. Soon after this, the then Archbishop of York, John Habgood, stressed the need for 'a new moral heart for Europe'. Adopting perhaps a more positive view of plurality than Hume, Habgood claimed:

> A pluralism in which there is also a seeking for common values, a pluralism in which there is also a sense of responsibility towards the whole, a pluralism set within the context of defined obligations, seems to me to provide the materials out of which Europe will rediscover its soul.[3]

'The Common Market has nothing to do with religion.' One person who would dissent from this view is Jacques Delors. It is significant that Margaret Thatcher should have – correctly – identified Delors as her principal ideological opponent. For these two figures represented different traditions and interpretations of Christianity in its social expression – Thatcher reflecting the individualism of English Protestantism aided by the self-help philosophy of Samuel Smiles and the economics of Smith and Malthus; Delors the social theology of Catholic Action and the thinking of Emmanuel Mounier. It was Delors who wrote:

> Liberal individualism has done immense harm. True, we have talked a lot about human rights, but we have forgotten about the other side of the equation: the solidarity that comes from shared experience.[4]

'Solidarity' – here too is a word which, like subsidiarity, does not belong to the current vocabulary of British governments. It comes straight from the mainstream of European Catholic social teaching. The Jesuit Heinrich Pesch wrote four volumes on it in 1920, and it has figured prominently in recent encyclicals of Pope John Paul. It is in fact to the social vision of John Paul that I now wish to turn.

John Paul II's European vision

John Paul would, of course, strongly dissent from the view that the European Community had nothing to do with religion. Indeed, it has been the collapse of the Communist regime on the one hand, and the movement towards European union on the other, which has led to his passionate concern for a spiritually renewed Europe, the theme of the European Synod held at the end of 1991. I want briefly to expound what I take to be the pope's vision of Europe, and to express both an admiration for it and some profound worries about it. I then want to look at some pressing problems within Europe which, I shall argue, call for a different – though not entirely different – form of response.

The key point to make is that John Paul's vision of Europe is of a united Europe, united across the old divides of wall and curtain. His eyes are on the East. In 1940 a book was published in Britain entitled *Poland, Key to Europe* by R. L. Buell. John Paul quoted it in the last article he wrote before he became pope, and it is clear that he does indeed see the developments in Poland as crucial to the spiritual renewal of Europe. He contrasts the spirituality, the devotion, the resilience under persecution and martyrdom, and the solidarity of Eastern European Christians with the materialism, individualism and secularism of the West. Indeed, a new heresy was identified at the Synod – the heresy of Westernisation, an umbrella-term for the culture of modernity.

Another feature of John Paul's vision is that it is a sacral vision – of a Europe marked by Marian shrines and pilgrimage centres, of a Europe resacralised, reconverted. So at Compostella in Spain in 1982 he quoted Wolfgang Goethe's observation that European unity was forged by pilgrimages on which Latins and Germans, Celts and Slavs, Angles and Saxons exchanged stories and songs. So the Church is crucial to his vision of European unity and identity. It is not a new vision, though it has been given a new impetus by recent events. In 1979 when he returned to Poland, he called for the 'spiritual unity of Europe'. However, recently he has been more specific. At Bratislava in 1990 he called for 'a united Christian Europe' and for the reconquest of the European mind – shades of Margaret Thatcher at Bruges in 1988? This leads to another crucially important point.

John Paul does not believe that Marxism is dead. He rejoices in the collapse of the Communist regimes, and sees this collapse as an answer to prayer. But Marxism as ideology is, in his mind, located not in the East but in the West. When, on 13 April 1980, he visited the shrine at Turin, he condemned both liberalism and Marxism and linked them with terrorism! More recently at the Synod of Bishops, the view was clearly expressed that 'the problem of Europe' was 'the problem of freedom', and indeed the choice between freedoms: the authentic freedom in community offered by Christ and the Church, and the bogus freedom offered by secularism. And in his thinking, secularism, liberalism, and Marxism are all linked. They are all aspects of the heresy of Westernisation, of the secular culture of modernity. And they all end in nihilism. John Paul clearly sees himself as entering the vacuum left by the collapse of Communist regimes, but he is also committed to an ideological war, a war of ideas, between his Polish Christian vision and what he sees as Marxist ideology.

It is not surprising that John Paul holds this view for he was deeply influenced by the French thinkers Emmanuel Mounier (whose personalist philosophy sought to offer a Christian social alternative to Marxism) and by Jacques Maritain, by the contemporary German theologians, Hans Urs von Balthasar and Joseph Ratzinger, and by the philosopher Rocco Buttiglione, who was quoted twice in his speech at Warsaw in June 1991. Buttiglione, professor of philosophy at the International Institute of Philosophy in Lichtenstein, is a very significant influence on the pope's thought. He sees Marxism as the culmination of a process which began with the Enlightenment, and whose end is spiritual bankruptcy. The choice before European culture therefore is very clear – in his words, 'Europe can choose between nihilism and the rediscovery of Christian faith'.[5] There is no doubt that this accurately represents the pope's view, and that the reconversion of Europe to faith and to theocracy is central to his project.

Christendom: a desirable model?

But this raises questions about this deeply Christian vision of Europe: Is it true? Does it take account of all the data? I want to suggest that it contains some profound flaws. Its triumphalist dismissal of the Enlightenment and the heritage of scientific rationalism is a gross over-simplification of a very complex history, arrogant in its simplicity. Its identification of liberalism, Marxism and nihilism is simply incorrect as a matter of fact, and defective in its lack of analysis. Its emphasis on Christian Europe ignores the contribution of the Jews – the entire cultural renaissance of 'Mitteleuropa' was, after all, due to the emancipation and urbanisation of Jewish people. It ignores both Islam and the role of post-Christian secular achievements. Even within the Christian framework it seems to neglect the role of the Protestant Churches in the West and of Orthodoxy in the East. Its philosophical underpinning is open to serious question.

We need also to ask: is this vision of a new Christendom a desirable one? Is this the kind of Europe we want? I am very sympathetic to the view that there is a spiritual emptiness at the heart of Western culture, though I think it can be overstated. In different forms, this view has been expressed by Christopher Dawson in the 1940s, by the Chicago philosopher Leo Strauss, and it appears today in the writings of Alasdair MacIntyre and John Milbank. These writers (apart from Strauss) look to some kind of revival of the Augustinian Christian tradition as a countervailing force to those of liberalism and secular reason.

I think we need to be extremely careful here. I am sure that we cannot go back to the model of Christendom which dominated Europe from the Middle Ages until the catastrophe of Nazism. It is simply not possible – and, if it were possible, it is not desirable. Whether we like it or not, the inroads made by modern secular movements (of which Marxism is only one) have been considerable. We have all been affected by European secular consciousness (some would say corrupted by it): we cannot go back. Nor do I think we can simply dismiss the Enlightenment and the achievements of scientific reason in so cavalier a way. In saying this I am not suggesting that either the liberal political tradition or the culture of scientific reason is adequate as a moral, philosophical or spiritual basis for the Europe of tomorrow. It is not adequate, but it is a necessary component. The idea of Europe as a monolithic Christian culture is dead. The future must lie with some kind of post-Christian quest for social democracy – post-Christian in the sense that it cannot be built on Christian foundations alone. The culture and spirituality of a new Europe is not a past which can be reclaimed but a future towards which we struggle.

Concerns about the future of Europe

In the second part of this chapter, I want to suggest that there are a number of very worrying aspects of the current European scene which the Christendom model would not do anything to resolve, and which to a certain extent have their roots in that model. I will point to six areas where I see serious cause for concern and for concerned action by Christians in the twenty-first century.

1. Refugees and migrants

The first relates to the position of refugees, migrant workers, asylum seekers, and stateless persons. They constitute a vast population who have been termed 'new untouchables'.[6] Of course there is great concern at the plight of the 1.3 million refugees from former Yugoslavia. But there are over 16 million migrants throughout the European Union who form a kind of 'thirteenth state', a captive labour-force. As internal frontiers are relaxed, the evidence strongly suggests that both external frontier-controls and internal surveillance will increase, and that these controls will have their most powerful impact on people of colour. Hence the frequently expressed fear of a 'fortress Europe', committed to keeping out the poor of the Third World, who are often the victims of past and present European policies.

In Britain the terrible position today is the culmination of legislation which began with the Commonwealth Immigrants Act of 1962. The recent Asylum and Immigration Act met with strong opposition from the Churches who are now heavily involved in feeding and supporting many refugees and asylum seekers who have been deprived of state benefits. For the first time in 50 years, at Christmas 1996, the Red Cross distributed food parcels in Britain – to asylum seekers in London. Government callousness and denial have reached an appalling state, and it seems unlikely that under a Labour government the situation will quickly improve. The Churches' role as advocate for scapegoats and victims of racist immigration policies will become more important as we reach the new millennium, and Christians will need to co-operate closely with Muslims who, in many cases, will be the victims of the legislation. 'The time of the End is the time of No Room', wrote Thomas Merton 30 years ago, and his words are certainly true now.[7]

Linked with the question of migrant workers is the massive upsurge of racial violence. Racial attacks are rarely out of the news. What is often forgotten is that they go back to the early years of the European Community – to Rotterdam in 1972, Marseilles in 1973. But the last few years have seen striking increases throughout Europe in racial attacks on Africans, Arabs, Turks, Asians (especially in Britain), gypsies and many other minorities. We have seen attacks on synagogues – attacks which are sadly reminiscent of the 1930s. There were over 400 racial attacks in Germany in the first eight months of 1991, mainly in the East where police estimated that there were around 1,500 neo-Nazis with perhaps 20,000 supporters. There have been thousands of attacks in France. In Britain, attacks have increased in areas which have hitherto not been markedly affected. Reported attacks in London grew from 5,124 in 1993–4 to 5,480 in 1994–5. My area, the East End of London, is said to account for one quarter of all racial attacks in the country, and, while we have seen a decline in some parts, this has been the result of constant vigilance and activity over many years.

Immigration is a world issue and Churches in the twenty-first century will need to respond on a global scale. One of the main arguments used in Britain to justify racist immigration controls is that control of numbers promotes racial harmony: racial discrimination at the doors of Britain is the way to reduce racial discrimination within Britain! In fact, concessions to prejudice and hatred have been followed consistently since the 1950s by violence on the streets, as politicians have given the green light to the expression of such hatred. In the United States the panic over immigration is reminiscent of what happened in Britain in the late 1950s, which eventually led to the increasingly restrictive immigration legislation for over 30 years. In the USA also there have been new and more violent forms of racist activity. There has been a resurfacing of fire-bomb attacks on Black churches in the south during 1995–6, taking forms reminiscent of the early 1960s.

There is a tremendous amount of work to be done in Europe to create and enforce just and compassionate legislation on racial discrimination and on the rights of minorities. This will involve amending the Treaty of Rome, and perhaps strengthening and expanding British race relations legislation on a European scale. European action so far has been poor. The Declaration Against Racism and Xenophobia, issued by the Maastricht Summit, was weak, and did not point to any real action. Meanwhile, since December 1991, the Maastricht Treaty has enshrined deflationary economic policies within European law, and this is bound to create conditions in which racism will grow.

Race relations will not improve automatically. Racial justice will be the result of a struggle involving commitment and political will. In Britain we have never had a government policy on combating racism (though there nearly was one in 1974 when Labour last came to power). The material base of racial inequality, residential segregation in housing, has remained essentially the same since the early years of Black settlement.[8] Yet Section 71 of the Race Relations Act 1976 gave local authorities a clear mandate to eliminate discrimination, and this needs to be used as a campaigning charter. Certainly the struggle against state racism will need to be a high priority for Churches in the early years of the twenty-first century. All the evidence is that this struggle will be hard and painful. Many Christians will bow their heads, not in prayer but in evasion, for it is evident that the seriousness of the issues are still not recognised in most Churches.[9]

2. *A Fascist revival?*

Associated with immigration issues is the rise of the racist, Fascist and neo-Nazi parties and groups, and this raises the question: are we seeing something akin to a revival of Fascism in Europe? There has certainly been a significant growth in parties of the far right – the Front National in France, the Republican Party, National Democratic Party and German People's Union in Germany, and so on. Alongside this there has undoubtedly been a reappearance across Europe, not least in Eastern Europe, of ideologies which are closely akin to classical Fascism. We have seen the return of the Mussolini family to the political scene in Italy, while Fascist bands play on Slovak State Radio and the Mlodziez Wszechpolska (Youth of Greater Poland) has grown in recent years.

The spread of historical revisionism and the Holocaust denial movement (a range of attempts to rehabilitate Hitler and to deny, or downplay, the Holocaust) is a continuing cause of great concern. This movement has spread in many places, not least in the Arab world, where *Mein Kampf* has been reissued in Beirut and many copies distributed to Lebanese bookshops. In Germany itself, *Der Spiegel* in 1989 claimed that 6.4 million people (14 per cent of the adult population) held a positive view of Hitler. Of course, it is easy to oversimplify and overdramatise these developments – but it is still easier and far more dangerous to ignore them. The pendulum of political orthodoxy has been swinging to the right, not least in Britain, since the 1970s, and positions on all kinds of issues have hardened in a markedly authoritarian direction.

In all these areas, the responsibility of the Christian Churches in the coming years is very great. The Christian contribution to the growth of anti-Semitism is well-documented, as is the collusion of many Christians with the beginnings of Fascism. Churches in Britain have often only noticed the racist dimensions of government policy when it was too late to affect them. The new millennium should be a time of vigilance and pro-active, not reactive, action.

3. *A culture of militarism*

We need to take seriously the continuance of the permanent arms economy and of whole cultures based on militarism. In some respects the possibility of serious armed conflict has become more acute. We have been pleased and relieved at news of cuts in nuclear weapons by the great powers, but we need to remember that nuclear stockpiles are still as high as in the early 1970s when serious negotiations began, and that neither France nor Britain are at present involved in any such strategic discussions. A nuclear-free Europe is still a long way off. The real risk for the future is not that of a major super-power confrontation using Europe as a battleground. It is rather of the multiplication of smaller tragedies, and of smaller countries acquiring nuclear weapons or using their existing ones. Iraq, Iran, North Korea – the list could be extended. Although France eventually signed the Non-Proliferation Treaty in 1991, there is a real danger of proliferation in the Third World, including countries very close to the European border, often under threat from existing nuclear states and using precisely the same arguments to support their stance as the nuclear powers have been using for years. As national and ethnic conflicts reappear, the possibility of more brutal and dictatorial military regimes cannot be ruled out. And what is to be the new Europe's contribution to the reduction of such conflict? And what is the role of the European Churches in conflict-resolution and in positive peacemaking? This leads inevitably to my fourth area of concern.

4. *The future of Ireland*

As we read of conflicts in Slovenia, Croatia and elsewhere in Europe, we need to remember that the longest-running conflict in Europe, possibly in the world, is on our doorstep – the conflict in Ireland. How does the movement towards European union affect this most British of all conflicts? The commitment to, and involvement of Ireland in the European Community is quite recent, and it has certainly helped to transform that society. Ireland is perhaps the most extreme example of the inadequacy of the Christendom model. For here, *par excellence*, the medieval, Catholic feudal culture has survived, with its paraphernalia of hierarchy, theocracy, censorship, repression, and so on. But now, that culture is rapidly breaking down in its last European stronghold (it collapsed in Spain and Italy long ago, the rhetoric notwithstanding). Under the impact of recent events, not least the surfacing of cases of sexual abuse by clergy, both the control and the credibility of the Roman Catholic hierarchy has been weakened dramatically and perhaps irretrievably, and the Christendom model seriously eroded.

Ireland has gained a lot from the European Community, but at the cost of the sacrifice of much of its Catholic culture. The question which is surely all-important now is: what effect will the moves to union have on the resolution of the conflicts in the north of Ireland? It may be that only a pan-European approach can achieve what Britain alone clearly will never manage.

5. The growth of Islam in Europe

Along with the growth of Islam in Europe is a parallel growth of anti-Muslim sentiments. It is nonsense to speak of 'Christian Europe' and to ignore the Muslim presence: there are probably two to three million Muslims in France, two million in Germany, six million in Western Europe, and probably 30 million in Europe as a whole (excluding Turkey). About half of them are in the former Soviet territories. European unity was originally forged in the context of defence against the Muslim threat – and today there is evidence that the role of 'enemy', played until recently by the Soviet Union, is now being played by Islam, and that Europe is once again closing ranks against the Muslims.

Today in the Spitalfields Ward of East London, around 80 per cent of the population is Muslim. Most of the older Jewish population has moved. The old synagogue at the corner of Brick Lane and Fournier Street, once a Huguenot church for the silk-weaving community, is now a mosque, one of eight in Tower Hamlets. The old East London Mosque – which I knew 30 years ago when it was an old house in Commercial Road, frequented by the small but concentrated Somali community – has now been replaced by a magnificent structure in Fieldgate Street. Thousands worship on Fridays, and the Young Muslim Organisation is the biggest religious youth movement in the

East End. The mosque is an important social and cultural centre, and has recently established an excellent reference library and bookshop, and a room where students can do homework and other studies.

My experience has been that, whereas much inter-faith dialogue tends to be a rather disconnected, middle-class activity without roots in the communities, a real and growing dialogue is more likely to emerge from concrete co-operative action. It is in this context that I view with some horror and alarm the Open Letter on inter-faith worship of 1992, and the launch of the Decade of Evangelism. Within days of the Open Letter, the mosque was daubed with the words 'Jesus has died and is risen'. Of course, it may not have been put there by Christians, and it could be that members of the Fascist organisations are learning new tricks. But from my knowledge of these people, I doubt that they would know a line from a charismatic hymn. The mosque, and Bengali families, are only too familiar with the 'Pakis die' and 'Wogs out' slogans – but this was new. I believe that, as the anti-Communism of some Christians gives way to anti-Islam, a climate is being created in which much of the most valuable work of dialogue and encounter between faith-traditions – most of it still young and fragile – will be undermined.

Nor is this merely my eccentric opinion. I was struck by a letter in *The Times* several years ago from Peter Berry, the provost of Birmingham Cathedral, who probably knows the Sikh community better than any other Anglican priest, and who has worked on inter-faith relations in the Midlands for many years. He wrote:

I am so afraid that rising tensions, exclusions and declarations in the inter-faith debate will stultify all dialogue and progress in understanding between religious communities here in the inner cities.

He went on to stress the need to 'overcome more than 1,000 years of polemic, distortion and prejudice' in Christian–Muslim relations.[10]

At about the same time, another old friend, a distinguished academic who has been involved with Christian–Jewish dialogue, wrote to me:

The Decade of Evangelism is having a severe blighting effect in these quarters... It is discouraging that a still-fragile bridge should be wilfully broken down just when it had started to bear some really rather interesting traffic.

As so often, Church leaders are being naïve, insensitive and foolish rather than sinister and malevolent. However, there is a sinister and malevolent dimension to this, and I fear that good people have helped to create a climate in which other, more poisonous and evil fruit will grow. So not only will much creative work be undone or frustrated, but the forces of bigotry and, in the specific context of today, of racism will be encouraged. That, at least, is how it seems to me from the perspective of East London. Needless to say, I do not believe that any of this is what Church leaders, evangelists, Open Letter signatories or many fundamentalists want or intend. Nevertheless I think it is what will happen in fact. As Pascal noted, evil is never so perfectly done as when it is done with good will and purity of heart.

The inter-faith dimension in the twenty-first century will be most urgent in Britain. I do not myself think that we can simply take the roads of syncretism and what is sometimes called 'multi-faith stew', on the one hand, or of a narrowly exclusivist and proselytising 'one way' theology on the other. We need to grapple with the difficult issues raised by such concepts as pluralism, fundamentalism, secularism, and so on – words which are often used to end discussion rather than enable it. Why are we not learning from those Christians, particularly in the Roman communion, who have for centuries been living in societies whose experience of inter-faith issues is greater than ours? There are vast resources in India which could be tapped. Have we forgotten the important pioneering work of people like R. C. Zaehner and Thomas Merton at the very point at which it has become relevant to our culture? We need a rich, deeply rooted and yet humble approach to our own faith-tradition if we are to counter the intolerant and damaging tendencies of much in the contemporary Church.

6. *Europe and the Third World*

My final area of concern for the future of Europe is the danger of the neglect of the Third World, and the real possibility that parts of the future Europe will themselves assume Third World characteristics. Indeed, this has already begun to happen. The worries about a 'fortress Europe' mentality and the forging of a white, Western 'Christian' unity are more than worries about increasing racism. They are worries that the new identity, the new European order, might be forged at the expense of the international community. This is a point made strongly by Pope John Paul in his encyclical *Centesimus Annus.*

> The western countries . . . run the risk of seeing this collapse [of Communism] as a one-sided victory of their own economic system and thereby failing to make necessary corrections in that system. Meanwhile the countries of the Third World are experiencing more than ever the tragedy of underdevelopment which is becoming more serious with each passing day.[11]

I am delighted to be able to agree with the pope on this.

A new Christian Fascism?

I want, in this final section, to return to the question of Fascism and to ask: is there a new religious Fascism? Specifically, is there a new Christian Fascism? 'Can a Christian be a Fascist?' is a question which is rarely asked, perhaps because it is feared that the answer might be 'Yes'. Historically the links between Christianity and Fascism are considerable, and there is no doubt that many thousands of Christians have been Fascists in the most rigorous sense of both words. The authoritarian structure of the Roman Church was part of the tradition out of which Mussolini's movement grew. Christopher Dawson pointed out that the social teachings of Popes Leo XIII and Pius XI were closer to Fascism than to socialism.[12] Mussolini himself claimed that he was simply putting Pius XI's encyclical *Quadragesimo Anno* into practice, while Pius himself, on 20 December 1926, called Mussolini 'the man sent by providence'.

There are features in Fascist and Fascist-like movements which make them extremely attractive to religious people, and maybe to Christians in particular: the belief in total certainty and total control; the contempt for the mind and the insistence on uncritical acceptance of authority from above; the belief that the world is decaying and must be rescued from nihilism and rootlessness; the emphasis on tradition, inequality, stern laws, warfare against decadence; the appeal to the heroic, nationalism and patriotism; the offer of security and stability in exchange for freedom and justice – and so on. While at heart I believe – as did Hitler – that Fascism is utterly opposed to Christianity, it is foolish to deny that there are elements in Christian tradition, both Catholic and Protestant, which are open to a Fascist development. The Nazi movement was steeped in religious ecstasy and mystical symbolism of great power.

I gave a lecture with the title 'Is there a new religious Fascism?' on 14 March 1978 to a group of Christian socialists at the House of Commons. It was published in my book *The Social God* in 1980,[13] and it provoked conflicting reactions. While John Austin, now Bishop of Aston, said that it was truly prophetic, Andrew Kirk suggested that I had taken leave of my senses.[14] What I was arguing then was that there was a real danger of creeping Fascism in the West, and that both the resurgence of the Catholic Right in Europe and of Protestant fundamentalism in the USA were likely to make their impact on the British scene. I saw a real danger in the growth of broadly right-wing moral crusading movements and in the collapse of a genuine tradition of Christian socialist thought. If anything, I believe I understated the seriousness of the danger.

Since 1978 all kinds of changes have occurred. Margaret Thatcher has been and gone. Pope John Paul II has built up the conservative forces within the Catholic world. Cardinal Ratzinger has done his best to undermine liberation theology. The Moral Majority, the Christian Coalition, and other right-wing groups have made their impact in the USA during the Reagan years and since. In the future we are likely to see new forms of totalitarianism combined with the free market and liberal democracy. Meanwhile the 'Christian Right' has grown throughout the world.

What is now termed the Christian Right is not a monolithic structure in either theological or political terms, and includes a wide range of groups whose concepts of Christianity and whose political positions differ greatly; it is easy to caricature and to blur important distinctions. If we exclude groups of a vaguely moral kind which have no particular connection with the Christian tradition, we can identify a number of strands: the Catholic Right, in its old and new forms, the groups set up to oppose the World Council of Churches, the explicitly racist and anti-Semitic groups such as Christian Identity, the 'moral right' formed around pornography, birth control and abortion, and, more recently, around anti-gay and anti-lesbian positions. There are a number of other formations: there are those liberals who have drifted to a right-wing position through lack of credible alternatives, and there are (particularly in Britain) the 'gut right' populists, who, while knowing little or nothing about Christianity, appeal to a crude type of residual folk religion, and find considerable support from the tabloid press.[15] I want here to look briefly at two major streams, that of the Catholic Right, and that of the new politicised fundamentalism.

The Catholic Right

The resurgence of the right wing in the Roman Communion has been strongly encouraged by Pope John Paul who has been busy appointing extremely conservative bishops in many key dioceses, including some in Latin America where Christians have been in the forefront of progressive action for justice. We have seen two broad types of right-wing Catholicism. There has been a revival, and in some places a strengthening, of the old European Catholic Right. This survived in the Lefevbre movement, now closely linked with the Front National in France, and has recently resurfaced in other forms. There are historical continuities with the Catholic Right of earlier times (much of which had close affinities with Fascism) – evident in such movements as Action Française with its origins in the work of Charles Maurras. Opus Dei and Communione e Liberazione are also part of this picture. They are rooted in a pre-Vatican II concept of Catholic Europe.

I have referred earlier to the influence on the present pope of such thinkers as Buttiglione and the Lichtenstein group. Of course these are not Fascist, but it does seem clear that, given the historical context of Western Europe, these positions are helping to reinforce the power of the old Italian male hierarchy, and to defeat those who threaten the *status quo*. It is fertile soil out of which a new Catholic Fascism could grow, and it links with those groups in the Catholic world who wish to go back before the Second Vatican Council to an earlier, more stable and more secure type of Catholic order.

But there is a new Catholic Right of an altogether different kind, whose roots are in the liberal, democratic capitalism of the USA. Associated with figures such as Michael Novak and Richard Neuhaus – both of them former 1960s' radicals – this movement is more ecumenical, making alliances with right-wing thinkers in other Churches, and strongly supportive of democratic capitalism and its embodiment in the American way. Novak, and his colleagues in the American Enterprise Institute, figure prominently in the opposition to liberation theology. Crucial to these groups is the role of the big foundations: organisations like the Institute for Religion and Democracy and the Ethics and Public Policy Center serve as think-tanks for this wing of the Christian Right. The same names constantly appear and the same foundations give support – Sara Scaife, Smith Richardson, John Olin, the Heritage Foundation, and others. There is a large and interconnected network of right-wing think-tanks funded by conservative foundations, and a good deal of this money has probably gone to help similar groups in Britain. The attack on liberation theology and the support for American foreign policy are central, but there is involvement also in the promotion of domestic policies. Here this network connects with the critique of 'welfare' by Charles Murray and those concerned with New Right social policies. Novak and his supporters claim that his writing influenced Pope John Paul's encyclical *Centesimus Annus* with its critical support for capitalism.[16]

In spite of the liberal approaches of its intellectual leaders (or some of them), in the USA conservative Catholicism is linked with intolerance and nostalgia,[17] and this seems to be true in Britain too. But while the present papacy has encouraged the emergence of these kind of reactionary movements, it is not at all clear that they will in the end prevail over the more radical and forward-looking vision of Popes John XXIII and Paul VI. Writing of the North American situation, Andrew Greeley has commented: 'They may fire theologians, ban speakers, harass priests, write letters to Rome, but their lay neighbours pay no attention to them and are not likely ever to do so'.[18] It is important to avoid complacency and to build up the progressive forces within the Catholic world, and radical

Anglican Catholics will have an important task here in the future, whoever the next pope turns out to be.

The Catholic Right is part of a wider network of interests, attitudes, theologies, alliances and movements, a broad and diverse cluster, comprising numerous organisations and tendencies. Generally they are marked by political conservatism, moral traditionalism, social discipline, a simplistic reading of the Bible and sometimes of other formularies, and by patriotism. They are committed to, and wish to promote, Western capitalism – the free market, established structures of power and wealth, and US foreign policy – and they relate this promotion in some way to the defence of Christian faith. They oppose socialism, liberation theology, and 'progressive' movements within the Churches and elsewhere.

Fundamentalism

As in the case of the Catholic Right, the Christian movement known as 'fundamentalism' should not be confused with Fascism, but neither should it be entirely dissociated, for the two streams have much in common. The New Christian Right which has surfaced in the USA since the late 1970s has close links, but also sharp contrasts, with the older Christian right-wing movements of that country. Its recent rise is also linked with the resurgence of millenarianism, and this will be examined in greater detail in Chapter 8.

The word fundamentalism is used very loosely, and, even when it is used with care, there are varied ways of understanding it. Historically, Christian fundamentalism is an American movement, arising before the First World War, though the word itself was not used before 1920.[19] It was associated specifically with opposition to Darwinism, rationalism, Bolshevism and socialism, immigration, biblical criticism, various current heresies, and liberalism. It was marked by a strong belief in biblical inerrancy, salvation through Christ alone, and his imminent return. The movement has always been strongest in the USA, but it has been increasing in Britain for some years. In the USA fundamentalist Churches are very large, white, wealthy, and politically significant. The Southern Baptist Church, for example, has 16 million members and has become more aggressively fundamentalist and conservative in recent years.

Historically fundamentalism often goes hand-in-hand with racism, extreme conservatism, bigotry and violence. But there are many gradations, and the English species is often more genteel and suburban in ethos, lacking the vulgarity and directness of some of its American forms. (I emphasise the word 'English', for there are variations within Britain. Ian Paisley received his doctorate from Bob Jones University in South Carolina, one of the strongholds of old-style fundamentalism.)

Christian fundamentalists have a strong belief in sin, in the need for strong laws based on moral principles, a rigid approach to sexuality, and a resistance to all forms of secularism. However, what is new in the recent fundamentalist revival is its explicit political role, which includes putting up fundamentalist presidential candidates and exercising significant influences on presidential thinking. Since the end of the Reagan regime and the sexual scandals of some televangelists, many have assumed that the fundamentalist revival has run its course and has now subsided. On the contrary, there may be worse to come.

American fundamentalism has always been a deeply conservative movement. It is only since 1967 that Tennessee schools have allowed evolution to be taught – and even now only as one theory alongside that of 'special creation'. But there have been two strands to fundamentalist politics. One is basically individualistic and other-worldly, dominated by a belief in individual salvation and in the imminent personal return of Christ. This often involves a lack of interest in 'worldly' affairs, leading paradoxically to a strong support for the *status quo*. While there has always been a selective involvement of older fundamentalists in the political arena, this tradition has been mainly separatist. However, since 1976, the more politically active type of fundamentalism has emerged – a fundamentalism which seeks to rescue the USA from the clutches of secular liberalism and to claim 'dominion' over the social order. Both types have always taken a strong and punitive 'moral' line, with a particular stress on homosexuality, pornography, the position of women, and, more recently, abortion. But in the last decade it is the militants who have become dominant.

There is no doubt that fundamentalism represents a major

force in the USA and a growing one in Britain. Much of it is unchanged in its theological essentials since the early years of the century. But some features are new. Not until the mid-1970s did fundamentalism assume a political role of the kind popularised by Jerry Falwell. The fusion of fundamentalism with, on the one hand, modern technology – massive computerised networks, bureaucracies, and TV channels – and, on the other hand, the insights and campaigning experience of the Civil Rights movement and of liberal Christians of the 1960s, has produced a new mutant of the phenomenon. Fundamentalism has always been very consumerist, has seen evangelism as a form of marketing, the gospel as a product, and much of its preaching style has been influenced by the world of entertainment. What is distinctive about the new politicised fundamentalism is its use of the technology of modernity to attack the spirit of modernity.

Recent forms of right-wing fundamentalism have tended to avoid explicit racism, though anti-Semitic utterances are not unknown, but it is important to remember that the racist Christian Right is by no means dead, and indeed has regrouped in the last few years in a violent and dangerous way. There has been a resurgence of the Ku Klux Klan in recent years, as well as more disturbing features such as the rise of the Christian Identity movement (to which I will return later).

It is often said that fundamentalists and evangelicals are quite distinct. But, as George Marsden, the historian of fundamentalism, once commented, a fundamentalist is simply an evangelical who is angry about something. Evangelical churches in general have tied themselves to the *status quo*, and abandoned any real prophetic ministry. The ties which link evangelical Christianity to political conservatism are so numerous and so pervasive that one can say that historically the two are yoked together.[20] Of course I am aware that, since the early 1970s, we have seen the growth of different forms of evangelicalism – radical discipleship, Sojourners-type groups, and so on. I have written about such groups, and have myself been greatly influenced, inspired and encouraged by them. But they represent a tiny minority within the evangelical world, and they are not the most significant tendency within it. The evangelical world has a long way to go before it can shake off the legacy of right-wing fundamentalism, and this is certain to be a major part of the agenda for the next century.

The debates around fundamentalism have raised various ways of looking at the movement. Some have argued that what is really important is not the theology of the movement but its mind-set. At the end of the day, it does not worry me all that much if people choose to believe that the world was created in six days, that Jonah was swallowed by a whale, or that Ahaziah died both at Megiddo (2 Kings 9:27) and at Samaria (2 Chr. 22:9). At worst, this is a mixture of intellectual stupidity and biblical illiteracy. (In fact, a major problem among fundamentalists is that many of them are biblically illiterate, a point noted in the Gallup survey of American religion in 1989.) But this applies to many other people and groups, and most of us are stupid some of the time.

What concerns me far more, and what seems to me to be the most worrying and dangerous feature of fundamentalism in all its forms, is its uncritical conviction of its own possession of the truth, its habit of portraying its critics in demonic language as not only mistaken but evil, its utter exclusion of doubt and darkness from religious life, and its built-in tendency towards a totalitarian style. I find myself in agreement with James Barr that fundamentalism is a pathological condition of Christianity. It is also extremely dangerous, and the persistence of it, and of attitudes associated with it, may well, as Barr also noted, determine whether or not the human race is destroyed in nuclear war.[21]

So how should Christians in the coming years respond to fundamentalism? The ability to respond in a positive and sensitive way is bound to be one of the key issues of the next century. It is necessary to realise that we are not talking about a fringe phenomenon which is peripheral to the future of world Christianity. In the USA, fundamentalism is the public face of Christianity. There, fundamentalists constitute about a quarter of the population. Elsewhere they are a major force within Christianity. So we need to begin by recognising that we are confronting a substantial section of the Christian community.

While I believe strongly that fundamentalism is a harmful mutant of the Christian faith, it does not seem to me that it is either sensible, ethical or correct to dismiss those drawn to this movement by seeing them as psychologically insecure or ridiculous. No doubt many of them are – but this would be true of many movements inside and outside organised religion.

Some of the attacks on fundamentalism are themselves rather wild and irresponsible. Thus Bishop Spong writes of 'hysterical literalism', of 'safe havens for the frightened and the insecure', of 'frantically insecure people who seek to live in an illusion because reality has proven to be too difficult'.[22] This is not helpful.

We need to treat fundamentalists with respect. They are not all irrational or unintelligent. In fact, part of the problem is that fundamentalists, like liberals, are often too rational. They want proof, and may find the darkness of mystery hard to cope with. In this they are not alone, not all that different from the rest of us. No approach which fails to recognise the humanity and seriousness of the fundamentalist can hope to have positive effect.

At the same time, we do need to be aware of how dangerous this tendency can be, and to be prepared to say so. We are entering a period when many forms of intolerance, bigotry and false certainty are likely to flourish. There needs to be a thoughtful, prayerful resistance to such movements, if for no other reason than that the movement from false certainty to utter desolation and despair can be a very swift one.

4

Despair and Desolation

The long-term threat to social stability today arises less from those who feel unjustly treated as from those, essentially the young, who simply do not feel part of society at all. It is among such people that mass movements led by visionaries and dedicated to the destruction of the existing order, have historically found their strongest support.

SIR MICHAEL HOWARD, 1984

For is not everything dark as night for a country in distress?

ISAIAH 8:23

Throughout my ministry I have heard repeatedly the phrase, 'It all seems so hopeless' – but never with such frequency, or expressed with such passionate distress and sense of inevitability as in recent years. Ministry in hopeless situations and in communities which have lost hope will be a major part of the pastoral task in the twenty-first century. (See Chapter 10 for some of the pastoral implications of this.) It seems to me undeniable that there has been a massive increase in hopelessness, despair and insecurity among many, perhaps most, sections of society in Britain in recent years. There is hopelessness about job prospects, while insecurity has risen among those who are economically active. Nor is this sense an irrational one. The Organisation for Economic Co-operation and Development has claimed that the chances of prime-age male workers becoming unemployed has risen in all major member-countries except the United States. For many people, the chances of ever entering into full-time employment are low, and for years now many young people have left schools without any hope that they will ever get a job. But this is not the whole story: there is also a loss of confidence in the ability of 'the system' to deliver the goods, a sense that things are falling apart.

I recently spent a weekend in Barnsley in South Yorkshire, where I visited Grimethorpe, a community which had been utterly dependent on its mine. Today, as the pit lies derelict and unused, and as unemployment stands at 95 per cent in some districts, the devastation is horrifying, with whole rows of houses vandalised, burnt out, or abandoned. The sense of being a community without future is palpable. Not surprisingly there has been a 300 per cent increase in heroin use in Barnsley between 1992 and 1995.[1] But Grimethorpe does not stand alone, and it is likely that we will see more and more British towns in conditions which resemble parts of Belfast. If we substitute 'docks' for 'pits' we have East London, and if we substitute 'cars' we have Detroit. Increasingly we are seeing what we have leant to call 'Third World conditions' in the towns and cities of the West. One of the best-known statistics is that which tells us that life-expectancy in Harlem, New York, is lower than that in Bangladesh.

Of course, it is argued, we are now a 'network society' and have moved beyond the industrial age.[2] Our major social institutions are being reorganised in network form with indefinite boundaries. The new post-industrial order, however, still depends on manufacturing, though the nature of the manufacturing process has changed. However, both nationally and internationally, the digital revolution and the spread of information technology, while it has offered access to 'information' to a wide range of people, has both reinforced and strengthened the inequalities in society. It has been claimed cynically that all that computers have done for the Third World is to document their decline more efficiently.

The shift to despair

The intricate relationship between the structural and the personal is brought out in this crisis, as more people experience depression. While depression is often associated directly and exclusively with personal distress, my experience leads me to the belief that depression is increasingly a social, and rational, response to the conflicts and upheavals within the culture. The absence of hope has corporate and even cosmic dimensions. The American psychoanalyst James Hillman has argued that the depressed person carries the repressed part of the culture, and that in a sense faithfulness to the depression has major political and cultural consequences. Certainly, more and more people seem to be suffering from depression, and it was responsible for 6,454 suicides in the UK in 1994. But what I am seeing more and more is a sense of corporate depression, a dark night of communities, or rather, of environmental entities which are euphemistically termed communities but where all cohesion, energy and hope for the future has been drained away.

So I see a widespread shift towards nihilism and despair. Some will say that there is nothing new in this. Certainly the idea of an age marked by meaninglessness and loss of vision is not new. George Orwell in the 1930s wrote about a civilisation in decay, a dead world. Writers in the 1940s and 1950s commented on the exhaustion and depression within the culture, and on the disillusionment with mass movements. In 1956 Alasdair MacIntyre described our society as 'a society without a metaphysics', and our age as one marked by a combination of liberal morality and metaphysical meaninglessness, while three decades later Sean Desmond Healy wrote of the growing metaphysical void at the centre of Western cultural life.[3] In the 1970s American culture was described as a culture at breaking-point.[4] Such ideas of emptiness, void, and loss of meaning are particularly common as people approach the *fin de siècle*, and there is a sense of being in the death-throes of a diseased or exhausted culture.[5] Associated with this sense of loss, collapse and emptiness is a prevailing sense of boredom – indeed, some writers have argued that boredom is central to the culture. The fact that people think this is so, and write about it, does not, of course, mean that it is so. Nevertheless, the belief and feeling that Western culture is a culture of meaninglessness and emptiness has now been around for a long time, and it needs to be taken very seriously indeed.

Again, we are told that we have become a culture of nihilism. Now nihilism is not new either. But there is something different about the nihilism of today. There was an older nihilistic tradition – that of Nietzsche, of de Sade or William Burroughs – which was an adversarial movement, a cry of outrage, a passionate polemic. Today's nihilism is more an expression of covetousness, lust, hedonism, and, increasingly, of chaotic and desperate rage. Take the film *Leaving Las Vegas*, a film dominated by the imagery of alcoholism, violence, and gang rape, including the rape of the hooker Sera. Michiko Kakutam wrote of what he termed the 'designer nihilism' exemplified by the film.

> Forty years ago Doris Day's rendition of 'Que Sera Sera' won an Oscar for Best Song – a soppy signature-tune for an era that tried to ignore the dark side of life. Today folks are flocking to see a woman called Sera – the heroine of a movie that has turned that dark side into a phony yuppie fashion.[6]

Nihilism is not just a philosophical doctrine or cultural literary style. It is a way of coping with hopelessness, loss of love, loss of point. My perception of the 1990s is that the culture of covetousness and of organised selfishness which was so carefully cultivated in the Reagan–Thatcher years has given way to a widespread sense of cynicism, paralysis and uncertainty. From time to time – and, in coming years, perhaps more and more – it expresses itself in the 'politics of rage'. Most of the time it shows itself in the retreat from conventional politics, and in the loss of trust in both the process and the people, loss of trust in politicians themselves being most pronounced. The increase in distrust of, and disenchantment with, politics, combined with the general collapse of any sense of a hopeful alternative to the present chaos, is extremely dangerous, and has already resulted in considerable social and moral breakdown.

There are no easy solutions to something which has been building up over many years. Nihilism is a disease of the soul and cannot be overcome by argument, only by love and care. But does the Church really understand what is going on? My sense is that many clergy, and many lay Christians, come from precisely those groups in society who have never faced despair, and have somehow managed to avoid the upheaval which the existential crisis of meaninglessness and hopelessness brings to individuals and communities. They are the very people who will not understand how to respond. Yet I hope that there will be some in the Churches who have faced the darkness of nihilism, and who have encountered it with radical faith. For them there is a major task as we enter the twenty-first century.

The sense of hopelessness has affected young people in particular. We are no longer talking about a minority whose 'problem' can be seen in terms of personal or family pathology; rather, the language has shifted to that of social breakdown. It is worth considering, as one facet of this change, the shifting patterns of intravenous drug abuse since the early 1960s.

Drug abuse: the changing patterns

I have been involved with problems of drug use by young people since the early 1960s. For about five years, drug-related issues took up most of my pastoral ministry, in the Soho district of London. Today I chair the Maze Project, a small drug-prevention project, based in Bethnal Green, which, like most voluntary projects, struggles for survival within the sea of rhetoric about the importance of preventive work. At the time of writing, we are in serious danger of collapse – yet our local drug problem is more serious than I have ever known it since I first got involved with drugs issues here in 1963. Many people are now waking up to the need for drug-prevention work. But such work has been going on for years, and more would have been done if the voluntary agencies had been properly funded to do it.

Our situation could be repeated in many urban and rural parts of Britain. (It is important to stress that serious drug problems are now also common in rural communities, in small market towns and villages.) Many agencies and disciplines are involved at the level of treatment, support and help for established addicts. My concern – which I have been stressing in talks, letters and articles since, at least, 1964 – is primarily with helping young people not to get to that stage, with prevention not cure, with education and help at an early stage. The problems are in our midst, and so are many excellent youth workers, but we cannot do the urgent work unless we are given the funds. Yet in December 1996 the East London and City Health Authority decided to cut the funding of projects working on primary drug prevention and youth counselling. They are typical of many authorities throughout the country, and they are storing up far more serious problems for themselves in the future. If this work does not occur, we will be spending billions on treatment, much of which will be wasted. Yet who will say this, openly and publicly? Most workers in the statutory, and often the voluntary, sector are sworn to silence for fear of funding cuts. It is a terrible, immoral and ominous situation. At least nobody can stop priests and pastors from speaking out. But most of the time priests and pastors do not notice.

It is, of course, cheering that, after 30 years or more, the government has finally come round to a recognition of the importance of preventive work. How much this is due to persistent and exhausting pressure from the voluntary sector, and how much to the fact that increasingly their own children and friends are affected, is hard to tell. But it is far too late now to prevent the escalation of serious drug problems which has occurred over these years, and so much outreach work now, and for the foreseeable future, is bound to be in the area of picking up the pieces, casualty work, 'crisis intervention'. I believe that the Churches will have to play a major role in this casualty area. It needs to be done, and I have no doubt that it will be done – and yet it could deflect them into being no more than what Tony Benn once called an intensive care ward for capitalism.

I do not believe that drug misuse will go away or that it is possible to find 'answers' or 'cures' to the reliance on psychochemicals in isolation from the wider malaise of which their use is symptomatic. Nor do I believe that responses which deny the enormous value of chemicals in improving human life and treating illness are commendable or Christian. It is possible, however, to help young people to distinguish between substances, to pursue forms of controlled use which will keep serious harm at a minimum, and to create structures of care, support and solidarity which will in time make reliance on chemical 'solutions' less appealing. I will return to this, for it will be one of the most pressing problems facing Churches and others in the next century.

Looking back at one's own previous life can be a depressing as well as an illuminating experience. Around 30 years ago, I wrote a number of letters on the subject of the developing British drug culture which were given prominent position in *The Times*.[7] One letter, which appeared on 9 November 1966, the first anniversary of the Second Brain Report, is worthy of reflection over 30 years afterwards. The Brain Committee had been set up by the government to examine the treatment of heroin and cocaine addiction in the light of recent increases, and its report appeared in 1965. In my letter I made a number of predictions, all of which have been fulfilled.

I asked the question: What has happened since the report? At one level, the answer was 'Nothing at all'. There had been a good deal of talk and an increase in writing about drug abuse. Treatment facilities remained inadequate, and no action had been taken as a result of the report's recommendations. There had been a statement about treatment centres by the Minister of Health in the House of Commons on 2 August 1966. 'There are already centres for the treatment of drug addiction', he claimed, 'and more beds could be made available if the demand increases'.[8] I was puzzled by this statement and wrote for clarification to the Ministry of Health, who replied saying that the Minister 'was not referring to any action that had been taken following the Second Report of the Brain Committee', but rather to some 'specialised units' which had existed for some time.[9]

In my letter in *The Times* I said that the Minister's statement had been received by workers in the field with 'cynical laughter or with despair'. I described our experience:

Those who daily face the problems of the young drug-taker are finding the obstacles almost insurmountable: hours and days spent ringing round hospitals for admissions; refusals, evasions and interminable delays; addicts whose condition deteriorates and parents whose hearts are broken; doctors who refuse to prescribe, and doctors who prescribe with almost criminal irresponsibility; and an overwhelming sense of hopelessness and despair among those who know the drug scene closest.

I went on to identify three areas where there had been significant changes during that significant year of 1966. First, the increased resistance of GPs to prescribe heroin and cocaine for addicts, even under carefully controlled conditions. From the end of the 1950s there had been a small group of general practitioners, known as the 'junkies' doctors', who had played a critical role in the management of addiction in Britain.[10] Although they had a bad press, and were undoubtedly a mixed blessing, they did help to keep the criminal market at bay and the 'grey' market under control. But by 1966 the number of doctors willing to take on addict patients was diminishing. This was hardly surprising since, not unlike today's situation, there was considerable official prejudice, hostility and venom directed against them.

The second change had been the escalation of the illicit market, itself in part the result of the withdrawal of the doctors. The 1965 report from the Home Office to the United Nations had noted 'the significant increase ... in the numbers of addicts who have obtained their drugs entirely from unknown sources'.[11] This was a more significant statement than perhaps even the authors realised, for by 1966 there was evidence that criminal syndicates had moved in on the heroin market. I lived within a few yards of Gerrard Street in Soho during these years, and saw the entry of the Chinese Triads into the traffic. Ironically, the first reliable news report noting the arrival of illegally imported heroin appeared in *The Times* on 26 March 1969, and its author was Norman Fowler, later to have some responsibility in this area in the government. But powder heroin had begun to appear as early as 1966.

Thirdly, there had been, during 1966, a shift in the character of the drug subculture itself, and this was to change even more dramatically during the Methedrine ('speed') crisis of 1968.

While E. M. Schur in 1963 had noted the total absence of any addict subculture in Britain, and David Downes in a study published in 1966 (though based on research from 1960) claimed that drugs played a negligible role in urban working-class delinquency,[12] by 1966 both these claims were being falsified. The division between the kids on the pep pill fringe and the intravenous users was becoming blurred, and the addict subculture was spreading to embrace a wider range of young people. Again, while 1968 was the major year of change in terms of the spread of intravenous drug use, the process was well under way by 1966.

I ended my letter with these words:

> The situation can be exaggerated and distorted, but it is serious enough. What is to be feared is that official reaction will be repressive and negative. So far the results of the Brain report have been almost entirely negative and bad. Since Brain, the situation has got worse, not better. And, perhaps most frightening of all, is the fact that many of our best workers in the areas of infection are coming to feel that they are banging their heads against a brick wall. Paralysis, like addiction itself, grows like a cancer, and destroys.

Could any of this have been avoided? Was our heroin problem necessary? It is difficult to be certain 30 years on, but my suspicion is that, had there been encouragement rather than calumny towards doctors who were willing to treat addict patients, both the concentration of prescribing in the hands of such a small number and the reluctance of most GPs to have anything to do with addicts, could have been avoided. There was certainly a direct relationship between the rapid reduction in heroin prescribing and the escalation of the criminal market. What happened was predictable, and was indeed predicted.

But the most dramatic change has been in the whole economic and political climate, the environment of the growing drug culture. Just as the inventor of the glazed ceramic sewage-pipe did more for the health of nineteenth-century London than all the charitable endeavours of dedicated social workers, so the spread of the drug economy is more likely to be halted or controlled by changes way beyond the field of drug use. But we cannot ignore the damage done by ill-conceived policy changes. Whereas in the 1950s, the pattern of addiction in

Britain was the reverse of that in the USA, by the 1980s we were moving more and more in an American direction: not only in the increasing correlation between addiction and high unemployment, poverty and youth hopelessness, but also in the unintelligent following of American approaches to many areas of urban policy and penal affairs. It could be said that Britain has followed American practice in the field of drug abuse in all those areas where the Americans have most conspicuously failed.

Governments never apologise, so it is left to the voluntary agencies to point out that many of the disasters of the last few decades could have been avoided, and that much of the mess that we now deal with – not least the escalation of the criminal market in heroin and cocaine – is the direct result of ill-thought-out policy.

Replying to my letter of 9 November, that remarkable London GP, the late Dr A. J. Hawes, in *The Times* of 15 November 1966, made the same point in a more direct way.

> The most threatening portent is that addicts are telling me that there is plenty of the stuff to be had on the black market even though the source from over-prescribing doctors is drying up. It looks as if big business, which has been waiting in the wings for so long has now taken over the stage and is playing the lead. So we may look for an explosion in the teenage addict population as the months go by. One can only write to the press, which most of us 'junkies' doctors' are always doing. What else can pull the public ostrich head out of the sand? It could never happen to my children! Oh, couldn't it? Just wait.

In the 1950s and 1960s, and for some time beyond, it was possible, and even common, to see drug addiction in terms of the personal psychological problems of the individual addict – but what has happened on a massive scale since then is that heroin and cocaine, and other substances, have become common currency within depressed and devastated communities. Increasingly, addiction is correlated with high unemployment, deprivation, and social breakdown. Increasingly the criminal syndicates have taken over the market. And increasingly the addicts are becoming more and more 'normal', more and more like everybody else. Heroin has classically been the drug of despair among the youth of urban

96

society, the ghetto drug, the powerful analgesic that kills both physical and mental pain, even the pain of a futureless community.

Drug use exists throughout the class structure. For many years in Britain heroin and cocaine were the drugs of the upper classes and the aristocracy. Today there is still considerable serious drug use (including alcohol) in the City of London, among company directors, and among the hangers-on of the monarchy and the nobility. There are serious problems here. But my experience is among poor people, and it is here that drug use is spreading in the context of unemployment and an alternative criminal economy. It is here that we see young people without hope turning to drug-dealing as at least a way to manage. It is here that we see despair seeking chemical solutions. It is here that we see how poverty corrupts good people.

But poverty is indivisible, and it is important that the Church in the twenty-first century sees its response to poverty as a gospel imperative. Already, the work of groups in Britain like Church Action on Poverty has been extremely effective, but this needs to be expanded and developed in the coming years.

Poverty and persons

It is impossible, as R. H. Tawney saw, to deal with poverty apart from wealth. What thoughtful rich people call the problem of poverty, he noted, thoughtful poor people call the problem of riches.[13] Today, on a world scale, the wealth of some 338 billionaires is greater than the combined incomes of countries with 45 per cent of the world's population. The World Bank's approach to 'structural adjustment' makes the situation worse, while free trade based on authoritarianism and central control imposes a monoculture on the Third World.[14] The seriousness of the global food crisis has still not penetrated to many people in the West, though now the World Bank recognises that world food-stocks are dangerously low and that over 800 million people do not get adequate food to meet their basic needs. What is true on a global scale is repeated within countries. In the USA 10 per cent of households hold 70 per cent of the country's wealth. The conditions of the poor in American cities is terrible. Under the recent welfare 'reforms' implemented by President Clinton, it is likely that an additional million children will be pushed into poverty.

It would be insulting to my readers to develop at length the fact that there has been a massive increase in poverty in Britain in recent years. That reality is beyond dispute, in spite of the specious attempts by government ministers from time to time to question the data. Indeed no intelligent person who is not a government minister, or one of their paid lackeys, would question it. The growth of poverty has been thoroughly documented, and only a broad summary of published research data can be attempted here.[15] Undoubtedly the coming to power of the Thatcher government in 1979, and its commitment to the redistribution of wealth in favour of the rich and the better-off, was a turning-point. Between 1979 and 1983 the numbers of people living on or below the Supplementary Benefit level rose from 6.1 million to 8.9 million. By 1986 it was estimated that around 18 million persons were living in poverty. The numbers of very poor people increased in Britain during the years 1980–5 faster than in any other European country. In 1991–2 it was estimated that 13.9 million people (25 per cent of the population) earned below half of the average income. Families living below the poverty-line grew from 14.3 to 17.2 per cent between 1983 and 1993.[16] By 1996 it was estimated that one in three children in Britain was born in poverty.

With the increase in people living in poverty has come a sharpening of disparities between rich and poor, and between wealthy and poor neighbourhoods. Today the gap between rich and poor is higher than at any time since 1886 when records began. In 1989, 1 per cent of people owned 18 per cent of marketable wealth. Unfortunately many of the changes in conditions brought about in the Thatcher years are irreversible. Social divisions have stiffened, and class differentials have reappeared in sharper forms. What are the implications of these developments for the Christian Churches in the next century? The worst scenario – but I fear a likely one – is that the Churches will ignore poor people and will look rather to the affluent suburban middle class as a more likely source of custom. We have learnt many wrong lessons from Uncle Sam, and this is certain to be another one.

Poverty and health

The question of poverty raises the related problem of health. Research has shown the strong links between income and health. Health-care in Britain was at its least unequal in 1951, but equalities have been increasing since then. As the gaps between communities have grown wider, so the incidence of ill-health has increased. It is clear that the more equality and cohesion there is, the more likely it is that the population will be healthy.[17] The Christian Church is concerned with health, wholeness, fulness of life – all of them parts of the meaning of the word 'salvation'. The struggle for equality of health, for just health-care, and for the ending of the present injustice will be a major part of the Church's task in the coming years.

Let me return to my home territory of Tower Hamlets, the heart of London's East End. In terms of multiple deprivation, of the ten most deprived wards in London, six were in Tower Hamlets. Thus in Spitalfields Ward, at the time of the 1991 census, unemployment stood at 32.5 per cent and over-crowding at 29.8 per cent, while people not owning their own home was 83.8 per cent in St Dunstan's Ward, 82.2 per cent in Weavers Ward, and 81.9 per cent in Spitalfields Ward.[18] Using the government's Index of Local Conditions, Tower Hamlets ranks as the fifth most deprived borough in London, and the seventh in England. However, on the basis of smaller-scale research, when ward scores are aggregated to borough levels, Tower Hamlets becomes the most deprived borough in England. All wards in the borough have higher levels of deprivation than most wards in England.

As a theologian working in these neighbourhoods, I find it constantly being driven home to me that the material circumstances of life are integral elements in the dignity of persons made in God's image. There is an old Anglican maxim, attributed to various people including Henry Scott Holland and Father Dolling, which locates a concern with drainage within the framework of the theology of the incarnation. That maxim comes from the nineteenth century. I am aware that in many districts of Britain, Dickensian conditions and diseases are returning. So in the East End, problems of damp housing are very serious. Health visitors report high incidences of tuberculosis: TB notifications here are seven times the national rates. Living in the most overcrowded ward in the UK, I see the problems of poverty and deprivation in a most acute form – although in many respects, other parts of Britain are far worse off than London. I see no evidence that conditions here, and in similar areas elsewhere, are likely to improve, and this must raise major questions about the Church's pastoral, prophetic and political role in the coming years.

As usual, the East End of London is a microcosm of the country as a whole. We are seeing a 'hardening of class inequality' as we move towards the twenty-first century.[19] As the benefit safety-net has unravelled, questions around nutrition have again assumed great urgency. Work by the Low Income Project Team of the government has confirmed what those in poor areas already knew, the fact that there are serious problems of inadequate food and consequent ill-health. According to a recent survey by the School Milk Campaign, the deregulation of school meals has led to poorer nutrition and poor growth rates.

The 'disposable poor'?

As I look towards the future, one of the most horrifying prospects is of a whole section of humanity being consigned to a state of uselessness, being treated in effect as refuse. Again, what we are seeing in Britain is an aspect of a global problem. It is estimated by the International Labour Office that throughout the world some 800 million people are underemployed. Ian Angell, Professor of Information Systems at the London School of Economics, sums up my fears in a disturbing way.

> We are entering an age of hopelessness, an age of resentment, an age of rage. Whole sections of society who previously felt their future secure can see it slipping away. Dissent is fermenting, and normally law-abiding citizens, who have nothing to lose, are being sucked into a culture of protest and crime.[20]

It is of the utmost urgency that the roots of gross inequalities of wealth and poverty are tackled as the twenty-first century dawns. If they are not, not only will there be social upheaval on a scale hitherto unheard of, but the corrupting power of this dehumanising process will have disastrous effects on rich and poor alike. But this raises a major question which I do not think the Churches are willing to face: can this be done within the framework of capitalism?

The Churches have a long record of concern for 'the poor'. They have done good to 'the poor'. They have fed and clothed 'the poor'. They have campaigned on behalf of 'the poor'. They have been advocates for 'the poor'. But 'the poor' have always remained 'out there'. The well-used term 'out there' is a significant one, and has become part of the jargon of the liberal intelligentsia. It implies a population who exist somewhere else, for whom the jargon-users, be they Church or journalists, have care and concern. And this does actually sum up the situation accurately. The relationship between the Church and poor people has mainly been an 'I–It' relationship. This is more than a semantic quibble, indeed it is becoming more serious as the years go by. We are increasingly labelling whole sections of society by use of terms such as 'the poor', 'the underclass', and so on. It is a dehumanising mechanism with built-in elements of condescension and at times contempt. It destroys human relationships and encourages the worst kind of paternalism.

The 'underclass' debate

This brings me to the current 'underclass' rhetoric. In recent years the debate on poverty has taken a new twist through the popularising of the term 'underclass'. No Christian social ethic or pastoral praxis for the twenty-first century can ignore the developments to which this concept refers, and I want both to outline its main features and to raise some warnings about the continued use of the term. It has become a common usage among sections of the population who rarely see eye to eye: I feel that, when a term is used by Shirley Williams and Peregrine Worsthorne, Cornel West and Ray Honeyford, A. Sivanandan and Charles Murray, Peter Hall, David Duke and Robert Moore, it is right to raise some questions about it. More seriously, I think the term has some substantial conceptual difficulties and I hope to give attention to these.

The antecedents of underclass discourse lie in the rhetoric of 'the mob', in the anti-Irish polemic of the nineteenth century, the myth of 'the great unwashed', the unregenerate, the depraved. Charles Booth wrote of 'a large class who must be regarded as outcasts', and the term 'outcast London' became common after the appearance of *The Bitter Cry of Outcast London* in 1883. Marx spoke of the 'lumpen', while John Bright's term 'the residuum', which he first used in a debate on parliamentary representation in 1867, was taken up by Booth.

In the late nineteenth century, this kind of rhetoric acquired more directly anti-immigrant facets with the warnings of 'criminal aliens', while the eugenics movement raised the spectre of degeneration, a theme which was to dominate much writing in this period. *The Times*, on 6 February 1886, spoke of those who had 'fallen out of the ranks of respectable society'. In 1904 the Interdepartmental Committee on Physical Deterioration warned of 'an undesirable class . . . steeped in every kind of degradation and cynically indifferent to the vile surroundings engendered by their filthy habits, and to the pollution of the young brought up in such an atmosphere'.

All this is part of the prehistory of the current underclass debate. The actual term 'underclass' was first used by Gunnar Myrdal in 1964, but seems not to have been picked up for some time. Today it is used by thinkers of left and right, by academics and by popular journalists. In the USA, where the term is used virtually exclusively about poor Black people in urban ghetto districts, there is now a whole industry of writing and research around this theme. Two main figures have captured media attention – Charles Murray of the American Enterprise Institute in Washington DC, and William Julius Wilson, formerly of the University of Chicago. Both recognise a serious problem in the existence of an urban underclass, but while Murray stresses the damage done by welfare, the creation of a dependency culture, and the moral irresponsibility of single parents, Wilson lays more stress on the need for economic restructuring, and his recent work has been concerned with the disappearance of regular employment. While Murray has reverted to nineteenth-century language, and speaks of a 'new rabble', Wilson looks less to moral degeneracy than to social isolation, the shifts in the urban economy, and the social incoherence and moral disorganisation of the ghetto culture.

Use of underclass language in Britain goes back to John Rex's work in the Midlands in the 1970s. Writing in 1979, Rex defined the underclass as a class which was cut off from the main class-structures of society, not only in quantitative terms but also in structural and qualitative terms. As such it could not simply be seen as an underprivileged part of the British labour movement.[21] Rex's former colleague Robert Moore devoted the whole of his inaugural lecture as Professor of Sociology at Liverpool University to the idea of an underclass, finding it a useful concept.[22] In Britain, underclass writing has also come from writers such as Ralf Dahrendorf and Frank Field (who, basing his work on experience in Birkenhead, makes no reference to Black people).

These writers have in common a concern with poverty, low pay, unemployment, and the conditions of the urban society. They tend also to associate the underclass with crime, especially violence and drug use, single mothers, welfare dependency, Black males (though this is not true of Field), and the fact that the underclass condition is permanent.

Criticism of the term has come from Ruth Lister – who sees it as imprecise, emotive and value-laden, and believes that its use is likely to weaken the claims of poor people to citizenship – and from Bea Campbell who sees it as a way of attacking single mothers. In the USA the sociologist Herbert Gans has made some sharp criticisms, to which I will return below. I believe that there are some valuable insights in much of the writing about an underclass, including one which is of abiding importance. It does convey, and does not seek to play down, the sense of hopelessness and corporate despair. This certainly tallies with my own work among heroin and cocaine addicts and dealers, where one sees a strong combination of enterprise and nihilism, an oscillation between energy and lethargy, a survival culture and a kind of lumpen Nietzschianism.

However, I wish to express my unease with the rhetoric of the underclass and to issue some warnings to the Church not to accept it without reservation. Indeed I believe that its uncritical acceptance by sections of academia and the media is disturbing and unhelpful for at least four reasons.

1. Its use is imprecise and conceptually sloppy, and encourages the notion of an undifferentiated and homogeneous society of cultural poverty, instead of a range of groups and individuals with overlapping needs and problems – as well as potential. Its use for social policy is extremely limited, as Gans has shown. Gans argues that the term is dangerous as a planning concept, and gives ten reasons why it should not be used. They include

its flexible character, its function as a stereotype, its tendency
to interfere with anti-poverty policies by focusing on aspects
such as mental illness rather than the central issues of poverty.
But he also believes that it is a buzz word with moralistic
overtones, that it is racially coded, and that it has a sinister
tendency to expand its meaning according to convenience. It
is a stereotype or label which reduces both self-respect and
clarity of thought.

I find myself very much in agreement with Gans. Having
analysed the uses of the term in the British media since it
became popular, I have found it used about poor Black men
in ghetto districts, about poor white youth in the north of
England, about vagrant alcoholics, one-parent families, the
long-term unemployed, the elderly, homosexuals, skinhead
attackers of homosexuals, European migrant workers, young
beggars, drug addicts, and members of Fascist youth movements. Can such a slippery and all-embracing concept really
be of use to us?

2. There is no doubt that the underclass notion is being used
by neo-conservative ideologues to resuscitate the centuries-old
theme of a cancerous and dangerous mass of poor people, an
outcast group which eats away at the fabric of civilised society.
The 'Black underclass' in particular is seen as the new form of
the undeserving poor who are associated with crime, drug
addiction, teenage pregnancies and female-headed families,
and who are largely dispirited and disenfranchised. It is the
presence of such people that makes an area 'bad'. 'I see you
live in a bad area', said the taxi-driver when he drove me into
47th Street in Chicago. What provoked his comment was not
the structure of the buildings but the presence of Black people
in the street. Such usage obscures the diversity within Black
communities, as well as the immense variations between urban
neighbourhoods.

3. I believe that the idea of an underclass obscures the need
for serious attention to class as an analytic tool. Ironically it is
in the USA, where there is no serious attention to class-struc-
ture and virtually no class analysis, that we now have discovered
one class – the underclass. In fact, in both countries race and
class are intertwined in more complex and subtle ways than
allowed for by this concept.

4. My main objection to underclass language is that it is loaded with contempt and with the philosophy of abandonment. The underclass are seen as riff-raff, scum, beyond redemption – along with certain neighbourhoods where 'they' live. And the reinforcement of such attitudes can become internalised, as Fanon showed, and become a self-fulfilling prophecy. While for many on the right, the urban poor have no future and simply have to be controlled, walled off, so that they do not contaminate civil society, for many on the left the urban poor are a political embarrassment. They have no direct relationship to the means of production. And while the white poor may be a recruiting ground for Fascist activities, the Black poor are just a mystery in political – particularly electoral – terms. The Labour Party, at least at the official level, seems more concerned with cultivating the middle-class vote, and can no longer be regarded as a movement of poor people. Yet this is in part one of the effects of creating a form of labelling which makes people the objects of rhetoric, polemic, even 'concern' rather than the subjects of creative agency and action. It is a dangerously unhealthy basis for a social agenda which is meant to represent poor and oppressed people.[23]

The rhetoric of the underclass seems to me to be part of a return to the attitudes of a previous era. Of course there have been many improvements in the lives of poor people, but I fear we are in some areas experiencing a return to Victorian (and pre-Victorian) conditions without Victorian concern. I see this, for example, in the field which takes up so much time at St Botolph's, the field of homelessness. Here, the revival of the concept of 'Victorian values' is not only rooted in historical ignorance but is deeply insulting to many Victorians whose sense of outrage, compassion and social responsibility stands in stark contrast to the cruelty and coldness of today's market.

What is particularly sad is that key figures – government ministers, members of the Royal Family, and sometimes bishops – have colluded with popular prejudice and ignorance, and therefore helped to reinforce them. The style of rhetoric is fairly easy to summarise, and has three major features. First, it lectures from afar. We are being told about begging or poverty by those who do not experience them. Secondly, it oversimplifies complex issues with a combination of arrogance and glibness, a style of delivery which is staggering in its lack of self-awareness and self-scrutiny, and which appeals to a mood of gut populism. Thirdly, it colludes with a national mood of complacency and of blaming victims. In a sense, one expects politicians to reinforce stereotypes and illusions, and to appeal to the kind of prejudice that will be electorally advantageous. There has been plenty of this in the career, for example, of Michael Howard, the Home Secretary in John Major's government.

However, Prince Charles's concern about the inner city and inter-faith relations, and Princess Diana's commitment to the work of Centrepoint among young homeless or to the care of people with HIV and AIDS, stand as something of a corrective to government attitudes. So it was sad to find the Duke of Edinburgh, in a speech to the Charities Aid Foundation in June 1994, playing into the hands of the complacent and the callous. There was no 'absolute poverty' in Britain, he claimed, no one was starving in the streets, and the welfare state offered a safety-net. In fact, over 600 people had died on the streets in the previous year, while high unemployment combined with tax and benefit changes had left many people in desperate poverty. The use of the word 'absolute' was a classic evasive tactic. There is no such thing as 'absolute poverty' anywhere; all poverty is relative to the conditions of place and time. The duke could have used his privileged position to arouse consciences and awaken outrage. Instead, he went along with the conventional response to poverty. So while there was some truth in his comments on 'absolute poverty' (when looked at from Africa or India, for example), the overall effect of his intervention, in its context, was utterly appalling, and his simplistic view of poor people was absolute nonsense.

What do I mean by 'the conventional response'? I see it as marked by five characteristics which Churches need to examine and critique very strongly.

1. The view that poverty is not connected with wealth. Tawney's comment – that what thoughtful rich people call the problem of poverty is what thoughtful poor people call the problem of riches – has been forgotten. Today, poverty has become severed from justice, and is seen as an accidental oversight, an unfortunate occurrence, rather than an inevitable result of certain approaches to, and understandings of, social and economic life.

2. The view that the poor are poor through their own intrinsic defects. Poverty is seen in terms of personal pathology, an approach which one associates with Sir Keith Joseph's infamous 'remoralisation' speech of 1974, and numerous speeches since then. So now we are told that homeless people enjoy being on the street.

3. The view that it is the Church's task to care for the poor but not to raise questions about why they are poor. (It could be added, the view that it is the government's task to ensure that there are enough poor people for the Church to care for!) This has already led to a new version of the soup kitchen, food pantry, elastoplast role for Churches. It is vital that they do not accept it as an adequate model of Christian practice.

4. The view that the poor are not actually doing too badly anyway, that they share in the rising prosperity of the population. By a clever use of general statistical observations, detached from their context, the impression is given that poverty is not a serious problem, and its elimination is only a matter of time. This, more than anything, leads to what has been called 'a nation in denial',[24] and once this process of denial has really set in, it perpetuates itself.

5. The view that, at the end of the day, poor people do not matter very much. If individuals are valued as consumers, customers and units of labour, but not as persons, then people who do not fit these labels, no longer count. Thus dies the human future.

The Churches' role?

The Churches in the twenty-first century will be in a crucial position to influence opinion, and to awaken hope. But 'hope is a piece of work, not a state of mind'.[25] The nurturing of hopeful commitment requires effort, prayer, struggle, and persistence. In their response to poverty and despair, the Churches need to reject the widespread assumption of a general goodwill, the idea that most people – including the government – are on the same side, and that, if only the evidence were presented, all would be well. *Faith in the City* seemed to assume this, and it may therefore be the last document of its kind. I have never believed it, and see it as one of the most fatal naïveties of the liberal tradition. The sooner we realise that people and groups have conflicting values and interests, the better.

The Churches in Britain on the whole are not marginal, not poor, not desperate. They hold a very privileged position, their voices are heard (though there is a selective deafness). But this situation is probably ending, and Churches in the next century are likely to become more marginal. They will need to earn the right to be heard by the intrinsic sense of what they say, and by their own integrity and credibility. This could be the salvation of the Churches, but we will need to develop new and far stronger forms of solidarity and sustenance. We are probably entering a new desert period, a dark time, in which our own ability to cope with despair and desolation will be tested and purified.

5

Spirituality and Narcissism

In our society, that feels at times so adrift from its moral, historical and institutional roots, I detect an increasing desire in people to find a spiritual home.

GEORGE CAREY, ARCHBISHOP OF CANTERBURY

Spirituality can simply become a search for the alternative feel-good factor or an escape into a purely personal pietism, wholly directed towards one's own self-fulfilment, and based largely on feeling and emotion. Darkness and evil are never very far from us, nor is the darker side of our human nature.

DAVID HOPE, ARCHBISHOP OF YORK

At various points during the late nineteenth and the twentieth centuries there have been periods of spiritual renewal, both inside and outside Christian and other 'mainstream' religious traditions. At the same time, there have been periods in which commentators have pointed to the lack of spiritual depth and insight, to a prevailing confusion and perhaps decadence. Often these two features – the appearance of movements of spiritual renewal and the identification of a spiritual malaise – have coincided. One group is worried, the other is excited, and no doubt a lot has depended on the point where one stands and the perspective from which one views the events and takes the temperature. Thus some Christian thinkers in the 1930s saw that period as one of spiritual decadence, while for others it was a time of immense spiritual striving. Thirty years later, there was a similar conflict over the significance of the movements of the 1960s. For some, the decade was dominated by promiscuity, drugs, rock music, anarchy and irresponsibility; while for others it was a time for seeing visions and dreaming dreams, a time of wonder, spiritual enlightenment and transcendence.

Spirituality and the 1960s

My view, looking back at the 1960s, is that it was an important epoch when those with eyes to see witnessed an amazing resurgence of concern about spiritual experience and spiritual renewal. It is a quarter of a century since I wrote a study of the youth counter-culture in Britain in the late 1960s.[1] Re-reading that text now, I am struck by the similarities to the present day, with how little has changed, and with the overwhelming evidence of continuities, as well as conflicts and upheavals, within the spiritual ferments and awakenings of the years since that formative period. Yet while there has been continuity, there has been a strengthening of some themes and a clear focusing on some areas which were in their infancy 30 years ago. That there was a real 'spiritual awakening'[2] in this period seems to me beyond doubt, and I am appalled at the lack of intelligence and perception among politicians, journalists and commentators who trivialise this period by slogan and cliché.[3]

It is essential to reclaim the 1960s as a time of progress – but we also need to move beyond it, building upon its insights and often half-digested approaches. So many seeds were sown in these years: it was a time of immense vision and creativity. Out of these years came much radical action, much of it of Christian origin. Shelter, the national campaign for the homeless, grew out of work done by the Notting Hill Social Council. Centrepoint, the emergency shelter for young people, was created at around the same time. Earlier the Simon Community had begun, inspired by the Catholic Worker movement in the USA. In the Church of England, these were the years when Michael Ramsey was Archbishop of Canterbury. Ramsey was perhaps the greatest spiritual leader among all archbishops of the twentieth century. More than any other Anglican figure, he constantly drew the Church back to prayer and spiritual discipline, and insisted that contemplative union with God was available to everyone. The Second Vatican Council, which has transformed the face of Western Christendom, occurred during these years. The Civil Rights Movement, under the leadership of Martin Luther King, provided both inspiration and long-term change. This was a seminal decade, and we are still working through its insights.

The 1960s was also a time when the idea of spirituality became popular, initially outside the Church. It was clear in the kind of songs which dominated the charts in these years. The teenage love-lyrics of the late 1950s gave way to Simon and Garfunkel, the Beatles and T. Rex with songs which reflected a concern for the deepest things in life. The movements of social protest, such as the anti-bomb movement, had also sparked off a wider search for new values and a new world. Bob Dylan embodied in his songs the move away from old-fashioned protest towards a concern for the inner world. Many young people in these years were seeking spiritual experience and transcendence, and were looking for it everywhere – except in the mainstream Churches.

The spiritual quest today

Today, as we approach the twenty-first century, 'spirituality' is in again with a vengeance. There is a lot of it about. It is a growth-area for the book trade. Nor is this now confined to non-Christians or to people outside the Churches. The Church has become *very* 'spiritual', often at the cost of abandoning its commitment to justice in the world. There is a resurgence of interest in prayer, devotion, techniques of meditation, ascetical practices, retreats and the 'inner life'. Yet, as in the 1960s, it seems that the majority of the young, and not so young, continue to seek their spiritual nourishment outside the mainstream Christian tradition.

Of course, institutions rise and fall, decay and are ruined, experience revival and transformation. Some become extinct, others survive in a condition of virtual extinction. The death of the Church of England in particular has been proclaimed regularly, and the cry 'Church in Danger' seems to have been heard several times in each recent century. Nevertheless, there does today seem to be a real 'dark night of our institutions' of a more serious kind, perhaps of a terminal kind. It is not necessarily to be identified with the collapse of all institutional life since, as mainstream religions decline, newer – and some older – institutional forms are being revived and renewed. Nor is there a simple correlation, as some have argued, between 'liberalism' and decline, or 'conservatism' and growth.

Yet one of the elements of continuity from the 1960s to the present has been the general decline of mainstream Christian institutions. In 1995 in Britain, while 60 per cent claimed to be Christian, only 14.4 per cent claimed to be church-members – a situation which has been described as 'believing without belonging'.[4] Of course, it is not a new experience for the Church of England. Its claim to be a truly national Church was questioned by Manning in the 1860s who pointed out that it contained only half of the English people. In fact, the position was worse than Manning believed. In 1851, 21 per cent of the English people went to the Church of England. By 1958, 67 per cent of the population had been baptised, but of these only 45 per cent were confirmed and 23 per cent of those confirmed received holy communion at Easter. Between 1960 and 1980 Easter communicants fell from 7 per cent to 4.7 per cent of the adult population. Some studies show increases, but only within the context of long-term decline. One survey suggested that on 15 October 1989 only 2.9 per cent of English people attended Anglican churches. Between 1975 and 1990 adult membership of the Church of England fell by 19 per cent. Though 46 per cent of the population claim to belong to the Church of England, on an average Sunday it has been claimed that only 2.4 per cent of people attend an Anglican church and less than 4 per cent attend at Easter.

There have been patterns of decline in the other mainstream denominations, the steepest being among Roman Catholics where the decline was 23 per cent. In fact, in Britain, the decline of the Roman Catholic Church has been most dramatic. Here, Sunday Mass attendance has fallen by 13 per cent since 1980, while seminaries admit fewer and fewer students, and defections from the priesthood continue to increase.[5]

One factor which is also clear is the continued and intensified drift of young people from mainstream Churches. Even where there has been evidence of growth, there has been little growth among teenagers, and rapid decline among those aged 20–30. The loss of young people in all the major denominations has been striking. Between 1987 and 1996, for example, the Church of England saw a drop of 34.9 per cent in attendance among 14- to 17-year-olds.[6]

It is easy to offer simple and one-dimensional reasons for the decline in the mainstream religions. Two world wars, the coming of the welfare state, increased migration and affluence, the impact of modern knowledge – these are all produced as explanations, and undoubtedly they all play a part. One important factor has been the disappearance of familiar reference points. The residual folk religion, so much prized by many Anglicans, is less strong today, and it is not clear if it can survive the disappearance or decline of stable, local residential communities. But from my experience of young people in particular (though not only the young), a major cause of decline is the sheer mediocrity and dullness of the religious life of the mainstream. Frankly it is boring. It opens no windows in the soul. Often its members exhibit no evidence of transformation or insight which might attract and draw people. As Nietzsche once observed, they do not *look* redeemed. It is not surprising that, for many years, our most creative minds have found it unattractive and devoid of life. Thus Samuel Beckett

113

gave up his faith on the grounds that, at the moment of crisis, it had no more depth than an old school tie; while Alan Bennett said that he could not enter the Christian community because its jollity, triviality and half-truths would deprive him of his power to write.

The mainstream religions seem to be marked by moderation, compromise and loss of confidence. However, it would be wrong to say that most of those who have moved away from them have moved towards fundamentalisms or forms of spirituality which seem to offer more direct experience of the divine. This is certainly part of the story. There has been massive growth not only in Eastern non-Christian traditions and what is often loosely termed 'New Age' spiritualities, but also in other forms of Christian presence – restorationist, charismatic, Black-led churches of African origin, mega-churches, non-denominational house churches, and so on. But it is clear from research in the USA (and I suspect that it is true here also) that the fastest-growing religious group is that of the unaffiliated – people who have abandoned the mainstream Churches, not for fundamentalism but for nothing.

Drugs and the spiritual quest

Since the 1960s at least, most young people have never been inside a church in the first place. Their quest of the spirit has always taken unorthodox routes. And in the main, these routes have followed the same lines as those I outlined in 1973. While the drug cultures (for there are a range of them, not one) have changed and expanded, for many young people they still remain a major form of ritual, ecstasy, and what must, without exaggeration, be called spiritual experience. The 'rave' is for many a new form of church, a place of 'ecstasy' – the choice of name for this most popular amphetamine derivative is not accidental – and of temporary transcendence of the conventional. Drugs seem to offer a way of losing oneself, of letting go, of experiencing that wildness and freedom, that sense of the 'beyond' which religion once offered.

Timothy Leary died in 1996. Today most young people and most drug users have never heard of him. But for some years

114

in the 1960s Leary was the guru of the spiritual quest through the use of drugs. It was he and his colleagues – along with the ex-Anglican priest turned Zen teacher Alan Watts – who placed the use of psychedelic (or mind-expanding) drugs firmly within a religious framework. Leary has been misrepresented a good deal by his critics: he never claimed that drugs were an automatic gateway to mystical experience. At the same time his claim was quite extreme: he saw the LSD trip as the classic visionary voyage, and believed that the levels to which LSD leads people are those which have been called the confrontation of God. The LSD trip was for Leary the contemporary form of mystical experience.

The claim that drugs can induce religious experience was not new. Benjamin Blood in 1874 and William James in 1902 had made the same claim about nitrous oxide. James believed that his experience with nitrous oxide had led to a kind of insight to which he ascribed metaphysical significance. The key aspect was reconciliation, the melting of opposites and contradictions. Later, Aldous Huxley made similar claims for the use of mescalin. Meanwhile, research had been continuing on a possible chemical basis for psychosis.

What was new about Leary was the centrality of LSD to his world-view, and his suggestion that what conventional psychiatry described as psychosis, and conventional religion saw as irresponsibility, might well be more accurately seen as the resurgence of the quest for mystical experience which both had suppressed. It was Leary too who located 'ecstasy' at the heart of politics.[7]

Within a few years of Leary's early work with psychedelics, the hippy culture was born in the Haight-Ashbury district of San Francisco. Haight-Ashbury was of critical importance for the spread of psychedelic drug use into a popular movement. A whole universal youth culture was created whose fruits are still with us. Out of Haight-Ashbury came the San Francisco sound, acid rock, and a musical tradition which shook and transformed American rock music, with groups like Jefferson Airplane and the Grateful Dead. But beneath the hair-styles, the music, the drugs, and the art forms was a movement of spiritual transformation. Charles Reich, in a work of some exaggeration, termed it 'the greening of America'.[8]

There have been two main ways of looking at the link between drug use and what was increasingly termed 'spirituality'. The first sees a straight causal connection: psychedelic drugs opened up human consciousness, broke through the doors of perception, and led directly to spirituality. It is certainly true that the ingestion of psychoactive chemicals can change, and has changed, the way in which human beings process data, see reality, and experience themselves and the universe. LSD and related drugs, in particular, can trigger a depth-charge into the unconscious, and all kinds of material are brought to the surface. It was the recognition that the human brain was capable of unlimited new dimensions of awareness and knowledge which was central to the spirituality of the drug culture. So there was much talk about a 'new consciousness' and about 'ego-transcendence'. Michael Hollingshead, the Englishman who introduced Leary to LSD, argued that we in the West were witnessing a change in the nature of human beings, and a shift towards a more mystical consciousness beyond the limitations of subject and object; while William Braden connected this with the 'death of God', the shift away from conventional theism.[9]

The second view, which I have always favoured, is cautious of too simplistic a connection between chemicals and enhanced consciousness. At best, chemicals can be an aid, just as fasting or breathing exercises can be an aid. I have never understood why, in principle, mind-altering chemicals should not be used in the context of the spiritual journey. However, I would interpret these developments in the 1960s by saying that there was a rebirth of spiritual need which, for a period, was sidetracked into the methods and techniques provided by materialistic technology, that is, chemicals. The 'psychedelic revolution', at one level, was no more than the application of the highly respectable 'better living through chemistry' thesis to the realm of the spirit. Or, as the Indian mystic Meher Baba put it in 1968, 'God in a pill'. Theodore Roszak was scathing in his critique of this reductionist model of the spiritual quest.

> The gadget-happy American has always been a figure of fun because of his facile assumption that there exists a technological solution to every human problem. It only took the great psychedelic crusade to perfect the absurdity by proclaiming that personal salvation and the social revolution can be packed into a capsule.[10]

So, while the pharmaceutical industry offered hypnotics and

minor tranquilisers for the treatment of sleeplessness and anxiety, Leary offered psilocybin and LSD for treatment of spiritual sickness and deprivation. From the perspective of pharmacology, Leary and the psychedelic crusade were the exact opposite of Dr William Sargent, the high priest of chlorpromazine (Largactil), who had argued that under chlorpromazine the patient should be more immune to the spell of religious revivalists.[11]

I have written extensively over the years about the relationship between drugs and the spiritual quest, and I do not wish to extend the discussion here. But it is necessary, in the climate of the 1990s, and as we move towards the year 2000, to emphasise that the range of chemicals available now is a good deal greater than in the 1960s, as is their geographical spread in terms of availability. In 1967 it was mainly middle-class dropouts who used LSD, while working-class communities were less affected; today, by contrast, many thousands of young people use drugs such as Ecstasy and the anaesthetic Ketamine in the belief that these will enable them to attain deeper levels of experience. We should not be surprised that many young people seek in drugs a way to those levels of transcendental experience which organised religion seems unable to provide. There are dangers, and they can be serious dangers – but for many people risk and danger are preferable to boredom and convention. Yet this seems a lesson which Churches are slow to learn.

The search for an authentic spirituality moved beyond the drug route many years ago. As early as 1968, Allan Cohen, who had worked with Leary at Harvard, was talking about the 'meta-hippy' quest, and the 'journey beyond trips'.[12] I worked with Cohen in the early 1970s. His argument was that the drug route to spirituality was the result of a culture which had come to see the solution to internal problems in the use of external agents. But, he argued, drugs simply did not work in terms of spiritual progress. His path from drugs to Eastern mysticism was one which was to be followed by many in the coming years.

These years have been marked by the rediscovery of some ancient paths – Zen, Sufi mysticism, pagan religion – and by the creation of new syncretisms in which diverse elements of a variety of spiritual traditions are mingled together, often haphazardly and promiscuously. So we have witnessed a renewed interest in schools of meditation, while bookshops offering approaches to spiritual awareness have multiplied around the country. It is clear that there is a widespread 'rediscovery of the sacred'.[13] While this has been most clearly documented in the USA, it is evident elsewhere. In the spiritualities of the 'New Age' we find a fusion of pantheism, gnosticism, and deep ecology. Most of these movements have antecedents, not only in the 1960s' counter-culture, but also in the theosophical and related movements of the late nineteenth century, in medieval cults, and in the gnostic movements of the ancient world. In 1892 W. B. Yeats said that the mystical life was the centre of all that he did, and he saw this as the advancing edge of an emerging mass-consciousness. So, later, did C. G. Jung who believed that the spiritual currents of his time had close affinity with gnosticism. The new seekers of the post-1967 generation have looked in many places for spiritual nourishment. But, with a few significant exceptions, they have bypassed the Christian tradition.

The attraction of the occult

One area which has increased tremendously is that of the occult and the various magical traditions. These have ranged from theosophical and esoteric approaches to consciousness, to contemporary forms of Satanism, black magic and witchcraft. Many conventional American young people, after entering the psychedelic drug culture, developed a magical belief-system. By the early 1970s there was evidence of a widespread interest in astrology and the occult, with an estimated 40 million people dabbling with astrology in the USA.[14] Since then, interest in the occult has spread way beyond the confines of the older cultic enclaves, and bookshops in most towns display vast amounts of material of this kind under the heading of 'spirituality'. Very little of the material is Christian, and one would have thought that this might have led some Christians to wonder why, or to raise questions about it. But this questioning does not seem to have occurred. Instead we see what Andrew Brown has called 'shelves of astrology, homeopathy for cats, the tomb of Jesus found in the Dordogne, or aromatherapy for dolphins'.[15]

Modern Satanism is linked with the figure of Aleister Crowley, and, more recently, with Anton La Vey who sees the Satanic Age as beginning in 1966. La Vey was a consultant to the influential film *Rosemary's Baby* in 1968. More recently, Satanism has grown in Germany: one estimate claims that one in four pupils in Berlin is involved with the occult. In the north-west Ruhr region, an area of high unemployment, it seems that unemployed young people in particular are attracted to Satanism and other forms of occultism.[16] Meanwhile, in the USA there has been an increase in interest in 'aliens'. In Florida, it is now possible to take out insurance policies against being kidnapped by aliens. According to *Newsweek*, 48 per cent of the population of the USA believe in UFOs.[17]

There is much sensational writing about this area, and an important task of the Church in the coming years will be to sift through the material and try to develop an approach which is serious and avoids hysteria. For example, it seems clear that most modern witches are middle-class professionals, not deranged psychopaths. It is not clear that Satanism is directly linked with child sexual abuse – although there is no doubt that some element of ritual plays a role in some cases. It is not clear that black magic in the strict sense occurs much at all, not least because, for its efficacy, it requires a priest in valid orders who has been 'unfrocked'. All these claims need to be examined, scrutinised, and not accepted without great care. Many of the claims made by Christians lack any real statistical basis. For example, Billy Graham was quoted in 1971 as saying that 80 per cent of young people in Britain had been in touch with a witch or a wizard![18]

A major factor here is that the area of the occult and the demonic seems to have an unhealthy attraction for some Christians, who become obsessed with it and deranged by it. The recent history of exorcism is full of examples of this, and points to the need for spiritual stability, rootedness and immense care. So it is not surprising that, with the recent revival of the occult, we have seen also the revival of crude forms of opposition to it. By 1993 many fundamentalist Christians no longer saw the Soviet Union as the enemy, but rather the Devil. The influence of works such as Frank Peretti's novel *This Present Darkness* has not been healthy and has helped to damage the credibility of the Christian Church, as has some of the writing and rhetoric about 'spiritual warfare', which lacks both theological balance and pastoral sensitivity.[19]

However, I fear that part of the problem here is that many mainstream Christians are so removed from these areas of exploration that all response has been left to fundamentalists, who are often the mirror-images of the groups they oppose. But at least they are there! We saw something like this happen with drugs in an earlier epoch, and it is well beyond time that orthodox Christians learnt the lesson. Christians of an Anglican type, for example, really have to abandon their concern with respectability and safety, not to mention intellectual arrogance, and take these areas seriously and responsibly. It is all very well for academic theologians to issue statements condemning the abuse of exorcism, but there needs to be a much greater involvement of Christians on the ground with people who are involved with the occult, the demonic, and what is broadly termed 'the irrational'. If the academic theologians can help us, as I think they can, fine – but the crucial issue is pastoral care at the points of involvement. I have no doubt whatever that these fields of activity, and the problems associated with them, will increase in the coming years, whatever happens to the Church's own spiritual growth.

Spiritual quests: the new gnosticism

One continuing trend since the 1960s has been the thirst for the mystical, often vaguely defined and conceived. The mystical quest was already well under way by the 'summer of love' in 1967. Since then, there has been a growth in gurus, a proliferation of forms of 'salvation by technique', and a tremendous yearning, craving, thirsting, for mystery, affecting thousands of people who are not attached to any 'school' or religious group.

But these years have shown what classical spiritual writers have consistently emphasised, that spiritual growth without cultivation can be dangerous. Roszak, in a study in 1976, drew attention to the rising curiosity in the West concerning the marvellous, concerning mystical experience – a curiosity which has been driven into unorthodox channels by the rigidity and spiritual narrowness of mainstream religion. He called this

120

movement 'the biggest introspective binge any society in history has undergone'. But he warned, as I have warned, that this could become no more than a quest for private spiritual experience, a new narcissism, 'the weary businessman's late afternoon pick-me-up, a sort of Yogic Martini'. Roszak went on to attack what he called 'Flash Gordon religiosity', in which signs and wonders replaced love, compassion and justice, and he described the current cult of Uri Geller as 'the lumpen-occult version of Abbot and Costello meet Jehovah'. At the same time it was important not to despise this explosion but to help to give it direction, to create a 'healthy ecology of the spirit'. For 'where fertility is not matched by careful cultivation, it yields no livable human habitat, but instead the deadly luxuriance of swamp or jungle'.[20]

It was the widespread concern for self-cultivation which led Christopher Lasch to speak of a 'culture of narcissism'.[21] Lasch saw a loss of historical continuity in American culture, so that individuals lived for the moment and for themselves alone. This waning of the sense of historical time was the central feature which distinguished the contemporary spiritual crisis from earlier outbreaks. From a theological perspective, I have preferred the term 'gnosticism', and in fact Lasch, in one of his lesser-known articles, agreed with me, claiming that gnosticism was 'the characteristic form of contemporary spirituality'.[22] By the early 1970s I had become aware of the emergence of new forms of gnosticism in both Christian and non-Christian forms. Historically, there have been three features of gnostic spiritualities. First, a concern for enlightenment, self-awareness, *gnosis*, involving the acquiring of insight and spiritual power. Indeed the gnostic sees salvation primarily in terms of enlightenment, and tends to be more concerned with spiritual technology than with God. Secondly, the division of humanity into the initiates – those who are 'in the know' – and the rest of us, the common herd. This elitism is deeply embedded in the gnostic traditions. Thirdly, a deep suspicion of the flesh and of matter, and a tendency to locate the source of evil in the material world and its structures. We see each of these features in many of the new movements.

There is a great deal of confusion between the psychic and the spiritual – a tendency to despise and ignore the body and the material world, and to withdraw from human, not least

121

political, struggles into an inner search for peace, contentment and illumination. Of course, there are profound contradictions here, since neither the body nor the material world can be ignored in practice, and so gnostic groups are often a curious combination of unworldliness with sexual, and sometimes financial, excess. There is a dangerous concern with spiritual technology, with method and technique, the carrying over into the spiritual realm of the corrupting effect of consumer capitalism. So we see spirituality sold as a commodity, a technique to increase efficiency, relieve stress, get the kids off drugs, make better soldiers, increase conformity, or whatever. In recent years, it seems to me that the gnostic resurgence has been much more pronounced, an increasing amount of it now taking place within the Christian Churches.

This has done great harm to the whole notion of 'spirituality'. Within parts of the Christian Church, spirituality has come to be seen as somehow different from being a Christian, or from being human. And in a culture like ours, which is obsessed with privatisation and consumer choice, spirituality is in danger of becoming an essentially private pursuit. We only need to visit any secular bookstall to see the range of spiritualities which are on offer on the consumer market. This way of conceiving the life of the spirit is very different from that of the New Testament, where virtually no interest is shown in the inner life of the individual. Indeed, the whole notion of an 'inner life' is a post-Reformation development. Today, at least in evangelical circles, we talk about 'bringing Jesus into *my* life', whereas the New Testament speaks of bringing us into Christ's life. The entire thrust of the New Testament is the new creation, the new humanity in Christ, the building up of the body of Christ, the coming to the fullness of God. Being in Christ, *en Christo*, is so important that the phrase occurs 164 times in Paul's letters. But the focus is never on the individual in isolation. By contrast, much of what is called Christian spirituality today has little to do with Christ or with building up the Christian community. Rather it seeks to promote forms of personal wholeness, inner peace, and enhanced consciousness – all of which may be desirable goals, but they are not what Christian faith is about.

At heart, what we are witnessing is a view of religion or spirituality as an essentially private activity, another aspect of consumerism to be catered for by the 'providers'. And they do indeed provide – cassettes, oils, candles, and, in American bookstores, books termed 'inspirational'. When I asked a priest in one American city what the label 'inspirational' meant, he replied that it was a euphemism for 'second-rate'.

In her book *Searching for Lost Coins*, Ann Loades has a chapter entitled 'Why certain forms of holiness are bad for you'.[23] I want to suggest similarly that much in the contemporary spiritual quest is unwholesome and possibly damaging. To put it very crudely, I am not at all sure that the present resurgence of spirituality is to be welcomed. I say this for two reasons. The first is that it is not clear to me that an increased interest in spirituality is synonymous with a deepened sense either of communion with God or of a more faithful following of Jesus. I often recall the comment of Graham Leonard, former Bishop of London, who, after visiting a particular American city, commented, 'I have never been in a place before where I heard so many people talking about spirituality, and where I never saw anyone on their knees'. An interest in spirituality can be yet another way of avoiding the actual encounter with the living God, another excuse for not praying, another way of putting a screen between us and reality – in other words, a diversion.

The second reason is that it is not clear that a resurgence of spirituality is necessarily either Christian or wholesome. I do not wish to be misunderstood here. Many forms of non-Christian spiritual practices are extremely helpful, just as many Christian spiritual practices may be unwholesome. My worry is that there is much in the contemporary quest which is neither. The very word 'spirituality' is a bit of a worry. It is not an ancient word, and does not enter the Christian vocabulary in any significant way until the eighteenth century. Its use, according to Simon Tugwell, is modern, and the confident use of the term is very, very modern.[24] More important, however, than the word, is the suggestion behind the word. It tends to suggest a separate realm, a kind of compartment of Christian life, a dimension which can be kept apart from other compartments and other dimensions.

Grace Jantzen has recently pointed out that prayer, meditation and even books on spirituality may simply be helping people to cope with the distresses of life which arise from unjust social conditions without challenging those conditions themselves. To that extent, these 'spiritual aids' are acting as a sedative which dulls the awareness of the need to dismantle the structures which perpetuate the distress.[25] Jantzen is one of a long line of writers since Marx (and indeed well before Marx) who have made the same point. Her point, however, remains a valid one, and there is considerable evidence that, while many people and groups within the religious world have become more socially and politically conscious during the last 30 years, the reverse process, towards an escapist and neutral spirituality, has also gathered ground.

The world of contemporary spirituality is complex, full of ambiguity and mixed messages. There is much, for example, in New Age spirituality which is of great value – its spontaneity, creativity, its emphasis on healing and renewal, its use of the 'new physics', its openness to new insights as well as to old wisdom. It certainly manifests a greater concern with the created world and its future than did some of the earlier movements, and, it must be said, than do most Churches. It is important that these positive elements should be warmly welcomed.

But at the end of the day I believe that gnosticism is a barren path leading to nihilism and world abandonment. It may well be that today gnosticism is more of a danger inside the Church than outside it, as we see the increased attraction of ministries based on power, 'miracles' and dramatics rather than on love and justice. Just as Ignatius of Antioch attacked those who neglected the Eucharist and the common life, had no care for widows, orphans, the afflicted, prisoners, and the hungry and thirsty, so it is necessary today to issue a warning against false spiritualities wherever they arise.

The Pentecostal revival

It would be impossible to conclude a chapter on the changing face of spirituality without mentioning Pentecostalism. It is almost 40 years since H. P. van Dusen called the Pentecostal movement the 'Third Force in Christendom' and saw its emergence as a 'new Reformation'.[26] The Pentecostal movement is now so strong that it must be seen as a distinct species of world Christian presence, alongside Roman Catholicism, Orthodoxy, Anglicanism, and post-Reformation Protestanism. Indeed, it overlaps with them all. Pentecostalism is probably growing at a rate of 20 million new members per year, and its world members number over 410 million. It is the main Christian group in Africa and in parts of Latin America, Korea and China. It is very important to note that it is not only the charismatic renewal movement or neo-Pentecostalism – the movement which has affected the mainstream Churches, not least the Roman Catholic Church, since the 1960s – which is growing. It is classical Pentecostalism, the movement with its roots in the early twentieth-century revivals in California, Wales and elsewhere. It is the Black Pentecostal Church movement – for Pentecostalism was in origin a Black movement. Thus in the USA recently, the Church of God has grown by 147 per cent, the Assemblies of God by 116 per cent, and even the Church of the Nazarene, one of the Holiness Churches which (reluctantly) gave birth to modern Pentecostalism, by 50 per cent.[27]

Theologically, Pentecostalism has its roots in the Wesleyan and Holiness movements with their concern for sanctity and sanctification. Early Pentecostalism was concerned with the recovery of the 'full gospel', with a stress on the fundamentals of faith, on wholeness, and the recovery of apostolic gifts. Since the 1960s, the movement has spread within the Roman communion, which was seen, in classical Pentecostalism, as the Antichrist and the great whore of Babylon. This has thrown the older Pentecostal groups into confusion. Either their original theology was wrong, or the manifestations of the gifts of the Spirit among Roman Catholics are fraudulent. The spread of Pentecostalism within the Roman Church has many peculiar aspects, and they will have to be struggled with in the coming years. It is not at all clear, in spite of many positive statements from the hierarchy, that Pentecostal theology fits well with traditional Catholicism. Many Roman Catholic Pentecostalists tend to ignore some of the key elements in the classical Pentecostal tradition, such as the 'second blessing', biblical literalism, the centrality of speaking in tongues, the need for conversion of the Jews, and the imminence of the Second Coming.[28]

The Pentecostal revival is important in relation to some of the issues which I have looked at earlier. Pentecostalists reject the dualism of spirit and body, believing that the Holy Spirit is shown in physical manifestations – so the use of the body, the emotions and feelings, is central to Pentecostal worship. This does not necessarily mean that they have broken with the anti-incarnational trends within the Church, but it does mean that there is the potential for change.

And change there certainly has been. One of the effects of the Pentecostal revival has been to throw conventional Church divisions into confusion. For example, Latino evangelicals or 'evangelicos' are the fastest-growing section of North American Protestantism, particularly in states such as California, New York and Texas. Conservative in theology, they have been described as 'a wild card on the religious right', for they are likely to judge political candidates less for their views on abortion or homosexuality than for their position on immigration, health-care and housing, and they tend (correctly in my view) to see much of the white religious right as racist.[29] The growth of the Pentecostal movement is worldwide. For example, in Papua and other countries of the Pacific, evangelicals, Pentecostalists and Seventh Day Adventists are the groups who are advancing most rapidly.

Western Christians have tended to look at these groups through their conventional wisdom, that of psychology. There have been numerous studies of the psychology of those attracted by Pentecostalism. Since the numbers in this group run into millions, whatever characteristics they may have must be extremely common. It has been claimed that Pentecostalism appeals to 'uncommonly troubled people', people with a low frustration-tolerance, people with an inability to cope with ambiguity, and so on. If this were true, it would certainly make sense of the undoubted success of the work of Pentecostal Churches with drug addicts. There is probably some truth in these claims, but they need to be looked at in the context of wider cultural changes. Purely psychological explanations of social and cultural shifts are rarely satisfactory.

One major change has been in the area of political involvement. The dominant view among mainstream Christians has been that Pentecostalism is politically reactionary. By its other-worldliness and concern to appease 'the powers', it has offered neither threat to, nor critique of, the dominant regime within which it exists. As a result, it has become one of the more acceptable forms of Christianity in the world. But this is changing: there has been a fusion of Pentecostalism with political action, as in the case of Herbert Daughtry, pastor of the House of the Lord in Brooklyn. The Black-led Churches in Britain are almost certain to break with the reactionary stance of the Church of God of Cleveland, Tennessee, the mother of their main denomination. Pentecostalism in the Third World has also shown signs of radicalisation, and there is widespread discussion of a Pentecostal theology of liberation. So, while the major, white American Pentecostal denominations will probably remain agents for capitalism, this cannot be guaranteed as a permanent Pentecostal position. In fact, the radicalisation of the Pentecostal movement which some of us hoped for in the 1970s seems to be coming to pass, at least in some places.[30]

In recent decades we have seen many new forms of Christian presence. We are seeing the appearance of what are called 'new Christians', publicly manifested in the annual Greenbelt festival, in which there is a fusion of fundamentalism, ecological concerns and radical streams.[31] There is a whole range of movements which now use the prefix 'post', including the 'post-evangelicals'.[32] Again, in many of these movements there is a belief in 'restoring the Kingdom', and the theme of 'restoration' recurs throughout.[33] Throughout these groups, there is much extremely superficial religiosity, including much which seeks to fuse elements of neo-Pentecostalism with aspects of youth rave-culture. This was evident in the Nine O'Clock Service in Sheffield which led to accusations of sexual abuse. It is evident in a different way in the so-called Toronto Blessing in which some of the worst features of spiritual immaturity seem to have resurfaced in a bourgeois form.[34] There is much evidence of extreme authoritarianism in the form of 'heavy shepherding', with a call to absolute obedience. But we should not see these developments purely in terms of their problems. It is far more important that the potential and the positive elements within them are guided and strengthened.

A major factor in the growth of spiritual renewal movements is their position in relation to the principalities and powers, to the structures of injustice. In the face of the trends towards fragmentation and the intensified privatising of spiritual life, it is surely a matter of the greatest urgency that Christians build communities of resistance to the forces which are working against human communion. Such communities may form around specific issues or areas of witness – peace and justice, housing, the environment, minority rights, and so on – but they must not be merely movements of protest. The

Christian witness is an extraordinary one, one of testimony against the spirit of the age, witness to the alternative life of 'the world to come'. In fact, I believe that the only effective resistance to the corrosive individualism of the age is the renewal of authentic contemplation linked to political commitment. This will involve the formation of networks of communities committed to politics and to prayer.

Discernment – the Churches' response

If I am only partly right in my analysis of our predicament, then at the heart of the Christian task as we approach the *fin de siècle* is the work of discernment, *diakrisis*. *Diakrisis* is the key word in the ministry which is called 'spiritual direction', a ministry which has been rediscovered in recent years throughout the Christian world. However, this ministry, particularly in the USA, has to some extent been co-opted by the very forces of capitalism and consumerism which I have described. Discernment therefore must begin with a rigorous process of spiritual disentanglement, and this calls for political perception.

There are immense spiritual needs within the mainstream Churches. Yet sadly many sections of these Churches, including parts of the retreat movement, have not resisted the narcissistic trend but have colluded with it and reinforced it. Much contemporary spirituality within the Church itself is highly individualistic and directed more at self-cultivation than at communion with God. Part of the work of spiritual direction is to take seriously the actual process of sanctification, to discern, and to struggle with, the actual mechanisms and movements of the Spirit in the life of one person. There has to be a focusing – for religious life cannot exist at the level of ideal and abstraction: it has to be realised in concrete and particular acts and practices, if it is to continue to live and grow. There has to be a 'scaffolding of Spirit' if we are to make progress beyond the foundations.[35]

I devoted a good deal of my book *Soul Friend* to pointing out that spiritual direction was different from pastoral counselling, and I will return to the current popularity of counselling in

Chapter 10. Sadly the two are still widely confused, and the models of secular professional counselling and clinical pastoral care have made such deep inroads into the Church's life that many people have lost a grip on the wider tradition. So, in one study of clergy of the Episcopal Church in the USA, 46 per cent thought that counselling and spiritual direction were the same thing.[36]

How should Churches try to respond to the new spiritual movements? I wrote a final chapter of *Youthquake* on this question, and it is worth re-reading it in the light of the changes which have occurred since. I remain convinced that, at the end of the day – and indeed at the end of the century! – what will determine the Church's credibility is its utter commitment in faith and rootedness to its own spiritual tradition. It is out of this rootedness that an authentic response which is thoughtful, prayerful, humble and, in the best sense of the word, critical, can arise. Of course, there is an immense amount in the new spiritual movements which is good, wholesome, wonderful and creative. But it would be a serious mistake for the Church to latch uncritically onto them, as it is often prone to do when it does not go to the opposite extreme of seeing them as uniformly demonic. In fact, I see two kinds of Christian response to New Age and similar spiritual movements. The first is the wholesale onslaught from the fundamentalist wing. For them it is all devil-inspired, demonic, and so on. A second, and more nuanced response, is illustrated by a recent Church report *The Search for Faith and the Witness of the Church*. Here there is a critique of pick-and-mix religiosity, our old friend syncretism. It is even argued that such a consumerist approach to religion could lead to the collapse of civilisation. It was interesting that, within weeks of the publication of this report, the cliché 'pick-and-mix' became part of the standard rhetoric of bishops' addresses. (Perhaps they are all written by the same person?)[37]

Two comments seem necessary on this. I have consistently attacked the idea of spirituality as yet another consumer product in the hypermarket. Yet there is something hypocritical and lacking in honesty for Churches – which have themselves colluded with consumerism and the capitalist approach to religion to a far greater extent, and for far longer, than the new religious movements – to turn and attack this collusion when it is New Age spirituality which is involved. The maxim, 'Physician, heal thyself', comes to mind. But, secondly, it needs

129

to be remembered that Christianity, particularly Catholic Christianity, is itself syncretistic and inclusive. Indeed, the syncretism is most evident (and most harmful) when it is unrecognised, as in forms of fundamentalism which have absorbed more of secular ideology and of the culture of modernity than they realise. The issue is one of discernment. There may well be elements from New Age spirituality which are needed for the renewal of the Christian tradition – though it is also true that Christian tradition may have words of wisdom which may prevent New Age spirituality from certain deviations. Lasch believed that New Age is to gnosticism what fundamentalism is to Christianity – a literal restatement of ideas whose original value lay in their imaginative understanding of human life.[38] I am not impressed by warnings of the collapse of civilisation, particularly when they come from an established Church. Some civilisations ought to collapse, and it may be the role of the Church to aid that collapse. Again, discernment is needed.

It is always tempting to be so pleased that there is spiritual life somewhere, and to rejoice in the fact that, in P. T. Forsyth's words, a living heresy is better than a dead orthodoxy. But we need to be careful here. The growth of religion and of spirituality is not in itself benign. It is not to be a matter for rejoicing. Esoteric spiritualities and experience-centred movements have a great appeal. It is, however, part of the task of the Church to earth the spiritual search in the concrete, the ordinary, the common. We need to remember that Christianity is not an idea but a living body, a Church, with warts and wrinkles, heavy with imperfection, ambiguity and mess, stained with human sin and oppression. For all its frustrations, we must never abandon the common life for the advanced purity of the *illuminati*.

Christianity is concerned with the particular and the material, the specific and the concrete. It is rooted in the particularity and materiality of incarnation, resurrection and Eucharist. If this is so, there is bound to be a somewhat paradoxical relationship between the gospel and the various elitist, esoteric and inward spiritual currents which appear in similar forms in each generation, and which tend to assume particularly bizarre forms as we approach the *fin de siècle*, the end of the age. For the gospel calls into question and undermines all approaches to the spiritual which play down or deny the material, fleshly and social dimensions of human existence.

Spirituality can be a form of activity which takes us away from the commonness, the earthiness, the concrete crudity of our lives together. Much spirituality, some of which purports to be Christian, is in fact profoundly anti-incarnational, very elitist and obstinately apolitical. We need urgently to recover a tradition which avoids these dangers, and we will not achieve it by colluding with the notion of spirituality as merely a dimension of Christian life, or with the cult of experts and gurus – the high priests of salvation by technique.

As long ago as 1952, Julian Langmead Casserley predicted that the retreat *into* religion would be the most profound and most enduring form of the retreat *from* Christianity. Our age, Casserly suggested, was likely to be one which was prolific with new superstitions and myths.[39] A major cause of this retreat, I believe, has been the exclusion of the mystical from mainstream Christianity. It is the mystical element which gives warmth, humanity and tolerance, and without which religions can grow hard, inflexible, and cruel. It is the mystical element which integrates theology, action and prayer. Of course, the classical mystics would probably never have seen themselves as such. As Denys Turner points out, the notion of mysticism as a separate area of Christianity is a nineteenth-century invention.[40] The very fact that we need words like 'spirituality' and 'mysticism' indicates the extent of our loss of these realities.

It is important that the coming Church calls into question the idea that the spiritual and the mystical are sections of religion which are concerned with inner or peculiar experiences. We need to assert that all theology is mystical or none is. Indeed, many of the classical mystics make no reference to unusual experiences, or, if they do, attach no special significance to them. What is vital is that all our action, all our striving, is rooted in our prayer, our mystical union with God. For, as Walter Wink has warned us,

> Unprotected by prayer, our social activism runs the danger of becoming self-justifying good works, as our inner resources atrophy, the wells of love run dry, and we are slowly changed into the likeness of the beast... Prayer, in short, is the theatre in which the diseased spirituality that we have contracted from the powers can most directly be discerned, diagnosed and healed.[41]

6

Society and Sanctity

There is no holiness but social holiness.

JOHN WESLEY

The fate of the soul is the fate of the social order.

THEODORE ROSZAK

The Gospel is indeed a social gospel ... The good news of the Gospel is imparted to the individual only as a member of a society ... The most fundamental heresy of all is to imagine that the gospel is given to individuals or received by individuals or apprehended by individuals.

ENOCH POWELL

I began to write this chapter on the Feast of the Visitation of Our Lady, when the Church celebrates Mary's song, Magnificat. God, she proclaims, has torn the imperial powers, the *dunastas* or *potestates*, from their thrones, and has exalted the lowly, has filled the hungry and sent the rich away empty. The song is a celebration of reversal: not simply of justice for the down-trodden, but of the removal of the oppressors. Liberal Christians are, in my experience, more committed to the former than to the latter, wanting justice without threat to their own position, or that of those who support them. A related characteristic of liberal Christianity is the desire for change without conflict. Conrad Noel once said that Anglicans in particular imagined that the mighty would be put down from their thrones so gently that they would not feel the bump when they hit the ground;[1] while Saul Alinsky defined a liberal as a person who leaves the room when an argument becomes a fight. Others have found the sentiments of the Magnificat illusory. Thus Tom Thomas, who founded the Workers' Theatre Movement, in a talk to History Workshop in the 1970s, pointed to the daily recitation of the Magnificat as his reason for leaving the Church in favour of political struggle. He had sung in the choir for years about the putting down of the mighty and the raising of the lowly, and it had become perfectly clear to him, as he looked at the congregation, that God had done nothing of the kind, and that it was high time someone else did.[2]

It is clear to me that much, perhaps most, of the disorder in the world today is related to the existence of structures of domination, to the *dunastas*, the *potestates*, who are firmly in position; to the systematic oppression of the lowly and weak; to the persistence and promotion of hunger and poverty; and to the growth and persistence of concentrated wealth and power. While there are many examples of Churches and individual Christians who struggle to shift these structures of domination, the main role of Churches and of other religious groups has been to reinforce and uphold them. Within that accepted framework of reinforcement, the religious task is seen as one of limited reform, attitude-changing and spiritual renewal. As soon as there seems to be some progress towards a more radical critique, the hierarchy rushes to distance itself and return to the safe world of 'general principles'.[3] It is widely taken for granted that the structures as a whole, 'the system', cannot be changed; that the best we can hope for is to 'humanise' them, to deal with the distortions which have 'crept in'.

We saw this theological approach in the report *Faith in the City*. It was, on its own terms, an excellent report, its excellence reinforced by the trivial and ill-researched responses from the British government. But it stood firmly within the reformist tradition. The authors began by telling us of the 'basic Christian principles of justice and compassion which we believe we share with the great majority of the people of Britain'. This in itself was a profoundly theological and sociological assumption, and highly questionable – but clearly the basis of the report, as indeed it has been of much Anglican social thinking. Individualism has 'crept into both public and private life', as if, having crept in, it could just as easily creep out. It was unreasonable, the report argued, for Christians to offer more than a critique of the present system.

> Christians can hardly be expected to propose a realistic alternative to the entire economic system, but there is ample precedent in the Christian tradition for exposing the system we have to moral judgment.[4]

Capitalism and society

I want to put a contrary view. Although it is a view which I have held since the age of 15, when I became a Christian and a socialist, I find it is still not an acceptable one within most sections of the Church or 'society'. I want to suggest that the features hinted at in the Magnificat – the oppression of the lowly, the promotion of hunger and poverty, the persistence of concentrated wealth, and so on – are not accidental aberrations within capitalism, but are central to its character and vital to its success.

The fact that capitalism seems to demand the existence of oppressed and deprived groups within it has raised yet again the question: is capitalism compatible with society in any meaningful sense? Many years ago, Karl Polanyi answered this question in the negative. Capitalism, he argued, by its very nature had destroyed the whole idea of human society.[5] In Britain and the USA, as well as elsewhere, there has been for some years a sense of alarm about the erosion or collapse of society. Certainly, from the situation I know best, that of the East End of London, the belief that society has disintegrated seems to be vindicated. Here, we live on the underside of capitalism. Of course, it is possible to exaggerate, and I do not believe that things are beyond repair (though certainly not within the present system), but it does seem to me indisputable that we have entered a world in which any sense of social cohesion, common commitment, or common values, has been destroyed. Mammon has gained the victory. And this has raised the question: if society has collapsed, what is left?

The curious factor here is that writers continue to use the term 'society' – a term which has no meaning apart from a sense of corporate unity and solidarity – to describe our fragmented existence. Allied with the word 'society' are words like 'age' and 'culture'. So we have been called an unprincipled society, a careless society, an irresponsible society. We are urged to become a decent society, a good society. We are said to live in an age of anxiety, the psychic postscript to the affluent society of which we were told earlier. We have been told that we are a culture of contentment, or, if not, a culture of separation, or a culture of complaint.[6] All these slogans suggest something which is deeply wrong, disturbed, frayed, diseased – a society whose *raison d'être* has been eroded. While I do not believe that this is of recent origin, I am sure that it has reached an extreme point of decay since the coming of the Thatcher and Reagan regimes. Thatcherism, which purported to exalt and defend family values, in fact undermined economically what it espoused ideologically. The post-Thatcher regime presided over by John Major is no more than a modified, slightly more genteel, form of the earlier phenomenon.

So the question arises: do we have a society at all? In Britain particularly, has society survived the Thatcher years? Many commentators have suggested that the breakdown of any sense of solidarity was so serious that nothing was left. Certainly, the damage done by these terrible years has been immense, and it is by no means certain that a decent society can again be built. The seriousness of the Thatcherite revolution is difficult to overestimate. So much has been destroyed, so much has been lost. The sense of evil embodied in a programme has acquired a vivid and awful meaning. It is here, when confronted by monsters, that one sees the uselessness and unreality of the 'general principles' approach to Christian social witness. The demons must be named.

But the Thatcher years were a symptom of decay, not its cause. At a deeper level, there was a sense that there was no moral core. In spite of claims that there should be a consensus of values and a common moral vision, this does not in fact exist, nor can it be produced out of nowhere. The current rhetoric about family values is illiterate and meaningless. The truth is that we are in a state of spiritual and moral incoherence.

Christians and society

The erosion and disintegration in Britain and elsewhere in the West has coincided with a deeper concern and commitment among Christians in relation to social and political structures. While I am pleased at the renewal of Christian social action, and impressed by the thoroughness of some Christian social thought, I believe that much of it suffers from serious weaknesses and inadequacies. If Christians are to move into the twenty-first century with a realistic and effective social and political witness, some important shifts will be needed.

For example, I am not convinced that we can any longer speak of 'a Christian society', except as one social formation within the larger national or transnational ones. T. S. Eliot wrote about the 'idea of a Christian society', and many Christians of varying shades of political alignment, from socialist Christians in Britain to the Christian 'reconstructionists' in the USA today, have argued for a kind of 'dominion', rooted in biblical principles, in which Christians exercise a social and moral leadership over nations. A society based on Christian principles has been central to much social thought among Anglicans in England since the time of the Christian Social Union of 1889. But can it be sustained today as an intelligent or theologically defensible option? I think not. Whether we like it or not, we are not a Christian society but a plural one, involving a variety of people and communities of different faiths and of no faith.

Much of the rhetoric about Christians and British society seems to be based on some kind of notion of what C. S. Lewis called 'mere Christianity'. However diverse the interpretations of Christianity may be, it is argued that there is a general Christian basis or foundation for our society. So when politicians and others tell us that we are a Christian country, they usually mean that our actions and mind-set are based on these general beliefs. I have never found this argument convincing, either in Lewis's form or in the current, more incoherent form. There may be assumptions derived from a kind of folk memory of Christianity, but they are so vague as to be at best of little use, and at worst dangerous.

This is not to say that Christian social thought is irrelevant to our present predicament. If Christian social thought is rooted in a sacramental theology which is world-embracing, it can surely envisage and prepare for a society which embraces different communities, and yet within this context testify to its own distinctive beliefs. The ability to do this will be a major test, perhaps the major test, for the Christian Church in the coming years.

My view is that the idea of a Christian society is mistaken, but that we can and must speak of a Christian testimony to, and within, social structures. At times that testimony may demand, and contribute to, the overthrow of these structures. Never will it uncritically endorse them. Christian social hope and social vision is rooted in Jewish tradition, with its insistence on justice, hospitality, reverence for land, and belief in the presence and action of God in history. Christian social ethics, which also grew from Jewish soil, place particular stress on the centrality of love, on non-violence, on the presence of God's Kingdom in our midst, and on the commitment to those whom respectable society rejects. These are the biblical foundations of the Christian social tradition, and, to the extent that they are embodied in a society, we could call it a Christian society. But I would be reluctant to do so if it conveyed some sense of arrogance and implicit imperialism, and I cannot see how this could be avoided. For this reason I want to speak of the Christian witness to society.

In the quest for such an entity we are not without guidelines. There is a significant body of Christian discourse about the gospel and human society. Much of it is 'implicationist' – the notion that the gospel is one thing, and its social implications are something else, derivative perhaps, but essentially an offshoot. This view was criticised many years ago,[7] but it seems to reappear regularly today. In fact, there is no distinction between the gospel and the vision of a transformed human society. Jesus was far more concerned with the coming of the Kingdom of God than he was with the shape of the Christian community in this age. Nevertheless the Christian community, what we call the Church, has a significant role to play as a social organism which seeks to prefigure the shape and form of the Kingdom in which God's justice and compassion will be manifested in terms of human society. The proclamation of that reality *is* the gospel, 'the good news of the Kingdom of God'. To speak (as, for example, *Faith in the City* did) in terms of a gospel which is primarily concerned with personal salvation, and the implications of that gospel which are social, is to do violence to the Scriptures and to the Christian tradition. *Faith in the City* speaks of the 'social and political implications' of the faith which is actually about 'personal relationships and individual responses'.[8] This implicationist rhetoric is deeply ingrained within the Anglican hierarchy, and it is reproduced regularly in the media and in sermons – but it really has an extremely weak theological base. The proclamation that God was in Christ reconciling the world to himself, the vision of a transformed society – the Kingdom of God – and the commitment to work with the incarnate, crucified and risen Christ to achieve it, through the power of the Spirit and nourished by word and Eucharist, *is* the gospel. There is no other.

Equally, it is not intelligent in today's world for bishops and Church leaders to think of themselves as spokespersons of societies or nations as a whole, though they may well have important insights and contributions to make. The more I listen to bishops speaking on national political issues, the more convinced I am that they are, in the main, suffering from a certain self-deception and self-delusion. First, they imagine that they are somehow politically neutral and can address political issues without taking up party political positions. There is a failure to grasp political reality and to recognise that the notion of a neutral, objective position above party politics is a mystification. South American theologians perceived this years ago, pointing out that the difference between their position and that of most Western theologians was not that they were biased and we were not, but that they recognised their bias while we failed to recognise ours. This is not to say that bishops should become lackeys of political parties, any more than they should be lackeys of any other pressure group. But the whole issue of their own class and ideological position calls for a greater sense of self-awareness and political discernment than they seem to show.

Secondly, they seem to have an unreal estimate of their own relevance as moral leaders. When bishops of the Church of England address the nation, they seem to see themselves as leaders of the national Church (as they are in law) rather than the representatives of one minority among others (as they are in fact). It is vital for all Christians to learn not only to live with, but to value, the position of being a minority. This may mean that in *sociological* terms, Churches will be seen increasingly as 'sects' – but this is quite different from adopting a *theologically* sectarian posture.

The thought of the late Juan Luis Segundo is important here. According to Segundo, Christianity is by its nature minoritarian. The normal condition of the Church is that of a creative minority within society – as indicated by the symbolism of leaven, whose purpose is to transform the piece of dough into bread. Similarly the symbol of salt, the purpose of which is to improve a meal. If we were to produce nothing but leaven and salt, it would not be success but disaster. I believe that the awareness of this minority role, and the development of strategies based on it, will be crucially important in the coming years.[9]

I want therefore to argue for a critical recovery of the Christian social tradition. Of course, recent changes and insights have called many earlier positions into question and made much earlier thinking irrelevant. I have always been wary of the theme of 'Christendom', and certainly its Islamic equivalent is no better. Such sacral models of society, if they grow and acquire wide acceptance, are likely to release dangerous and even demonic forces upon us. Here is where spirituality and politics come together, and the issue of holiness becomes central.

Holiness and justice

That God is a God of justice and holiness is central to the
Jewish and Christian traditions, just as a division between justice
and holiness is utterly alien to those traditions. In the coming
years, it is almost certain that a commitment to justice will be
seen by many Churches not only as an evangelical imperative,
but also as a political necessity as inequality, poverty and
dehumanising tendencies increase throughout the world. What
is not so clear is that they will connect the struggle for justice
with lives of holiness, spiritual discipline, virtue and purity of
heart. Yet the two areas cannot be severed without great harm
being done.

Sanctity, or holiness, is more central to the New Testament
than is morality. Christians are called not to be moral but to
be saints. The term 'saints' is in fact a synonym for Christians.
The whole idea of morality apart from sanctification is
unknown to classical Christianity. I believe that, in the midst
of the current rhetoric about morality, the call to Christians is
to assert the centrality of holiness. For without holiness there
can be no authentic Christian witness. To engage in moral
crusades is a very dangerous exercise, potentially corrupting
for all involved. Unless those who do so are also involved in
the most profound and rigorous encounter with their own sins
and with God, there is likely to be a hardening of moral posture
of a very harsh, judgmental and unchristian kind. I will return
to this towards the end of the chapter.

Holiness was originally about separation, and this separatist
emphasis should not be entirely abandoned. I believe that
many Christians, particularly in what are misleadingly called
'mainstream' or 'liberal' Churches, have tended to operate on
a minimal basis of ethics: low expectation combined with high
tolerance and compassion. While I am entirely in favour of
compassion and of supporting people in their struggles and
trials in a spirit of gentleness and understanding, there is an
element in the gospel which speaks with a different voice,
issues a different call, and articulates a different hunger. This
is the voice of holiness, the call to heroic discipleship, the
hunger for God. Separation from 'the world' – in the sense of
the sinful and unjust demands and structures of the fallen

141

world-order – remains a requirement for us if we are to follow the call to be transformed, not conformed.

Yet the specific thrust of the Christian sacramental tradition is to bring together the holy and the common. 'Holy communion' is not only the name of the central Christian act of worship; it also sums up the whole meaning of Christian life, which is the practice of the holy in the midst of the common life of humankind. As we move into a new century of inequality and privilege, the authentic celebration of the Eucharist, and its testimony to sharing and equality, will become more and more important. But it needs to be extended and made real in our social life.

Holiness is inseparable from justice, or righteousness. Here I want to put in a plea for the recovery of the biblical concept of righteousness. While it was right for translators and theologians to stress the word 'justice' at a time when 'righteousness' had become desocialised and was widely seen in individualistic, forensic or moralistic ways, I suspect that we now have a different problem which calls for a different response. The word 'justice' tends to be seen as meaning fairness, a careful balance between this and that, impartiality, a minimal requirement; and it is seen as existing in a state of objectivity which has nothing to do with the personal qualities of its practitioners. But in the Christian tradition we can only *behave* justly if we are on the way to *becoming* just persons. To restore the use of the word 'righteousness', emphasising the social and political dimensions of the idea, would bring back the extreme demand embodied in the word, and its connections with the holiness and righteousness of God. Gerard Manley Hopkins's phrase, 'the just man justices', draws out the connection between interior, habitual righteousness and its external practice. We may see holiness as the habit which issues in actions of justice. Certainly justice cannot be externalised except in the most minimal way, unless there is a process of change within persons and their communities.

This raises the critical issue of humanity within politics. I am more and more worried at a creeping dehumanisation and ruthlessness aimed at the most vulnerable sections of our society, a process which must call into question the ability of modern politicians to cope with the ethical area. What happens to politics when it loses its heart, its bowels of compassion, its sense of outrage and its spirituality? A good example of this is the question of homeless beggars, and the response of the Labour leader Tony Blair. In a recent interview he supported the police 'zero-tolerance' approach, including zero tolerance for beggars.[10] It is not so much that his sentences, taken out of context, are perverse (although for someone to think that saying we should be 'intolerant of people homeless on the streets' is the same as being 'intolerant of homelessness' gives a clue to what is wrong). It is naïvety of an alarming kind.

It is now fashionable to attack beggars, perhaps because they have highlighted the problem, forced the issue upon the politicians. I am grateful to them. There has been research on homelessness since the 1950s. Many of us have documented the issues, well before *Cathy Come Home*. The politicians have taken little notice. Now they are on the rampage, and we have the beggars to thank for this. But there are years of disbelief, of incredulity, to make up for. To understand and respond to this calls not for clichés, but for humility, willingness to learn, and a degree of imagination which seems to be missing. And it is the profound imaginative failure which is most difficult to deal with. But what is equally worrying is that we now have – and have had for some time – a large number of people who are politically homeless, who cannot with integrity find a home in the Labour Party, not least because they are socialists, people who will probably vote Labour but with no great enthusiasm. It is not a good recipe for the future. These are people who are really committed, who know the streets better than the politicians do, who have been involved in struggling for justice for years. They can be ignored – but they will be a major loss to political life, and they have been trampled down in the frantic electoral rush of the Gadarene swine.

I cannot see that any humane politics can be built on the basis of contempt or the failure to respect the dignity of every human person. Certainly no politics which fail at this fundamental level can hope for Christian support. A central task of the Church in the coming years will be to strengthen and nourish the humanity – and, in theological terms, the deified humanity – of those involved in the struggles of the political order. This task is dangerous, it is full of risks, and it is essential if a Christ-centred politics is to be sustained.

What does holiness or sanctity mean today? In 1955 Alasdair MacIntyre deplored the lack of contemporary writing in moral and ascetical theology, and raised the question: how do we learn to live as saints in contemporary terms?[11] The work of trying to lead holy lives in the midst of imperfection, corruption and mess will be frustrating, but frustration itself is an important, sanctifying experience.[12] I feel that the Churches of the future need to take much more seriously their role as laboratories for the nourishing of saints, and I believe that three streams of Christian tradition can help us in this task. We can learn from the Catholic and Orthodox traditions of spiritual direction, and the monastic movement out of which spiritual direction developed, which have always emphasised the nuts and bolts, the actual details of the process of sanctification. We can learn from the Wesleyan and Holiness movements, which have laid great emphasis on holiness of life, purity of heart, and entire sanctification as the call of every Christian. And we can learn particularly from the revival of interest in the Anabaptist and Mennonite traditions which, more than any other Christian group, have stressed discipleship, the creation of committed, holy and righteous communities, and the need for a social expression of the character of the Church. The idea of 'community' raises important questions for the future.

What is 'community'?

'Community' is a warm word. Nobody is supposed to be against it. Yet there is a bewildering range of uses of the word. In recent years, we have heard of community development, community studies, community policing, youth and community work, community care, community health, the Community Charge, community organising, and even community theologians! In 1955 George Hillery listed 94 uses of the term, the only feature they had in common being a concern about people.[13] A feature which was not included was that of decline, although this seems to be the central theme in current discussion. Concern about the decline of community in Britain is not new. The 'peril of England', according to Disraeli's novel *Coningsby*, lay in the 'decline of its character as a community'. Today much of the language used suggests nostalgia and a lost world.

Indeed, much talk about community seems to be based on an idealised model of village life.[14]

The recent revival of the theme of 'community' has been associated with the American communitarian thinker Amitai Etzioni. However, there is much confusion about 'communitarianism'.[15] There is certainly a tendency in some communitarian writing to see community in a homogeneous way, and to be blind to issues of gender and economics. Etzioni tends to stress responsibilities in contrast to rights, ignoring the crucial place of rights in any just society. Civil liberties are under threat in many places, and do not exist at all in others. To call for a moratorium on most, if not all, new rights (as he does) is irresponsible, and will play into the hands of the most backward elements in our societies.

The communitarian ideas expressed by Etzioni seem quite benevolent in contrast to those, for example, of Mussolini. Yet we are right to be suspicious of these ideas when they arise, as they invariably do, in the context of dissatisfaction with liberalism and a concern for common values. In such a context, it is all too easy for critical faculties to be put to sleep beneath the hypnotic power of the charismatic word or the demands of law and order. In fact Etzioni's ideas have been picked up and popularised in rather crude form by politicians such as Tony Blair and Jack Straw, while the rhetoric of community has been taken up by others, sometimes with explicit reference to Etzioni. Thus the Bishop of London seems to have aligned himself with Etzioni's thinking.[16]

So what are the problems associated with this kind of thinking? There is a danger of creating a normative view of sameness, an organic community which rejects diversity. There is a danger too of a designer philosophy with questionable goals. The litany of community, Bea Campbell has claimed, has become a kind of new religion. I want to suggest that 'community' and 'communitarianism' may be mixed blessings, and need critiquing very carefully. Much of the rhetoric of community, and many communities in practice, have been strong and supportive at the cost of high rates of exclusion. Much current communitarian thought is very anti-feminist and pays little attention to the role of women, apart from regular attacks on single mothers. Many of the tightly-knit urban villages of London – such as Hoxton, Bethnal Green and Notting Dale (all of them areas where I have worked) – were districts with low rates of movement, strong patterns of kinship, and fierce levels of xenophobia and racism. It is not surprising that it was in these areas that Sir Oswald Mosley found much of his support for the Fascist movement, and the first two are still targets for Fascist activists. Community can turn to Fascism very quickly if it does not connect with other values such as diversity and minority rights. Yet Etzioni wants a moratorium on civil rights, and much of his thinking seems to assume a normative view of sameness. Nor are these thinkers strong on economics. Yet it is the globalisation of capital which is the biggest threat to community.

This is not to deny that the communitarians are addressing real issues: the moral confusion and fragmentation, the sense of hopelessness, the rising crime-rate, the influence of individualism (in part sponsored by recent governments). But to recognise problems is only the beginning, and some 'solutions' can make the problems worse – as Germany in the 1930s saw. The Church has a tendency to latch uncritically on to some new movement in each decade. Before it latches on to Etzioni (who is hardly new, in fact), it is right to urge caution and critical scrutiny.

There is a really big problem here in relation to East London where there is so much nostalgia and talk of a lost world, the true spirit of the East End, Wilmott and Young, the collapse of community, and so on. The language of 'community' evokes sentiments and memories of both a real and an idyllic past, and may be the precursor of a real regeneration of corporate life, or of something resembling a grass-roots Fascism. And how does the Church relate to all this? This was the central issue in the recent crisis about the nature of the Church *vis-à-vis* community on the Isle of Dogs in the build up to, and the aftermath of, the election of Derek Beackon of the British National Party. There is a lot to be said on this, and I have a sense that the recent rhetoric of community, which has been transmitted across the Atlantic from Etzioni to Tony Blair, will find an uncritical audience in some sections of the Church which have a strong sense of incarnation and presence but not much sense of redemption, judgment and struggle against 'the powers'.

Perhaps we need to remember the words of Martin Buber:

Community should not be made into a principle; it should

always satisfy a situation rather than an abstraction. The realisation of community, like the realisation of any idea, cannot occur once and for all time: it must always be the moment's answer to the moment's question and nothing more.

As 'community' becomes popular as a concept, 'Utopia' becomes a term of abuse. What do we mean by the use of the term 'Utopian'? It is used conventionally in a pejorative sense, to indicate unreality, illusion, fantasy. The socialists of the Utopian type – Fourier, Saint-Simon, and others – gave no indication of how the vision might be realised. Indeed, William Morris said that he had no desire or energy to put things right, and that his task was to dream. I want to insist against the pragmatists and reformers that the Utopian vision, the dreaming of dreams, is a necessary part of politics. Of course, it is not enough, but it is still necessary – and 'practical' men and women who ridicule it are on dangerous ground and risk destroying that which gives their own work any real rootedness and foundation.

Yet it is not enough to dream. Politics is also about implementation and action. For Christians, this world matters. This world matters in any case, as a site of tremendous change and progress. More occurs every year in one rainforest than has occurred, for example, on Mars during the last million centuries. But within the Christian framework of understanding, this world matters because God created it, loves it, has redeemed it in Christ, and seeks to transform it into his likeness. Christian people are called to co-operate with God in this work, and this involves a concern with politics. But it involves also a dissatisfaction with the conventional models of the political.

Liberalism – and its limitations

Within the overall framework of capitalism, most forms of political life have been to a large extent affected by the liberal tradition. However, in recent decades many thinkers have come to see liberalism as defective. The anti-liberal rhetoric is linked to a general attack on what is termed the 'Enlightenment project'. Of course, there are a range of positions which tend to be lumped together under the liberal umbrella, including the moderate leftish version of neo-conservatism known as neo-liberalism, which supports free trade but is rather more pro-welfare and pro-state intervention than other conservatives. Although they share a concern for individual freedom, there is nevertheless a vast difference between free-market liberals and social liberals, some of whom probably think that the Labour Party under Tony Blair is too sympathetic to market capitalism. Certainly the failures and inadequacies of economic liberalism are evident on all sides, and the shift to a more authoritarian position is evident in various parts of the world. It is worth noting the diminishing number of political parties which now use the label 'liberal'. The attack on liberalism could take some very sinister forms in the coming years, and Christian critics of liberalism (such as I myself) need to be extremely careful that we do not end up in some strange alliances.

It is important to recognise and defend the positive commitments within political liberalism – the concern for civil rights, personal liberty, the dignity of individuals. Yet there are serious weaknesses. Many social liberals are far too optimistic about the role of law and of the state – part of their overall excessively optimistic view of progress. Much Christian social thought, influenced by a liberal reformist tradition, has had a very high view of the state, based more on Aquinas, who saw the state as part of the created order, than on Augustine, who saw it as a result of the Fall. Both liberals and those Christian social thinkers who have inherited liberal assumptions seem to have little taste for conflict, and wish to effect social change without any major disruption. As I have suggested, this possibility may well turn out to be a mirage.

Equally serious is the liberal understanding of the self and its neglect of the social context of selfhood – again, a defect shared by many Christian thinkers. Liberalism has worked with a disembodied, ungendered, view of the autonomous self, a self which is not socially grounded. Most liberals do not understand (or choose not to recognise) the social construction of self, issues of class position and class conflict, and the power relationships which are involved in personal life. Atomistic and shallow individualism is deeply ingrained in liberal attitudes.

Christians in the future will need to question many of their liberal assumptions, and the grandiose claims which are made for liberalism – even to the extent of rooting it in the Hebrew prophets and the Sermon on the Mount![17]

Christianity and capitalism

Liberal economic and political thought has grown out of the capitalist order. Again, most Christians in the West take capitalism for granted, either as part of the way things are, the best we have, or (very often) as the neutral context of their activities which they do not even think about or examine. In recent years we have seen numerous announcements of the triumph of capitalism. Ironically the publication of Francis Fukuyama's book, arguing that there was no alternative to Western capitalism, coincided with the reappearance of others looking at the nature of alternatives to the capitalist economic order.[18] In whatever areas contentment may be found, contentment about the stability and permanence of capitalism does not seem to be universal.

There are still people who hope for capitalism with a heart, a human face, but it is questionable whether this is possible. In Britain, the years since Margaret Thatcher came to power have been marked by increased division, by a divided nation, by the growth of the 'overclass' (the very rich), and by the polarisation of the prosperous majority and an increasingly embittered minority. It is a highly dangerous condition, and if the Conservative Party is torn apart and disintegrates, it will be to some extent the result of this process. No party can survive without some social vision, and if it is a vision which effectively casts off whole sections of the population, its fruits will be very bitter indeed.

The future of world capitalism – the global economic order and its political structures – must be of major importance to Christians in the coming years. An area which is the subject of constant discussion, and which will remain high on the agenda of the next century, is globalisation. It seems to me that, while there is much oversimplification here, there is a basic truth which is unassailable: that decision-making, and economic and

149

political trends, are determined now, and will be in the future, more and more along transnational lines. The globalisation of capitalism has rightly been seen as a new Leviathan. Global capitalism since 1945 has increasingly assumed the status of a belief-system, a Mammonite theology, with the World Bank as the key group in a hierarchy.[19]

The global political process has become increasingly dangerous to social and physical health, not least because developments in science, technology and banking have led to vast international power-systems which are not political in the traditional sense but which override political systems. The power of the multinational conglomerates creates unemployment, wage-cuts, and widespread vulnerability all over the world. We need to guard against simplistic ideas of globalisation, and the language of 'world capitalism'. Capital and investment-flows around the world were greater before 1914 than they are now. Robert Reich has written of the rootless firm with no national identity which roams the world for cheap labour but in fact, most multinationals are American, Japanese, German or British, and are very much locked into their specific culture. However, I do not think this undermines the globalisation thesis, though it refines it and modifies some extreme claims about it.[20]

In Britain, neither deferential hierarchical capitalism nor the newer versions of unaccountable quangos, managerial elites and bureaucratic empires are particularly stable. They have not led to the 'culture of contentment' identified by Galbraith, but rather to a culture of insecurity. Galbraith's thesis contrasted the simmering discontent of the 1930s with what he called a culture of contentment today. Yet it is not as simple as this: clearly there is a good deal of discontent. Indeed, it would seem that we live in a profoundly discontented and insecure age at many levels – as even the Royal Family has realised. One of the most worrying aspects of current capitalism in Britain and elsewhere is the rise of the unaccountable quango, and the breakdown of accountability. Decisions affecting human lives are increasingly made by remote bodies over the heads of local, democratically elected councils. The history of the London Docklands Development Corporation is a classic example, where the Toronto-based property developers Olympia and York were selling property in New York in order to pay for developments in London's East End. In spite of the rhetoric of 'consultation' and the commitment to 'social housing', this movement of 'regeneration' has been dictated by international developers accountable to no one.[21]

Local churches have played an important role in resisting these forces: for example, the record of the Anglican Church in Docklands at the time of the election of the Fascist councillor Derek Beackon in 1993 is excellent.[22] The seed-plot of unaccountability and of contempt for local residents is classically ideal soil on which grass-roots Fascism can grow and has grown. In the future, the relationship of local churches with the revived 'community organising' movement will be extremely important. But it will not touch the structures of international capitalism, and serious attention must be paid as to how we can move beyond the role of achieving small victories. It must also be said that the Church is far better at spotting and fighting injustice outside itself than it is at dealing with the unaccountability, the secrecy, the authoritarianism, the old-boy network, and the capitalistic ethos within its own walls. Hence the need for social holiness and the equivalent of Trotsky's doctrine of permanent revolution within the Church. It is of vital importance that Anglicans in particular struggle to bring an end to the unjust forms of hierarchy and bureaucracy at national and diocesan level. In this struggle, political realism is vital, for the Church, as institution, fears all threats to its power and security, and will only share power when it is in jeopardy.[23]

I do not believe that any challenge to injustice within the Church will be effective unless it is grounded in a wider political awareness and commitment. Injustice within the Church is one aspect of social injustice which, in global terms, is part of capitalism. Trotsky, and others within the Marxist tradition, held that there were contradictions within capitalism which would lead to crises and collapse, and, while their specific predictions have often been mistaken, their general assessment is correct. The gross inequalities which are essential to capitalism lead inevitably to social conflict, while the enforcement of the law to defend inequality and injustice leads to upheaval and perhaps to revolution. Within Western cities, the capitalist economic order combines massive concentrations of wealth with the most appalling – and increasing – poverty. Nowhere is this seen so starkly as in Chicago, where the towers of Michigan Avenue stare aggressively and insolently across the lake at the wastes of the devastated South Side. Here, on the South Side, inequality mounts to new heights, and many commentators believe that the degree of inequality may be unsustainable. What we see in Chicago is repeated in most American cities, and it is a recipe for total social collapse. One third of all American Blacks between the ages of 18 and 30 are now in prison awaiting trial or on bail. It is no basis for a healthy society.[24] The future of Western cities must be a high priority for Christians in the coming years.

Yet I have always believed that the fundamental critique of capitalism is the moral critique. As a system it may work for a time, may lead to the kind of crises predicted by Marx, Lenin and Trotsky. There is evidence for both the resilience and the crises of capitalism. But at heart, what is critical for Christians is that it is a system which is not only in fundamental conflict with religious values, but actually corrupts people and impedes the work of redemption. The classical Christian tradition has pointed out that the inequality and injustice are the results of *pleonexia* – a word which is usually translated as greed or avarice, but which in fact refers to that disposition towards acquisition which is essential to the working of the capitalist order. It is here that capitalism comes into fundamental conflict with Christian ethics and spirituality. Nowhere has this been put so clearly in recent years as by Alasdair MacIntyre in his account of the effect of capitalism on persons.

> What constitutes success in life becomes a matter of the successful acquisition of consumer goods and thereby that acquisitiveness which is so often a character trait necessary for success in capital accumulation is further sanctioned. Unsurprisingly *pleonexia*, the drive to have more and more, becomes treated as a central virtue. But Christians in the Middle Ages had learned from Aristotle that *pleonexia* is the vice that is the counterpart of the virtue of justice. And they had understood, as later theologians have failed to do ... the close connection between developing capitalism and the sin of usury. So it is not after all just human sinfulness that generates particular individual acts of injustice over and above the institutional injustice of capitalism itself. Capitalism also provides systematic incentives to develop a type of character that has a propensity to injustice.[25]

Traditional Christian socialism regarded capitalism as a faith rooted in devouring, overpowering lust, a form of Mammon-worship. The history of the consumerist ethos since Thatcherism confirms the truth of its view, for in this philosophy there is nothing except the satisfaction of desires, no sense of human life, only material and functions. But the cost of this is the death of the soul.

Christianity and socialism

If we are to move from death to life, from slavery to liberation, from acquisitiveness to holiness, we need to work both at the level of personal and corporate spiritual discipline, and at the level of political restructuring. And this must raise the question of the future of socialism. The struggle for alternatives to capitalism will occupy Christians and all people of moral concern during the twenty-first century. Socialism, as a political movement, is quite modern. In its origin in the 1830s, it was seen as the opposite of individualism. At the heart of the socialist vision was social or common ownership of the necessities of life. Common ownership and democratic control of the means of production was originally far more central than state control or nationalisation which developed later. Socialists have always recognised that there are many forms of social ownership, of which co-operative ownership is one. Nationalisation in itself has nothing particularly to do with socialism, and has existed under non-socialist and anti-socialist regimes. But throughout its history, socialism has been inseparable from some form of social or common ownership. Socialism by its very nature involves the abolition of private ownership of capital.

The Labour Party in Britain has never been a socialist party, but it has contained socialists and still does. Its commitment to common ownership was embodied until recently in the famous Clause Four, as well as in many other statements. The National Executive policy document *For Socialism and Peace* (1934) stressed the centrality of common ownership. Socialists, of course, have widely differing positions, not least about whether socialism can be realised by the 'parliamentary road'. As long ago as 1948 G. D. H. Cole warned British socialists that it would be impossible to win an electoral majority for socialism, while Sir Stafford Cripps believed that the Labour government should take emergency powers to force its pro- gramme through. Hence many socialists see themselves as 'revolutionary socialists', because they do not believe that socialism is possible without a revolution – that is, without a fundamental shift in economic and political power, a shift which is bound to meet with strong resistance.

However, in spite of these differences, all socialists until recently have agreed that socialism could not work simply by patching up the superstructure. So has there been a collapse, or decay, of the very concept of socialism? Certainly the lan- guage has largely been abandoned, not least in the Labour Party. Lenin's claim that socialism means nationalisation plus electrification might now be rephrased, in a Blairite way, as stakeholding plus computerisation. There is a great deal of what has been called 'angora jumper' politics – pink and woolly. Some have even spoken of the burial of socialism and of the need for post-socialist politics. The maintenance of a socialist philosophy, when the economic theory underlying it seems to have died, is a major problem. The Blairite position seems to be that socialist 'values' can be maintained without the socialist economic or social structure. This seems highly questionable, since values and structure are inextricably bound together. Can the vision be renewed? Can the project be restructured?

Undoubtedly, if there is a socialism of the future, it will have to be reshaped and reconceived in major ways. Much of what we have called socialism suffers from a narrowness of perspec- tive. It has been a European movement, a movement which grew up within Western Europe and the nation state. So we find today that on many crucial issues – sexuality, pornography, the Middle East, Ireland, not to mention vast areas of cultural politics – there is no identifiable socialist perspective. Socialism is also a product of the Enlightenment – yet it is the Enlighten- ment which is currently under question. Of course, socialist thinking and practice has been changed by the growth of the 'new social movements' – feminism, the green movements, and so on. A simple-minded adherence to notions of class and labour cannot be meaningful in the vastly changed societies of the future, thought this is not to deny the fact that class is still very relevant in our society.[26] I believe that a major problem for the left is its inability to respond to key issues of everyday life

– racism, sexism, the environment, sexual orientation, personal despair, and religion. There seems to have been a paralysis of the British left which has led to an increased concern about Third World issues – what Terry Eagleton has termed a 'stampede from Trotsky to Trinidad'.[27]

Many have seen the break-up of the Soviet Union and its satellites as evidence of the final collapse of the socialist enterprise. I have never understood the logic of this argument, and I suspect that it does not possess any. It is just as likely that the post-Soviet atmosphere will give new life to the socialist endeavour. Many writers have argued that some kind of 'new left' is urgently needed in the aftermath of the breakdown of the Soviet system. Whether or not this happens, it is important that the left does not lose its links with its own history, and, whether we like it or not, the Soviet Union is intricately tied up with that history. The recognition of mistaken paths and judgements is not to be confused with the abandonment of much that is important in historical development. It is, as Marx said, out of our old history that our new history will be made.

Perhaps what has collapsed is not socialism but the alliance between socialist economics and the repressive authoritarian politics of excessive central control. In many parts of the world (such as south-east Asia), we find a strong commitment to social ownership and co-operation. One of the important questions for the future is whether, and how, markets can be linked with a socialist society. Markets are not intrinsically inimical to socialism, though their dominance most certainly is. The idea of a market economy grew up alongside capitalism. But capitalism is primarily about ownership, while markets are allocating-mechanisms and are capable of existing within a variety of systems, including a socialist system. Markets can only operate within some social context. A major area which socialists, including Christian socialists, will have to work at in the coming years is the place of markets within a socially responsible order. There has been a good deal of talk about a 'social market', but much of the discussion remains vague and imprecise. It is not clear how social markets would work, how interest rates would be set, how public spending would be decided, and so on. The concept is a very general one, and has no solid body of analysis behind it, so that it is in danger of becoming a political slogan. What is clear is that society cannot survive subordination to market laws, and the whole issue of the place of markets within a socialist society remains an urgent one.

Whether or not the future of British politics lies with 'New Labour', the future of the Labour Party is of great concern to all people who are committed to justice. Yet I do fear that many of the New Labour activists, who seem often to have come from rather sheltered, middle-class backgrounds, do not mix easily with ordinary people. As Labour abandons socialism, it is likely that what is left of socialism will become no more than what Tony Benn has called 'intensive care units for capitalism'.[28]

The attack on inequality must remain central to any socialist agenda, and it is vital that we rescue the concept of equality from its not-so-cultured despisers. Much of the polemic against equality is in fact an attack on 'sameness'. Yet it is precisely because human beings are not the same, because of the immense diversity within human beings and societies, that we need the idea of equality at all. Here, in the commitment to the project of equality, Christians and socialists come very close. My own view is that some form of socialism is intrinsic to any progressive Catholic social theology. In spite of its crudity – all slogans are crude – I stand by the old maxim, coined first by Canon Lewis Donaldson, that 'Christianity is the religion of which socialism is the practice'. But even if this is not accepted, the affinities between Christian social thought and at least some forms of socialism are clear.

One of the most significant events of recent years has been the revival of the Christian socialist tradition, albeit in a particular reformist version. The Christian Socialist Movement, formed in 1960 out of two earlier groups, had for many years been a small and ageing organisation, dominated by elderly white men from Nonconformist backgrounds. In recent years it has grown enormously, and has attracted many young people – as well as a large number of MPs, including the two recent leaders of the Labour Party, the late John Smith and Tony Blair. The ethical socialism associated with Tawney and others seems to have returned in a modern form.

However, two cautionary words are important here. First, numerical growth in itself is not adequate unless there is also a growth in ideas, serious theological and political analysis, and commitment. Secondly, it is ironic that the revival of Christian socialism has coincided exactly with the virtual abandonment of the historic language of socialism within the Labour Party. Tony Blair stands within the venerable British tradition of social democracy rather than that of socialism. It is interesting, and to some of us depressing, that leading Christians such as the Bishop of Edinburgh have decided to join the Labour Party at the very point at which it has abandoned socialism.

If socialist thought is not popular within the Western Churches, Marxism certainly is not. Yet I believe that the neglect of Marxist analysis by Christians is a serious error, not because Marxism is adequate as a total theory of the world, but because there are insights here which are not easily available from any other source. Cornel West has claimed that Christianity and Marxism are the most distorted traditions in the modern world. He goes on to argue that an alliance between prophetic Christianity and progressive Marxism may be the last humane hope for humankind.[29]

I believe that Marxism and the dialectical materialist view of history remain an indispensable tool for Christians. Without contradiction and conflict there is no movement. Louis Althusser has said that Marx opened up a 'new continent' of thought – the historical dimension.[30] Among Marx's successors, Trotsky argued, (correctly, in my view) that the future lay in a movement towards socialism or a slide back into barbarism. But Trotsky saw also that, as capitalism was an international phenomenon, so only an international socialism could be effective. But neither Trotsky nor his followers gave enough attention to rethinking the whole concept of revolution, and the Trotskyist tradition is still to a large degree imprisoned within dated and increasingly sterile concepts about permanent revolution. Nevertheless, I do not think that socialists can afford to ignore the crucial insights of Marx and Trotsky in their analysis of the workings of the capitalist order.

A central task for Christian social thought in the coming years will be the encounter between Marxist analysis and the mainstream Christian social tradition. Much of the latter remains locked within thought – forms established by the social encyclicals since 1891. The most extraordinary feature of the debate around the Roman Catholic bishops' document, *The Common Good* (October 1996), is not the fact that they said what they did. Nobody familiar with the literature of Catholic social doctrine since 1891 would have been surprised at the general content, which stands well within the mainstream of the social encyclical tradition. Nor were the predictable responses of leading politicians surprising, however depressing one might find the lack of sophistication in debate on social ethics. What was surprising was the clear lack of awareness among many Roman Catholics that there was a body of social doctrine within the Catholic tradition at all.

The document was very much a traditional one. Since Leo XIII's *Rerum Novarum* of 1891 there has been a history of encyclicals, pastoral letters, and so on. The tradition of the social encyclicals is fairly consistent. Paul VI in *Populorum Progressio* (1967) – denounced by the *Wall Street Journal* as 'souped up Marxism' – described capitalism as a 'woeful system' in which profit was the key motive of progress, competition was the supreme law of economics, and private ownership of the means of production was seen as having no limits and no obligations.[31] Pope John Paul II has laid particular stress on the human dimension, as in *Redemptor Hominis* of March 1979.

Yet without exception, all the Roman Catholic lay people questioned by BBC Radio 4 in Coventry on the day of publication said that the Church had no business being involved in politics, and that the bishops should stay within their churches. The social tradition is, as the authors of a well-known manual call it, the Church's 'best-kept secret'.[32] Individualism has affected Catholic life, and many Christians brought up with a Catholic sacramental framework are as individualistic as the most committed evangelical of the 'personal pronouns' genre.

The Christian way forward

The notion of a common good goes back a long way, but its use does need to be questioned. It was used by the Conservative Prime Minister Anthony Eden in 1955, and has been taken up by many Anglican social thinkers. Thus John Atherton offered it as 'an important alternative to liberation theology'.[33] It is a favourite phrase in Anglican worship, and does tend to reflect a Church which is unfamiliar with, or removed from, social conflict and which thinks of itself as neutral and detached. However, in the current climate we need to ask: is the enunciation of general principles enough? Is there a 'common good'?

Is not this precisely the problem, that, in a class society, what is good for one group is bad for another? To assert a common good is as unreal as to deny the persistence of class. The common good is something which has to be struggled for, and, if my thesis is correct, it cannot be achieved within the present order of things.

The Anglican social tradition has not been encyclical-based, yet some of its governing features are similar – reports of Archbishops' Commissions, from the Fifth Report of 1919, *Christianity and Industrial Problems*, down to *Faith in the City* (1985).[34] Archbishop William Temple in his best-seller *Christianity and Social Order* (1942) began his first chapter with the question, 'What right has the Church to interfere?' The responses to Temple and his predecessors were at the same level of crudity as responses from some of the politicians of today – though it should be noted that some, notably John Selwyn Gummer, made it very clear that the Church's right to speak was accepted and that the disagreement was about the details. In fact, very little official Anglican social thought has been about the details. If we ask why this is so, the answer is partly cultural and partly theological. The cultural aspect is to do with the Church's place within the *status quo* and its unwillingness, at the official level, to disturb that order of things.

A major problem with much Anglican 'social concern' – and the depth of the 'concern' is not in doubt – is that it is top down. Much Christian socialism, like most Anglican social thinking as a whole, has been very patrician – aloof, genteel, polite, detached from the lives of working-class people, committed to the basic structures of society – not in fact socialist at all, certainly not revolutionary. We see this dramatically in the career of Mervyn Stockwood, former Bishop of Southwark, that most medieval and authoritarian of bishops who called himself a Christian socialist in spite of all the evidence that this was not so. As Valerie Pitt so perceptively explained:

Socialism is about the structures of society. Its aim is not only economic, that is the redistribution of the resources of a community from the rich to the poor, but political, the transfer . . . of political and social power from 'the governing classes' across the community as a whole . . . A socialist knows that the new wine of social justice will burst the old political bottles. He/she expects real revolution, the world turned upside down. There is no evidence that the Bishop [Stock-wood] wanted any such consummation ... It is ... not a moral defect not to be a revolutionary, only, if your intention is to bring new life to an ancient institution, it is a fatal obstacle. New wine will not go into old bottles. The Church of England couldn't and cannot sustain any real vigour of reform without a revolution, an onslaught not only on its centres of power but also on its inherited mind set. Unfortunately Mervyn Stockwood had himself inherited that mind set. It was a pity.[35]

Theologically, a major problem with Anglican social witness has been that it has tended to exalt incarnation and sanctification at the expense of redemption and judgement. A 'neat incarnationalism' has marked much Anglican thought. So there has been a tendency to bless and hallow communities, movements and individuals, in a fairly uncritical way. Charles Gore even spoke of the need for the 'sanctification of each new social order'.[36] In a similar way, the American social gospel movement argued for the 'Christianisation' of the social order. I think this idea is very questionable.

Can the hierarchies take up more partisan and biased positions? Some will say not. In extreme circumstances, it is agreed, it is legitimate and indeed obligatory to resist and call upon Christians to resist. However, it is interesting that, in recent months, the Bishop of Edinburgh has broken with the long tradition of 'general principles' and has advised the electorate to vote Labour. It seems likely that others will now follow. Yet within days of Holloway's very mild statement – and he is not even a bishop of the Church of England – the Archbishop of York was appearing on radio, on this occasion supported by his Archdeacon, to present what was in fact an extremely dated concept of the Church's social witness.[37] One step forward, two steps back. However, whether the hierarchy will grasp the nettle or not, a confessing Church of deviant minorities must do so.

While archbishops and bishops tend to be frightened of dealing with specifics, they are quite good, from time to time, at issuing calls for moral renewal. These are always safe, and can usually be guaranteed to win support from the government and opposition. Morality is, after all, what the Church is supposed to talk about – unless, of course, it is about the Falklands War or some national issue involving immoral public behaviour.

It is usually safer to stay with sex and family issues (avoiding, of course, comment on the Royal Family or government ministers), and to restrict oneself to general exhortations. I believe that calls for 'moral renewal' by archbishops and bishops are almost always misconceived and unhelpful. There have been two examples of such calls in recent years in England, one by Archbishops Coggan and Blanch in 1976, and more recently one by Archbishop Carey in 1996. Both were extremely sincere, both appealed beyond the Church to the nation on the basis of shared moral concerns, both were issued by men with evangelical backgrounds, and both, in my opinion, exhibited similar mistakes and muddled attitudes.[38]

This is not the way forward. The coming generations will only respect Christians if they can be shown to have thought deeply and reflected carefully about the issues and if their rhetoric is free from cliché, platitude and simplistic phrases. We have a long way to go. I want to suggest that the renewal of radical Christian witness cannot now wait on the hierarchy, nor can it be restricted to a trickle-down approach. What is needed, and indeed has already begun to happen, is the emergence of a confessing Church network, rooted in the communities of people who are most seriously affected by the injustices of the present system. The late William Stringfellow stressed four characteristics of Christian social ethics: realism about the world; inconsistency; radicalism; and intercession and care for the poorest.[39] I would like to add the need for serious analysis; the recovery and maintenance of outrage and passion; hope and vision; a point of leverage and a handle on the structures; and strong political commitment.

For this kind of witness we need a disciplined, prayerful, thoughtful, courageous, network of local-based Christian communities. We need a Church which does not simply deal with social ethics, but which is a social ethic. We need a recovery of social holiness and a recognition that the fate of the soul is the fate of the social order.[40]

7

Liturgy and Liberation

The world can be saved from political chaos and collapse by one thing only, and that is worship.

WILLIAM TEMPLE

The liturgy is the indispensable basis of Christian social regeneration.

VIRGIL MICHEL

Is the modern Christian capable of the liturgical act?

ROMANO GUARDINI

The future of the Christian community in the twenty-first century depends to a large extent on the quality, authenticity and power of its liturgical life, its worship – its corporate life of penitence, lament, praise and glory. All Christian life begins in liturgy, in the act of worship. Liturgy is the primary theological act.[1] As the Athanasian Creed puts it, 'And the Catholic faith is this: that we worship . . .' Liturgy is both a sacred act and a counter-cultural act. It points both upwards in adoring love to God, and outwards in disaffiliation from the disorder and illusion of the world. It seeks to create and manifest 'the life of the world to come' in the midst of the present chaos. No religious movement has ever existed without some form of liturgical expression. But where today is this expression? Is it even possible? The critical question today is that posed by Guardini: are we any longer capable of the liturgical act?

Liturgy is about stretching our human capacity for awe and wonder almost to breaking-point. It is about the *finitum capax infiniti*, the finite capacity for the infinite. Over many centuries in the West, our sense of the power, wonder and mystery of liturgy has been eroded. Yet I believe that there can be no deep renewal of Christian life which does not involve the rediscovery of the central place of liturgy. In this process of rediscovery we will be led into strange, confusing, messy and mysterious places, for liturgy reaches back to the origins of human life and human desire. It leads us into the worlds of sacrifice and of myth, of combat, and of death and resurrection. We need to visit these regions if we are to make sense of the liturgical moment and allow it to transform us.

Eugene Masure stressed the importance of going back to the ancient sources if we are to recover the real meaning of liturgical worship.

> At the risk of contamination, among these dark pools where our feet slip in the blood of goats and heifers, we must spend some time in this religious shambles if we are to understand it . . . Beneath the rubbish heap of myths, rites, systems, weird confusions and hideous practices, we must find the hidden line of Godward movement.[2]

Liturgy has its roots in ancient history. But it also reaches forward to the new world, and it sings a new hymn (Rev. 5:9). It is an act of yearning, of striving, of anticipation of a new world. Christian liturgy is the articulation of a new song, the song of a new humanity.

At its core, liturgy is praise. Praise is an emptying-out of self towards God in an act of utter uselessness. The quest for a 'relevant' liturgy is in a sense misconceived. Liturgy is irrelevant in the usual functional sense of the word. It becomes extremely relevant, but this occurs as a by-product of its action. But to make relevance the criterion of worship is fatal. Liturgy is useless in the same way that poetry is useless. Yet, as in poetry, the work of liturgical worship involves a quest for images and symbols which are adequate to our predicament. Like poetry, all it can do politically in the direct sense is to write in the sand, and yet this may well prove to be a powerful activity.[3] But liturgy is inherently and deeply political in its testimony against idolatry and oppression. It is a Godward activity, a turning to that which is beyond, in an act of praise. Praise is the heart of liturgy, the heart of theology. Praise constitutes theological reality. As a theologian, I believe that my primary theological task is praise and prayer.

Christianity: a corporeal faith

From its beginnings, the Christian community has worshipped. We get some sense of this in the Book of Revelation, which is to large extent an account of the liturgy of praise within the context of the conflict with oppression. At its heart is the dramatic vision of the slaughtered Lamb in Chapter 5. The Lamb has been murdered, but his sacrificial death brings about the emergence of a new people, created from all races, languages and nations, and constituted by worship. It has been suggested that the framework of the book is based on the paschal vigil.[4] Today, however, scholars are more reticent to seek such precise evidence of liturgical structures within the New Testament. What we do find there is the theological framework within which the early Christians saw themselves in relation to God and the world. This can be summarised as the solidarity of the body of Christ, the dying and rising in baptism, the feeding on Christ in the Eucharist, and the anticipation of the life of heaven.

The early Christian movement saw itself as the body of Christ, the *soma Christou*, created in the act of baptism and constantly renewed in the eucharistic offering. Throughout the Pauline letters the Church is called the body of Christ (e.g., 1 Cor. 12:27, Eph. 1:23). It is this sense of being the body of Christ, the organism of the crucified and risen Christ, which constitutes the primary liturgical consciousness. The community seeks the fullness of Christ in the building up of the body (Eph. 4:13).

The Christian looks back in awe to his or her baptismal incorporation. It is seen as *the* decisive turning-point in life. The ancient liturgy of baptism is now well-known and well documented. It consists, first, of a renunciation of the world and of Satan, a turning away from idols to the living God. This is followed by the baptismal promises, after which the candidate is plunged beneath the waters, symbolic of dying and being buried with Christ (Rom. 6:4), and anointed with the chrism. Numerous early Christian writers say that it is because we are anointed with the chrism that we are called Christians.[5] Finally, the candidate is clothed in a white robe, the robe of the risen Christ, and shares in the Eucharist.

I do not believe that we will recover the sense of being the body of Christ in our time until there is a revolution in our practice of baptism comparable to that which has occurred in the eucharistic celebration. The drama, the social context, the extreme character of the renunciations and commitments, the sense of sharing in the saving mystery of Christ – all this has to be enacted liturgically if it is to convey its transforming power.

The early Church was a eucharistic community. The apostolic group was united in the apostles' doctrine and *koinonia* (weakly translated 'fellowship', but better 'solidarity' or 'common life'), in the breaking of the bread, and in prayers (Acts 2:42). Liturgical scholarship has shown how rich was the eucharistic solidarity of early Christians, and it is good that we have recovered, through the new eucharistic prayers, some of that wholeness of vision.

At the heart of the Eucharist is the commitment to the material, and to the belief that spirit is mediated through matter. The physical crudity, materiality and even carnality, not only of the Eucharist but of the entire Christian world-view, was the key issue in the early conflicts with gnosticism. Thus Irenaeus stressed the centrality of the flesh:

> If our flesh is not saved, then the Lord has not redeemed us with his blood . . . There can be no blood without veins, flesh and the rest of the human substance which the Word of God actually became . . . How then can it be said that flesh belonging to the Lord's own body and nourished by his body and blood is incapable of receiving God's gift of eternal life?[5]

Irenaeus was attacking the gnostics who were very bothered by the body, and especially by sexuality, and his writing is typical of orthodox incarnational theology. 'The Word made flesh' and 'Christ is risen' are central to Christian faith. The flesh is holy and is the raw material of salvation: we should not be embarrassed by our bodies. Christians are by definition materialists and so art, image, bodily contact, sensuality, have a central place in liturgy. This was also the central theological issue in the iconoclastic controversy – the iconoclasts wanted to smash all the pictures! – and Catholic Christians are clearly on the side of the materialists.

So eucharistic liturgy is materialist. But it also looks forward to the messianic banquet, the feast in the Kingdom of God. All liturgy is eschatological in the sense that it seeks to image, to prefigure, the coming world. It is filled with wonder and with yearning, it looks forward in hope and joy. It is a festival. All our life is a festival, according to Clement of Alexandria.

The social nature of liturgy

It is impossible to recapture fully the worshipping life of the early Christians – nor would it be desirable if it were possible – but what evidence we have indicates something of the splendour and symbolic power of the liturgy. It is this which we have lost and need to recover for our own day.

Irenaeus was writing in the second century. He saw clearly that the whole eucharistic framework depended on a firm commitment to the goodness of the material. For if the creation is merely decay, ignorance and passion, then it would

167

be a sin against God to offer him the fruits of decay, ignorance and passion. The history of Christian liturgy is the history of offering material things to God.

The liturgy was the heart of the culture of the Middle Ages. The Christian community which arose from the ruins of the Roman Empire was based on the Mass. It was the inner principle of unity of medieval culture. The preservation of liturgical tradition was a major preoccupation of the Church in the Dark Ages, and was the way in which the vitality and continuity of life became the seed of a new order.[6] In the Carolingian period, civilisation was organised around the liturgy, though between 400 and 800 there took place a clericalisation of liturgy and a reduction of popular liturgical activity. The Roman rite *was* much more basic than earlier liturgies, and involved less popular participation. The readings were reduced, and preaching and intercessory prayer were omitted at an early stage. From the eleventh century the Roman rite was used throughout Western Europe, except in Milan and parts of Spain. We are still recovering from the effects of this process of reduction and of clericalisation.

In spite of this, it is still clear that medieval liturgy was profoundly social. Duffy has argued that, at this time, there was no great gulf between clergy and laity, and that the medieval liturgy was the main reservoir from which religious beliefs and practice were drawn.

> In the liturgy and in the sacramental celebrations which were its central moments, medieval people found the key to the meaning and purpose of their lives.[7]

Liturgy was a social act. The very language of the eucharistic offering was 'saturated with communitarian and corporate imagery'.[8] The medieval liturgy was a drama. Indeed, modern drama is derived from medieval mystery plays which drew on the Christian liturgy. Of course, we should not try to return to the Middle Ages – but we can find help, inspiration and resources in that period of Christian history in which the sense of being a community was far more deeply ingrained than it is today.

The Oxford Movement of the nineteenth century did look back to the Middle Ages for its inspiration. While much of the liturgical expression of the movement was influenced by the liturgical forms of contemporary Rome, there was a wing of the movement, often referred to as the 'sacramental socialists', who drew on medieval practices and linked them with current social and political struggles.[9] One element of this was the recovery of dance – a common feature of medieval worship. Among some early Christian thinkers, the whole work of redemption was seen in terms of dance. Thus St Thalassios ends one of his prayers with a reference to Christ's 'having risen from the dead and dancing with the angels in the blessed, eternal and indissoluble dance'.[10] The recovery of liturgical dance was an important element in the modern rediscovery of the liturgy. But it did not stand alone: it was part of a whole new awareness of the liturgy as sacred drama and creative act.

Liturgy as celebration

A key figure in the revival of corporate and democratic liturgy in the Church of England was Conrad Noel, parish priest of the Essex village of Thaxted from 1910 to 1942. Noel looked back to the Middle Ages because, as he argued, in spite of much oppression, there was a vigour and freedom which showed itself in communal life, glorious architecture and gaiety of colour. It was important to recapture that spirit and move forward to new adventures.[11]

Noel saw the liturgy as an expression in historical time of the life of the world to come. It was said, at the time of his death, that the celebrations of the liturgy at Thaxted were 'the most perfect, and, in all respects, the most typically English celebrations of the Holy Mass in the whole Anglican communion'.[12] Noel looked forward to 'a new social order inspired by Catholicism of which the Holy Sacrament of the Altar was its symbol and life'. The Thaxted movement was a deeply sacramental movement, rooted in splendid and colourful worship, as well as a prophetic movement, committed to a revolutionary vision of a new world. Noel wrote:

> We preach the Christ who all through his life stressed the value of the common meal, the bread and wine joyously shared among his people, the Mass as prelude to the New World Order in which all would be justly produced and

equally distributed. The Lord thus chose the human things of everyday life, the useful bread and the genial wine, to be the perpetual vehicles of his presence among us till his Kingdom should come on earth as in heaven.[13]

Noel's approach to liturgy was all of a piece with his understanding of theology. He saw that God was:

the maker of the sense of wonder, justice, love and worship; of the sense of colour which delights in the flowers, pictures, sunrises and gay fabrics; of the sense of justice which drives men to rebellion against tyrants who rob men's souls of vigour, their minds of leisure, and their bodies of nourishment; of the sense of smell which rejoices in roses and frankincense; of the sense of hearing which responds to poetry and music.[14]

So over many years Thaxted Church came to be a source of inspiration to thousands of people. Here they found the music of Gustav Holst, Morris dances and summer festivals, brilliantly coloured banners, and a liturgical space which encouraged expansion, freedom and festivity.

Noel was a country priest. His urban equivalents were people such as Etienne Watts in Manchester, Jim Wilson at Sneyd in the Potteries, and St John Beverley Groser in the East End of London. In these places too there was colour and festivity, processions, and a great spirit of joyful exuberance. A visitor to Sneyd church in 1937 wrote:

Outside the smoke banners of the pot-banks; inside the whitewashed church, the gay flags and ensigns of a different world. Just to step into Sneyd Church therefore is to face a challenge, for the two pictures do not seem to belong to the same order.[15]

The writer brings out the sense of worship as a counter-cultural activity, a prefiguring of the world as it could be, but particularly a manifestation of joy and wonder.

John Groser's ministry in the East End from 1922 to 1962 brings out the same stress on festivity. In contrast to much of the Christian left (which was grim and intense), Groser's politics were rooted in worship and dramatic celebration. He was profoundly influenced by Noel and the Catholic Crusade, and the Stepney chapter of the Crusade was based at Christ Church,

Watney Street. Like Noel, he saw the importance of festivity, of colour, music and dancing, in the creation of a Christian social consciousness. With Emma Goldman, he wanted no part in any revolution which did not include dancing. In some ways Groser's community at Watney Street was, with Sneyd, a kind of urban representation of what Thaxted was struggling to manifest in the countryside. Here too was the sense of a democratic Christian community; here too the stark contrast with the Romanising ritualism and clericalism of one wing of the Oxford Movement; here too the sense of the liturgy as a sacramental prefiguring of a liberated world.

Overlapping with Groser's ministry in Stepney was that of Stanley Evans at Holy Trinity, Dalston, where the life of the parish was focused on the parish Eucharist and the parish meeting. Celebration and debate, heart and head, were fully engaged in this dynamic Christian community. It was Evans in the 1950s and 1960s who helped me to understand the nature of liturgy in shaping the corporate identity of the Christian community. In an interview on BBC radio sometime around 1962, Evans spoke prophetically and with great perception about the future possibilities for a people's liturgy. Liturgy, he pointed out, had for many centuries been separated from the people, becoming something performed above the people's heads, by clergy or choir. A central problem for the late twentieth century was the lack of a common language and a common cultural form. Most thinking about liturgy had tended to focus on the rite rather than on the production of the whole liturgical act.

Evans emphasised that it is when people come together as a redeemed community that the whole body can be inspired and inflamed, and he went on to point out that:

> They are not ever an audience. They are an expressive community, if you like, an orchestra. Now this does not mean . . . that they all play the same instrument or that they all play all the time or at the same time, but they are an orchestra and everybody plays. While the audience-response in a theatre is something of great importance, there is still a distinction between the audience and the players. What I am trying to say is that this distinction does not exist in Christian liturgy. We have built up an area in which it does exist and we have destroyed Christian liturgy in doing so.[16]

171

I want, in looking at the prospects for worship in the coming years, to lay special emphasis on two phrases in that broadcast – 'expressive community' and 'orchestra'. Until we recover something of this sense of the worshipping community as an orchestra, we will not have liturgy at all, but rather a series of performances produced by the clergy for the people.

The eucharistic revolution

The emphasis on the centrality of worship, and on the need for a liturgical core for social action, goes back to the beginnings of the Anglican socialist tradition. Thus Stewart Headlam wrote in 1884:

> Restore the Mass to its true position as the one common necessary service and you preach a gospel which infidelity and plutocracy must give way to. We would urge upon our readers that there is no point in church reform of more importance than this of restoring the Mass to its proper central place.[17]

Donald Gray has argued that there was a close link between the spread of the parish communion movement and the growth of the 'sacramental socialist' tradition. The parish communion was already being celebrated in some 'advanced' parishes as early as 1909 and 1927. The East End was certainly one of its strongholds, and there is evidence for a parish communion at St Faith's, Stepney as early as 1890. Cosmo Lang, later Archbishop of Canterbury, was the first person to use the expression in 1905. In addition to the work of liturgical renewal through the parish communion movement, there was vitally important work going on elsewhere. Dom Prosper Gueranger, the nineteenth-century Abbot of Solesmes, was the pioneer of modern liturgical renewal, and was concerned to integrate matter and spirit; while in the USA, Virgil Michel of Collegeville, Minnesota (who died in 1938), was writing of liturgy as the basis of Christian culture. The journal *Orate Fratres* (now called *Worship*) was founded at St John's Abbey, Collegeville, in 1926. All these movements, and many others, formed part of the background to the Second Vatican Council and to the revision of liturgies within Anglicanism and other Churches.[18]

It is difficult to overstate the extent of the revolution which has been brought about. Today, the centrality of the eucharistic celebration and the coming together of the people of God in communion is taken for granted throughout the Church, in a way that was not common even 40 years ago. I certainly want to accept this revolution which has transformed the Christian world, transformed our whole understanding of what it is to be Church, and led to what Pannenberg has called 'a new eucharistic sensibility'.[19]

Let me be very personal at this point. I came to Christian faith as a teenager. At a certain point, around 1954, I wandered into a back-street Anglo-Catholic church, several miles from the centre of Manchester. The fact that I was able to do this at all brings home the first important fact about the church – it was open! I have been committed to keeping churches open ever since: had it been closed, I imagine my subsequent life might have been rather different. On entering, I was confronted by various ugly statues, and, apart from the Burne-Jones window, the church had nothing of great beauty about it. But I felt a strong compulsion to pray, and a very powerful sense that I was on holy ground. At the time I did not understand, and could not articulate, what any of this meant. It was some time later that I came to associate this experience with the reserved sacrament and with the fact that, over many years, a prayerful atmosphere had been built up. It was a place where others had knelt before me, a place where prayer had been valid.

When I later joined the worshipping community at this church, I found that, unlike most other churches in the area, the central liturgical act was the parish communion at which all received the sacrament. These were the years when Roman Catholics and Anglo-Catholics offered the Sunday Mass solemnly but only the priest communicated, and where evangelicals were very word-centred. Low-church Anglicans seemed rarely to celebrate the Eucharist at all, and Morning and Evening Prayer dominated (though only on Sundays – the notion of a daily office, although canonically obligatory, also seemed unknown). So, without knowing it, I entered the world of the liturgical movement, and the parish communion began to change my whole consciousness of what being a Christian was about. Only later did I come to see that I was entering into a long tradition.

Liturgical renewal

So the parish communion movement had already made considerable headway in the Church of England by the time the Second Vatican Council was convened in the early 1960s. The Council revolutionised the worshipping life of the Roman Communion, and, indirectly, of the whole Western Christian world. The liturgical reforms were taking place as I was preparing for ordination to the priesthood. I learnt to celebrate according to the old Roman rite, and had quickly to forget it and learn the new ways.[20] Since the 1960s Anglicans have also been involved in a process of liturgical renewal. We have had Series 2, Series 3, *The Alternative Service Book*, and a variety of supplementary volumes. Far more exciting and more ecumenical books have appeared elsewhere in the Anglican communion. By 1973 probably only 15 per cent of the Church used the 1662 or 1928 Books of Common Prayer. These changes have been basically good. Worship cannot be real if it is stuck in a time-warp, and, with the possible exception of the Royal Family and some sections of the Establishment, Anglican worship has moved on, theologically and pastorally, alongside the rest of the Western Church. It is sad, however, that there has been a loss of continuity, and that, by failing properly to revise the Book of Common Prayer and opt rather for an 'alternative' book, the Church of England missed the opportunity to achieve a real liturgical revision which maintained its place within a developing tradition.

I find *The Alternative Service Book* (ASB) a very odd and disappointing production. It is full of sexist language, even introducing it where it was not previously present, and its compilers seemed utterly insensitive to the fact – which is now so glaringly obvious if it was not at the time – that within a few years, it would be unusable by many people of integrity, male and female. Amazingly, it entirely ignored the most important week of the liturgical year and contained no paschal liturgy at all. It provided no rite of reconciliation at the very time when this was being revised and renewed elsewhere. It showed no awareness of the needs – or indeed of the existence – of the contemporary world, no recognition of such areas as human rights or other faiths. It contained no liturgy for peace and justice – though it did include prayers and readings for the consecration of an abbot, a fairly rare occurrence in the Church of England. Its collects were dreadful, didactic, often merely modernisations of Cranmer but keeping his bad theology. All in all, it was a disaster, and has made the Church of England unique in the Western Christian world. Everywhere else, there is a common lectionary, and common liturgical forms. Oh dear!

But the ASB is an aberration, and we are recovering from it. What is far more important is that there has been a major revolution in the approach to Christian liturgy. Frequent communion, the use of the daily office, new understandings of ways of worship, increased experimentation and flexibility at the local level: all these are now features of church-life at all levels. This process, while it needs guidance and direction, is unstoppable and good.

St Paul's, Bow Common: architecture and liturgy

During the years of liturgical change I found myself, at various points, associated with two parishes, one in the East End, the other in West London, where the liturgy made a powerful impact on my life and that of many others. The first is St Paul's Church, Bow Common, in the East End of London. Built in 1960, St Paul's is one of the few English churches which was built for the liturgical life of the future. The *Architectural Review* called it the most important church built in the twentieth century. Its theological and liturgical importance is manifested in the actual design of the building, which has been called democratic rather than hierarchical. All the seating is on one level, only the central altar being raised up. The altar is literally central, and is not separated by any altar-rail or structure. It is possible for people to stand on all sides of it. There are two small chapels in which there is provision for the eastward position at the Eucharist – something which should not be lost in the emphasis on facing the people. Both the reserved sacrament and the book of the Gospels are kept in one of the chapels, emphasising the equal importance of word and sacrament. There is no permanent special seating for special people, not even for the vicar – and clericalism in the liturgy is both discouraged and made physically as difficult as possible to express. (Robed clergy, apart from the vested eucharistic celebrant, do not appear at St Paul's.) The pew benches are easily movable, and there is a vast amount of open space. There are no permanent structures apart from the altars – no pulpit, no choir or other stalls, and the lecterns are movable.

From its early days, and indeed before the construction of the present building, the parish had been in the forefront of liturgical renewal, anticipating the Second Vatican Council's reforms by almost ten years. The daily office was sung for many years, even if only by two or three people, and there was a strong emphasis on the value of sheer adoration. Two distinctive features of the worship at St Paul's have lessons for the future. The first is its use of Gregorian chant, and its quest for simple forms of chant. There is an important principle here. The Second Vatican Council required that Gregorian chant should have the chief place in liturgical functions, and suggested that simpler melodies should be produced for smaller churches. This type of chant – from its use in primitive societies through early synagogues to the sometimes intricate and ornate styles of Gregorian plainsong – is monophonic, that is, based on one sound. Monophony is a universal style of singing, and perhaps the one musical practice which unites every human culture. It is purely vocal, and needs no instrumental accompaniment. It does not convey any message of its own, apart from the words which give it character and significance, and it acts as a kind of adhesive which locates key words and phrases in the corporate memory. The major twentieth-century rediscovery of the value of monophonic chants has been that associated with the Taizé community in France. On a smaller scale, the liturgical life of Bow Common has been for me a similar recovery of the need for discipline in liturgical practice. I believe that this small church in East London can teach us something about the vital role of rhythms, monotony and simplicity in worship. Without such rhythm and without the building up of a Christian memory, nurtured through loving repetition, liturgical worship becomes unstable and fragile to the point of collapse.

The second feature of St Paul's has been its stress on the

role of the liturgical hymn. Hymns shape theology, and most of it is bad theology. Most modern hymns are terrible, and reflect all the imbalance and disarray of the Christian world. Many are slushy, sentimental, sugary, otherworldly, individualistic, and so on. They feed the emotions with the spiritual equivalent of junk food, but they do not nourish the Christian consciousness in any healthy and nutritious way. The more modern the hymn books, the worse they often are – some of the worst examples being those associated with the charismatic renewal and with trendy evangelicalism. Sadly, many Roman Catholics have degraded their liturgy by the use of such hymns and songs, which contradict and undermine everything the liturgy stands for!

We need, therefore, to recover the theologically wholesome liturgical hymn, of which the early Ambrosian hymns provided the basic shape. The liturgical hymn avoids the use of the first person singular, sentimental piety, and subjectivity. It is theocentric, focused on God, and seeks to articulate the corporate identity of the Christian people. No more urgent task exists today than the creation of new liturgical hymns which can accompany, support and enrich the liturgical renewal of the coming years.[21]

St Clement's, Notting Dale: rooted in God and neighbourhood

The second parish I want to describe is St Clement's, Notting Dale, where during the late 1970s and 1980s the parish priest was David Randall. St Clement's is an old Tractarian parish located in a poor district of London, adjacent to some very posh districts. In an earlier period the parish provided the inspiration for Ernest Raymond's novel *The Chalice and the Sword.* During the years of David Randall's ministry, he led the most colourful and inspiring worship of any church in West London. The highlights of the year were Holy Week and Easter (with the Easter vigil at 5 a.m.), the Notting Hill Carnival Mass with steel band and fantastic costumes, and the Feast of Christ the King in November. In the preface for that feast, the Kingdom of God is described as 'a kingdom of truth and life, a kingdom of holiness and grace, a kingdom of justice, love and peace.' David was a 'kingdom priest', more interested in the struggle for the Kingdom of God than he was in the 'success' of the church. The parish was in the literal sense 'eccentric' – off-centre as far as the conventional structures were concerned, but truly centred on God and God's Kingdom of justice. David had an intense devotion to the Virgin Mary, and St Clement's was probably the only church in the world to have a shrine for racial justice focused on a statue of Our Lady of Fatima, beneath which was printed the Litany of Our Lady of the Freedom Fighters (written by some Catholic Worker activists in jail in Alabama). The liturgy at St Clement's combined the best of Anglo-Catholic splendour with a warmth and a crazy informality rarely seen in Anglicanism. But beneath the flamboyance and eccentricity, there was that same sense of celebration and festivity which we saw in an earlier period in Noel and Groser.

Every August, Notting Hill (Notting Dale being the district beneath the hill) is the centre for an enormous Caribbean carnival, the biggest street festival in Europe. David was a key figure in bringing church and Carnival together, and in making the church open to the community on the Lancaster West and Edward Woods estates. Unlike most churches, St Clement's church door was always open – indeed, at one point nobody had a key, and it could not be locked. In a neighbourhood marked by high crime, it was rarely vandalised because the community, Christian and non-Christian, saw it as their home. St Clement's combined warmth with the spirit of liberation, joy, and prayerfulness, from which flowed pastoral zeal and commitment to social justice. It was not respectable, it defied the establishment, it was a genuinely back-street church, rooted in adoration of God and commitment to the people.

These are the kind of churches which have nourished me and kept me in (albeit on the edge of) the Church of England. But I fear that such places may be diminishing, as 'middle Anglicanism' – the religion of the dull, nondescript, middle-class, boring, safe, clerical elites – takes over. I hope desperately that I am wrong. But I am sure that Anglicans need to lose most of the respectability, restraint and control which mark their worship and culture if they are to make a genuine contribution to the worship of the coming Church.

Art and liturgy

One central feature of each of the churches I have mentioned, and of St Botolph's where I work, is the role of art. I do not think that there will be any progress in our understanding and practice of liturgy if we do not develop a richer understanding of art, music and poetry. Salman Rushdie is one of many who believe that the language of orthodoxy has broken down, and that people are seeking a secular definition of transcendence through such media as the novel.[22] He may well be right – but my sense is that the Church may be one of the few remaining sites where art, imagination and ethics can come together, where the beauty of God and the world can be manifested, and where wonder and creativity can unite with justice. Much Christian liturgy is too word-centred. But many people are not word people, and express themselves through painting, music, poetry and sculpture.

This is a very important constituent in our worship and life at St Botolph's, and it needs strengthening in the coming years. For many years, St Botolph's has been a centre for exhibitions of painting and sculpture. It provides hospitality within the church for artists, and space for them to display their work. In the liturgical space, the celebration is surrounded by bright colours, powerful symbols, and images which help us to focus. The reredos is the Tree of Life, whose leaves are for healing, surrounded by the living waters which flow through the City of God. To the north of the high altar is a peace chapel, on the doors of which are the words for peace in a variety of languages. Nearby is a statue of Our Lady of Sorrows, gazing through the crown of thorns, at the pain of the world. Frequently a variety of images is erected around the walls, helping to create a context for worship. It is important that paintings, icons and sculpture do not deflect from, or divert attention from, the central focus on God. But, used carefully, prayerfully, and in a spirit of festivity, they can enrich the worship.

Simultaneously, for over ten years, there has been a resident artist in the Day Centre, and her work has been of absolutely central importance in helping people to understand something of their own inner potential. From this work has developed a good deal of thinking and reflection on the relationship between art, imagination and social ethics.[23] At a time when the visual arts are at a low priority for public funding, a new alliance between the Church and artists would have a number of benefits. It would provide space where artists could experiment and exhibit their work. It would help Churches to recover their medieval role of being centres of visual display; this would restore beauty and colour to buildings which are often drab and dreary. More profoundly, it would bring together two groups of people, two traditions of discourse and creative imagination, who are committed to the experience of beauty and truth for their own sakes, committed to something which is, in capitalist ideology, strictly useless.

In seeking to restore beauty and colour to worship, Western Christians have much to learn from the Orthodox Churches of the East. At the heart of Orthodox theology is the celebration of the liturgy. Indeed, in Orthodox thought, liturgical theology is the primary theological activity. The icon has been called 'theology in colour', and is rightly seen as a charism.[24] Of course, it would be absurd to imagine that we could, or should, reproduce Eastern styles of worship here, though the attraction and appeal of Orthodoxy to Western Christians is worthy of attention. (According to one recent poll, the Orthodox Church was the only mainstream Christian Church to show increases in membership.) At the same time, there is a real need for the restoration of a God-centred worship which involves all the senses, and invokes the experience of wonder. What is central is the understanding of the role of symbol. In the West we have to a great extent lost the sense of ritual and symbol, and this loss is really dangerous.[25]

The future of liturgy?

So what is the future for liturgy in the coming years? One major issue is acceptance. We need, in worship, to create an atmosphere where all are at home. One of the commonest criticisms of the new liturgical rites in the Church of England and in the Roman Church is their sectarian thrust, their closed character – evident in the fact that many occasional church-goers now feel lost, unfamiliar, cut off from access to the rite.[26] We need somehow to recreate a way of being the Church which does not exclude people, yet which is also a source of help and support as well as an ongoing discipline for the faithful. It is important to resist the tendency in many of the Churches to move in a sectarian direction.

A related problem is the fact that in many places, all worship now is eucharistic. We are told that the Church is in danger of becoming a 'eucharistic sect', and I believe there is some basis for this fear. Of course, the Eucharist is at the very heart of Christian worship – but it is not all there is, and we need to develop or recover ways of worship which allow other sources of life to surface. For a number of centuries, the Church of England was the only part of the Christian Church to read the whole Bible liturgically every year, and, while no one would wish to return to that lectionary form, the neglect of biblically-based daily offices is a cause for serious concern. The office is a form of prayer which demands no clerical presence, which is flexible, which does not rely on the emotional state of the individual, and which is firmly rooted in the Scriptures and in the rhythms of prayerful repetition. Anglicans were the pioneers of a democratic office for the whole people of God, and are now in danger of throwing away much of their heritage.

However, I see our major problem with modern liturgy as being the collapse of awe, wonder and the capacity for amazement. To stand in awe before God (Eccles. 3:14, NRSV) is basic to the human condition. But today, many no longer see the liturgy as a site of the holy. As I suggested in Chapter 1, much of the sense of the holy has shifted to the self and to the 'inner world'. Nor does much modern liturgy help to inspire awe, or point us towards glory. Today's official liturgy is in poor shape, lacking healing symbols. Liturgies are meant to quicken the spirit, not reduce it to the level of the pedestrian and the banal. Annie Dillard has suggested that people should wear crash-helmets at liturgical celebrations because they should expect trouble. To enter into worship is to expose oneself to extreme danger. In fact, Dillard says, liturgies are words which people address to God without getting killed.[27]

In recent years, sociologists, anthropologists and others have been highly critical of the banal and pedestrian language of liturgical revision. The modern rites have been said to speak 'the lingo of limbo and the dialect of Erehwon'. They have been accused of 'pious psychobabble'.[28] Ulrich Simon described the intercessions in modern Anglican rites as 'middle-class Baalism'. Simon complained that in modern rites we neither exult nor throw dust, there is neither laughter nor weeping, neither glory nor dread. Instead there is an absence of fight and the triumph of the didactic. Gail Ramshaw, herself a pioneer of progressive liturgical renewal, admits that most intercessions have more in common with personal therapy than with baptismal formation.[29]

The triumph of the didactic and the loss of the mysterious was part of the critique of the changes in the Roman communion in a study by Anthony Archer. He speaks of the 'pruned matter-of-factness' of the modern liturgy. One working-class Catholic layman had commented to him, 'It's just like a lecture, man, it just goes on and on'. In spite of the fact that modern liturgical revision took place at a time when non-verbal communication had been rediscovered, there seems to be no place in most modern rites for dreams or for silence, for gloom or for ecstasy. So it is that modern liturgies have helped to cut off many ritual streams of nourishment, areas to which people previously had access. Today the rite is pedestrian, lacking words of power, containing little that is memorable. One striking feature of most modern liturgies is their moderation and restraint. There is no excess in word or gesture, and only one clear meaning to the words. They are reflective of what Marcuse termed 'one-dimensional man', clean and functional, the expression of the middle-class taste of the 1960s.[30]

We see the reductionist tendencies in liturgical revision at their saddest in the 'reform' of the Easter vigil. Of course, the official liturgical texts of the Church of England contain no rite whatever for the most important moment of the liturgical year! But the vigil in the Roman rite was badly impoverished by Vatican II, and was a casualty both of the cult of shorter services and of the desire for one-dimensional clarity. The 1956 revision was full of very powerful sexual symbolism in its dramatic celebration of creation, resurrection and rebirth. The symbolic power, for example, of the plunging of the paschal candle into the water, accompanied by the words *'Descendat in hanc plenitudimen fontis virtus Spiritus Sancti'* ('May the power of the Holy Spirit descend into the fullness of this font'), is hard to exaggerate. Here the mysteries of birth and death, darkness and light, were re-enacted with the most fertile and moving imaginative power. Herbert McCabe called the 1956 revision of the vigil 'the greatest liturgical creation of the modern church' – by contrast, the new rite, McCabe sadly commented, looks as if Mrs Whitehouse has been getting at it.[31]

I believe, therefore, that we need to take the critiques of liturgical revision seriously in the coming years, in spite of the fact that this will seem to provide us with some strange bedfellows in the form of reactionaries, liturgical fossilisers, misogynists, and ultra-conservatives whose motivations may be nostalgia and incapacity for change of any kind. But the issues are too serious to be left to such people. It is important to attend to the critique made by Kieran Flanagan in his important and very neglected book *Sociology and Liturgy*. While the study is at times hysterical, shrill and full of over-heated rhetoric, its main argument is sound. Flanagan argues that those responsible for liturgical renewal simply did not understand the changes in social thought and in culture which were taking place at the time. The revisions of Vatican II, he argues, were based on inadequate sociology. There was too much stress on clarity. He refers to 'bare ruined rites and cold rational orders that freeze the soul'. Liturgical renewal took place at a time of profound cultural dislocation, which had led to disastrous results in art, architecture and urban planning. There was a loss of complexity, a rejection and exclusion of the lavish, the elaborate. The sense of the holy, the apophatic dimension of worship, was also under threat. These were matters which anthropologists and some sociologists recognised, but which liturgical scholars seemed to have ignored. Liturgy is rooted in symbolic complexity, in rites and ceremonies which quicken the spirit, in the dimensions of the timeless, of silence and the apophatic, the unknowable, the reality which can only be perceived through symbol and myth. Perhaps the most important part of Flanagan's work is his chapter on the place of the apophatic in liturgical worship.[32]

The liturgy is something which is done. It has a life independent of the subjective states of those involved. Frederick Hastings Smyth even compared it to a laboratory experiment, and, while this aspect can be distorted and exaggerated, it is important to stress the objectivity of the liturgical action. This is not to equate liturgy with magic. Magic locates divine efficacy outside the historical order. The Christian liturgy is a manifestation within historical time of the redemptive and sanctifying power of God to transform human communities. However, it is vital to create conditions which make the performance of the rite more authentic. Liturgical spirituality is rooted in human life. The liturgy draws its central symbolism from human life – birth and death, washing and feeding. It draws on impure materials and soiled language. It has been said that the best liturgies are messy, indeed that liturgical spirituality is only possible for those who are willing to let life be messy, language impure and God dangerously close.[33] Excessive tidiness, and the quest for purity and clarity, are alien to symbolic and sacramental action.

At the present time, partly because of the one-dimensional nature of much mainstream worship, there is a particular danger of the cult of the powerful leader, be he (and it usually is a 'he') preacher, healer or cultic guru. The saga of the Nine O'Clock Service in Sheffield, which led to serious cases of sexual misconduct and exploitation, brings out some central issues in the nature of worship: the danger of reliance on a 'charismatic' leader, the likelihood of disintegration and collapse if liturgy is disconnected from tradition, and yet paradoxically the importance and necessity of wildness and ecstasy in worship. It is unwise to panic in the face of such serious abuses, or to withdraw into a liturgical form which is safe and dull. (Sexual abuse by the clergy is not exactly unknown among liturgical conservatives!) How can these needs be reconciled? I believe only through ascetical discipline, personal holiness, and a structured liturgical ethos.

One of the most ancient images in Christian spirituality is that of 'sober intoxication' – a phrase made memorable by St Ambrose in one of his office hymns.

Laeti bibamus sobriam
Ebrietatem Spiritus.

'Let us joyfully drink of the sober inebriation of the Spirit.' In commenting on this, Stanley Evans described the Christian as a controlled drunk, purposively intoxicated by the Holy Spirit.[34] The expression of this in worship is really important, and, although it is filled with risks, it is preferable to its opposite – the repressive boredom of the dull and lifeless.

Christian liturgy is not an occasion for performance by some egocentric individual or for the experimentation in the latest trendy fad. It is a social act, the expression of the faith and commitment of a dedicated community. It is essentially a social

act. This is something which has been particularly stressed
by Anglican thinkers, and which is now being rediscovered
elsewhere in the Christian world. The late John Robinson,
when he was Dean of Clare College, Cambridge, pointed out
how central was the liturgy to all Christian action in the world.
The eucharistic action was the pattern of all Christian action,
the germ of all society redeemed in Christ.[35] In the Eucharist
we assert and enact our solidarity in Christ, our *koinonia* and
common life in him. The eucharistic action undermines all
pretentions of class and privilege – indeed, it is a powerful way
of creating the kind of social unit which can resist them and
destroy them.

The struggle against injustice in the Church has to be incorporated at the very heart of the liturgical life of the body. For
example, I do not see how we can witness effectively against
racism and social injustice by seeing these things simply as
matters for justice sub-committees and boards for social responsibility. As long as this attitude prevails, they will always be
tangential and peripheral to the central Christian task. The
resistance to racism has to be located where it belongs: at
the very heart of the liturgy, and specifically in the baptismal
covenant. The degree of this commitment comes out best in
liturgies from outside England – for example, in the American
Book of Common Prayer. Here, during the rite of baptism, the
candidate is asked:

> Do you renounce Satan and all the spiritual forces of wicked-
> ness that rebel against God?
> Do you renounce the evil powers of this world which corrupt
> and destroy the creatures of God?

A few minutes later the following questions are asked:

> Will you persevere in resisting evil, and, whenever you fall
> into sin, repent and return to the Lord?
> Will you seek and serve Christ in all persons, loving your
> neighbour as yourself?
> Will you strive for justice and peace among people, and
> respect the dignity of every human being?

In this baptismal renunciation and commitment, the Christian
community is formed, and regularly renewed, as a community
of resistance. Just as the worship of ancient Israel was an act of
'doxology against idolatry and ideology',[36] so our witness is

rooted in the adoration of the one true God who demands total obedience and who undermines the powers of this world. The liturgy is the heart of the protest against the disorder of the world.

8

Prophecy and the Millennium

We got into a conversation about how many of the prophecies concerning a Second Coming seemed to be having
their fulfilment at this particular time. [Billy] Graham told
me how world leaders who are students of the Bible and
others who have studied it have come to this same conclusion – that apparently never in history have so many of
the prophecies come true in such a short time. After the
conversation I asked Donn to send me more material on
prophecy so I could check them out in the Bible for
myself. You know I was raised on the Bible. I also taught
it for a long time in Sunday school.

RONALD REAGAN

I have read the Book of Revelation, and, yes, I believe the
world is going to end by an act of God I hope – but every
day I think that time is running out.

CASPAR WEINBERGER

Now all these things happened to them by way of example,
and they were described in writing to be a lesson for us,
to whom it has fallen to live in the last days of the ages.

1 CORINTHIANS 10:11

It is over 60 years since Nicholas Berdyaev observed that we stand not on solid earth but on volcanic ground. Berdyaev called his book, published in 1935, *The End of Our Time*.[1] Since then, the theme of 'the end' has increased to an extraordinary degree, and there seems to be a kind of inverted millen-arianism which sees only 'the end', with no vision of the future. The language of apocalypse is with us constantly. Film producers speak of 'an apocalyptic future for European culture'.[2] We are seeing a resurgence of religious movements of the end-time. As we look at the spiritual currents of our day, we see new-age themes, the return of the dispensationalists, millennial visions of all kinds, in the build-up to the year 2000 and the coming century. Nor is this phenomenon restricted to religious groups. There are 'millennium novels'. There is a kind of messianic conference rhetoric which affects political speeches, a millennium fever. We are being told that we are 'on the threshold' of a new age, and so on. Some writers have spoken of 'pre-millennial tension', and there are numerous attempts to examine the psychology of anxiety which surrounds expectation. We have been described as people 'living in the time of the parenthesis'.[3] While in South Korea, the Full Gospel Church expects the Antichrist soon, many Hindus believe that we are in the last days of Kaliyuga, and will move towards a deeper light. We are seeing true and false prophetic streams, and the issue of discernment of spirits has become increasingly urgent.

Early apocalyptic movements

The idea of apocalypse is closely associated with that of revolution. Indeed, revolutionary fervour has more in common with religion than it has with the calm, rational analysis which we associate with pragmatic politics. Historically, apocalyptic language is often linked to revolutionary movements. Norman Cohn and others have shown that millenarian movements are often associated with social upheaval and social struggle. Certainly disorientation is common at both the personal and cultural levels. Such movements are unlikely to occur among the secure and contented. Cohn went so far as to link millenarianism with megalomania, paranoia and conspiratorial approaches to history.[4] However, we need to be careful in our assessment of all this. The fact – even if it could be proved – that many, even most, movements rooted in millenarian apocalyptic beliefs attract unstable people, tend towards fanaticism and violence, and hold a view of the world which seems deranged, does not necessarily mean that all such views are to be abandoned. Religion itself, and the world of academia, attract some pretty odd characters, and irrationality is not a preserve of any one group. The truth is more likely to be that, when eschatology is isolated from a total picture and becomes dominant, it tends to unbalance and perhaps destroy the humanity and the wider grasp on reality of those who are caught up in it.

Strictly speaking, apocalypse and millennium need to be distinguished. Apocalypse means an unveiling, a revelation of something. Apocalyptic writing is visionary, full of symbols and images of the end-time, but looking forward beyond crisis and collapse to a 'good time coming'. This is the millennium, literally the thousand-year reign. Many millenarians interpret this literally, but we need to include under the broad sense of millenarian all those who look forward to some kind of Kingdom of God on earth. 'Soft' millenarianism, the belief in an earthly Kingdom, is present in a wide range of groups including many Christian socialists. 'Hard' millenarianism, which involves belief in the personal return of Christ, the rapture of the elect, and so on, is rooted in the adventist tradition and is usually linked to fundamentalism.

Millenarianism has a real appeal and meets some deep human needs. It provides a sense of security, of direction and of purpose. It provides a clear map of a future in which God is in control, and the chosen ones, the holy people, are sure of eventual bliss. It offers a demonology, the sense of a cosmic enemy, and this enables boundaries to be established and purity sustained. It gives a sense of urgency and crisis. Michael Barkun has suggested that much of its appeal lies in its ability to 'understand' and explain disasters.[5]

My impression, however, is that it is not the disorientated and desperate but the secure and contented who are involved in the planning of Britain's millennium festivities, which are likely, for this reason, to be superficial, tawdry and idolatrous. Yet few voices, other than that of Prince Charles,[6] have been raised in the interest of differing claims and visions.

Apocalyptic movements are ancient, predating and helping to shape the Christian movement. Jewish apocalyptic beliefs focused on cosmic conflict. God and the forces of evil were involved in combat. There was an eschatological catastrophe, as a result of which the 'age to come' would dawn. In the Maccabean period, the theme of holy war also became important. Violence, both divine and human, figures in almost all apocalyptic writing. Some have seen in apocalyptic literature a mood of world negation, fatalism and otherworldliness, an abandonment of earthly goals and of rational actions. All is left in the hands of God, and human beings have no role except patient expectation. In fact, there is a frequent element in apocalyptic writing which urges action and struggle. It is also assumed by many that millenarian and apocalyptic movements occur only among deprived and oppressed people. This does not seem to have been true in Old Testament times – Ezekiel, Zechariah and Joel were part of the elite priestly cult. However, it does seem that these movements are connected to insecurity and turbulence. It is not correct to see apocalyptic as utterly different from prophecy. In fact, apocalyptic grew from prophecy, and in such writings as Isaiah, Zechariah and Ezekiel, prophecy shades into apocalyptic writing.

While scholars disagree on the detail, there is no doubt that apocalyptic themes influenced the ministry of Jesus, and his teaching about the Son of Man and the Kingdom of God. Nor is there any dispute about the presence of millennial hopes in early Christian thought. The theme of a millennial reign is found, for example, in Papias, Irenaeus, Justin, and Tertullian – although Tertullian prays for the 'postponement of the End'.[7] Augustine reinterpreted the millennium as being a period from the birth of Christ to the creation of the Church, and culminating in the Second Coming, thus abandoning the notion of a literal thousand-year period. His view led to a tendency in the West to see the reign of Christ as exercised primarily through the Church. But in the Middle Ages millennial ideas resurfaced in the teachings of Joachim of Fiore, and they have continued to appear from time to time.

My view is that Christians should take millenarian ideas very seriously. However bizarre and strange they may appear to be, they do represent a recognition that this earth is the site of the divine presence and activity. They are a challenge to the Church to take both the earth and the future more seriously.

They are an abiding witness against pie-in-the-sky religion, even if they do locate the Kingdom exclusively in the future and often ignore the involvement of the people of God in the present. They are a testimony to the place of crisis, vigilance and expectation in religious life.

The second coming

A central theme of most Christian millenarian movements is that of a second advent, the followers of this view being known as 'adventists'. There is a problem here, for all orthodox Christians profess faith in the fact that 'he will come again'. Certainly, there is in the New Testament the theme of another event – the Day of Judgement, the day of visitation, the last day. The actual term 'second coming' is not biblical (though Hebrews 9:27f. refers to a 'second time'), nor is there any strong belief in Christ descending to earth. In fact, nowhere in the Old Testament, pre-Christian apocalyptic writing or in the Gospels is the word 'descend' used of the Messiah. The term *parousia* (coming) is only used of Christ's coming in a few New Testament texts and is not included among the foundational beliefs listed in Hebrews 6:1ff. There seems to be no reference to the return of Christ in the early apostolic speeches in Acts.

Nevertheless, what is certainly clear from the biblical material is the belief that, in some sense, 'Christ will come again'. But what does this mean? In what sense will this coming occur? It is clearly not seen as a repeat version of the incarnation, for the central emphasis is on the contrast – on the glory, on the bright light in the heavens, on the revelation of God and of God's purpose. The symbolism of the Day of the Lord involves the fulfilment of hope, the culmination of time and history. It belongs as much to the world of myth and symbol as does the account of creation. This does not mean that it is not real; but it does mean that it is a theme to which we hold but which is beyond our conceptual grasp. It belongs to the imaginative area of Christian faith. In a sense, it is the future dimension of our faith in God as a whole. We trust, in faith, that there will be a new day, that God will show himself in our midst. The power and meaning of apocalyptic literature is destroyed by a flat, literalist and one-dimensional reading. The prevalence of such readings, and the certainty of their multiplication and intensification in the *fin de siècle* period, has deterred many Christians from using this kind of material at all. This is a very serious mistake. Only through a sacramental and imaginative engagement with the realities of earthly struggle and the vision of God can religious life and political change recover its heart and its sense of direction. That is the heart of apocalypse.

Use and abuse of the Book of Revelation

To understand the place of apocalyptic thought in early Christianity, it is important to look at the Book of Revelation – that strange and much-misunderstood visionary text with which the Christian Scriptures close. The text is set within the context of upheaval, turmoil and oppression, but it is also a text filled with awe, wonder, and yearning for the City of God, the site of healing and renewal. As in all apocalyptic literature, there is a mingling of earth and heaven, of time and eternity. That Revelation has been the most misused text in the Bible seems indisputable. In the Nazi period it was seen as supporting the idea of a thousand-year Reich. Interestingly, some thinkers have seen it as a radical document. Engels in 1883 called it the 'simplest and clearest book' in the New Testament. It is certainly a political work, deeply seditious and subversive, perhaps the most political section of the New Testament. It is a polemic against the Roman Empire, against the inequality, injustice and nationalism of this powerful state. As we reach the climax of the text, there is a vision of the collapse of the oppressive regime, the fall of Babylon.

> How it is possible to read this and decide that the early Christians were not political it is quite impossible to understand. Here is a picture of the collapse of a city and an Empire in which is involved the mourning of the merchants. There is a careful and elaborate description of the consequent collapse of the world market in which everything was sold – and a long list is given, down to slaves and the very souls of men ... The collapse of the transport system is also involved, and at the sight of all this the saints rejoice! It is not our modern picture of Christianity.[8]

The Book of Revelation links worship and politics in a subversive way, opposing Jesus as Lord to the idolatrous claims of Caesar. The central question of the book is: who is Lord? The opposition to the Roman state is quite abusive. Indeed, as one commentator says, 'the literary attack on Rome is the most basic element of social radicalism in the Apocalypse'.[9] The Book of Revelation calls for the most thoroughgoing opposition to the Roman government. The mark of the beast (13: 16–17) is the technical term for the imperial stamp.[10] What we see here is an apocalyptic text which is a manifesto for radical resistance.

Unfortunately, much Christian use of the Book of Revelation misses its point. Evading the conflict, it uses the text simply as a source of prediction. The history of Christianity is littered with predictions of the end, and of the appearance of the beast. In much millenarian polemic, including that of the present time, the beast of Revelation is equated with Antichrist. The identification of 'the Antichrist' has become a major preoccupation, particularly in the USA. In fact, the image of Antichrist is based, not on Revelation where it does not occur, but on 1 John 2:18. The word is used three times in 1 John, once in 2 John, and nowhere else in the Bible. It has no definite article, and is also used in the plural, and so it does not refer to one particular figure but rather to heresy, false belief. According to most fundamentalist rhetoric, however, the Antichrist is a person who will lead a ten-nation confederation, will take control of the world, and insist that its inhabitants bear his mark. Thus Antichrist and the beast are fused. Eventually, according to this theory, Christ will slay the Antichrist at Armageddon.[11]

The precise dating of the end, of the decisive battle, and of the return of Christ, has been a topic of speculation for centuries. In the year 999 there were outbreaks of panic and wild behaviour as a result of a series of comets, natural disasters and other incidents, and it was believed that the end of all things was at hand. Wulfstan, Archbishop of York in the eleventh century, associated the appearance of the Antichrist with the arrival of the Danes in Britain. The end was predicted for 1033 in North France and Germany. The Apostolic Brethren fixed the end at 1300, and then at 1305, but they themselves were destroyed in 1306. The closing years of the fourteenth century also saw millenarian outbreaks and expectations of the end of the world. In Bohemia, 10–14 February 1420 were seen as the critical dates, while various Anabaptist groups fixed the end for 1534–5. Some early visionaries thought very far ahead. Mother Shipton, who lived in the reign of Richard III, predicted that the world would end in 1991.

Modern millenarianism

The major turning-point in modern millenarianism was the growth of a movement termed 'pre-millennial dispensationalism'. It is a movement which has had a profound impact in the United States. Not all millenarians are dispensationalists, but it is this movement which has provided the foundation for most forms of modern Christian millenarian groups.

The idea of dispensationalism arose in the nineteenth century with John Nelson Darby (1800–82), the founder of the Plymouth Brethren. Darby believed that Jesus Christ would soon return and would 'rapture' the Church, that is, draw it to himself while the world underwent the 'great tribulation'. The idea of a rapture is based on 1 Thessalonians 4:16–17. So, in Darby's view, there would be tribulation, followed by the return of Christ to establish the millennial kingdom. Hence the term 'pre-millennial', for these were Christians who believed that the rapture and return of Christ would precede the millennial kingdom. (Pre-millennialists sub-divide also into those who believe that the Church itself will go through the tribulation and those who do not: they are known in millenarian circles as pre-trib and post-trib.) Darby developed the idea of seven 'dispensations', and his ideas were taken up vigorously in the late nineteenth century by Cyrus Scofield (1843–1921) whose *Scofield Reference Bible* (1909) remains the standard text for all Christian pre-millennialists. The *Scofield Reference Bible* is without doubt the most important document in modern fundamentalism.[12]

Another key figure was William Miller (1782–1849) who believed that the second coming of Christ would occur at Dresden, New York, in 1843 or 1844. The Millerite movement played a crucial role in the formation of modern adventism, and both the Seventh Day Adventists and Jehovah's Witnesses can be traced to the Miller approach to prediction, specifically to his use of the Books of Daniel and Revelation. In view of the continued spread of Jehovah's Witnesses (a movement which was originally known as 'Millennial Dawn'), its neglect by Christian theologians is extraordinary. For here is the classic modern example of 'apocalypse delayed', predictions falsified, and yet the movement continues to survive and flourish.[13] Why is this? Surely because it offers precisely those features which I listed and which lead to the popularity of millenarian movements in all ages.[14]

As in earlier epochs, recent decades have seen the emergence of a variety of forms of millennial movement and of beliefs about the imminence of the end. It is believed that there are eight million millennialists in the United States. Elsewhere in the world, millenarianism is also alive and active. Lee Jang Lim of the South Korea-based Tami Missionary Church forecast the end of the world for October 1992, and 20,000 members of the Mission for the Coming Days met in South Korea in that year, waiting for the cataclysm to occur. Three years later 4,000 evangelistic leaders met there for the AD 2000 and Beyond Movement. Meanwhile, in the Ukraine, Maria Devi Khristos of the Great White Brotherhood argued for the 14 November 1993. But Paolo Farinella, a mathematician at the University of Pisa, has suggested that the end will come when the asteroid Eros swings out of orbit and crashes into the earth – in about 1,140,000 years' time![15]

Popular prophecy is particularly important in determining American attitudes to Israel and to nuclear war. Ideas of millenarian disaster were reflected in the speeches of Ronald Reagan – while Pat Robertson, who stood for the presidency, has worked out his narrative in terms of a global millennial apocalypse.[16] 'Armageddon theology' has played a key role in American foreign policy, and it is not inconceivable that it could do so again. It is a matter of the utmost urgency that we recognise how influential fundamentalism and millenarianism are in American life. We are not dealing with a lunatic fringe but with a mass movement involving very large numbers of people.

Nor should we forget that it is not only Protestant fundamentalism which provides the basis for millenarian visions. We find a form of millenarianism in the speeches and writings of Pope John Paul II – in his case nourished by the appearances of the Virgin Mary at Fatima, and her prophecy of the collapse of

Communism and the coming of an age of peace. At Fatima, the Blessed Virgin is said to have urged the consecration of Russia to her immaculate heart, but in 1929 she reappeared and complained that it had not been done. In 1978, just before he became Pope, John Paul spoke at Cracow of 'the final confrontation between the Church and the Antichurch, between the Gospel and the Antigospel'.[17] This is classic millenarian rhetoric. As the Roman Church becomes more authoritarian, so more bizarre forms of Marian millenarianism will flourish on the edge, sidestepping the magisterium. So Fatima and Medjugorje are likely to be the precursors of other movements of apocalypse, rooted in a curious fusion of adventism, visionary illuminism, popular Marian piety, and right-wing conspiracy theory.

Millenarianism: dangers and strengths

In the light of all this material, it is not surprising that many people regard all apocalyptic themes in negative terms.[18] Millenarian movements may involve a concern for social righteousness in this present world, though this is often neglected. After all, if we are in the final stage of history, politics is irrelevant. If Christians are to be raptured, what happens to the earth becomes unimportant. It is at this point that we need to recognise that there are conflicts among millenarian groups. The upheavals of the seventeenth century in England were full of examples of millenarians who took the struggle for righteousness on earth very seriously – Levellers, Diggers, Fifth Monarchy Men, and so on. In the nineteenth century, post-millennialists – such as the revivalist preacher C. G. Finney, for example – had a strong sense of the importance of working for that justice which was of the essence of the Kingdom of God, while pre-millennialists have tended to 'leave it all to God' to sort out on the Last Day. More recently, we have seen the rise of 'survivalism', a movement of 'holy war' devotees for whom the resistance against the demonic enemy (variously identified as Communism, the Jews, and Black people) assumes military dimensions. Not surprisingly, most survivalists, who are concerned about survival and safety on earth, tend to be anti-rapture and post-tribulationist.

An obvious danger is that eschatology, in the hands of fundamentalists – particularly those (and they are the majority) whose fundamentalism is inseparable from capitalist decadence – becomes crude and vulgar, and brings the whole Christian movement into disrepute. Take, for example, the words of the American evangelist and former presidential candidate Pat Robertson on his plans to televise the second coming of Christ.

> The greatest show on earth was in our hands. I wondered where we would put the cameras. Jerusalem was the obvious place. We even discussed how Jesus's radiance might be too bright for the cameras, and how we would have to make adjustments for that problem. Can you imagine telling Jesus, 'Hey, Lord, please tone down your luminosity; we're having a problem with contrast. You're causing the picture to flare'?[19]

There are other dangers. Millenarian movements have almost always, and almost inevitably, tended to demonise their opponents. Lacking any sense of self-criticism, they have assumed the status of the elect, the holy and righteous ones, the pure. Purity is at the heart of millenarian thought, and the quest for purity is the foremost concern of such fundamentalists.[20] There are problems of fanaticism, and of the obsessive concern with chronology. There is a more subtle danger (not restricted to Christians by any means) that some former confident Utopians, faced with the prevailing pessimism and despair, will turn to the language of apocalypse and disaster, claiming that the world faces a choice between superficial consumerism or materialism, and the darkness of doom-laden reality.

However, there is a more positive side to the place of eschatology in relation to social struggle. Apocalyptic faith may help Christians to resist totalitarian structures, and to maintain life in apparently hopeless situations. There are many situations where prophecy, and the exercise of influence within the framework of existing society, seem to have failed. In such situations, it seems to me entirely legitimate and necessary that Christians draw on the resources of the apocalyptic tradition.

I referred in the Introduction to an article by Gresham Kirkby, written in 1956. In 1983 Kirkby revised this article, arguing that Catholic Christians had much to learn from the millennial hope, which represented a simplified form of something really fundamental to Christianity: the vision of the Kingdom of God on earth.[21] The hope of the Kingdom of God is an otherworldly hope, but only in the sense that it involves the irruption into this world of 'the powers of the age to come'. Its roots lie in faith in the resurrection, a faith that things do not need to stay as they are, that transformation, transfiguration, are possible.

Violence: the apocalyptic struggle

Let me now turn to the links between certain types of eschatological expectation and violent movements. We have seen a number of examples of these in the last few years. On 19 April 1993, there was the massacre at Waco, Texas, of the Branch Davidians; in March 1995, the followers of Shoko Asahara's group, Om Supreme Truth, released poisonous gas in the Tokyo subway, killing twelve and injuring thousands; while one month later, on 19 April 1995, there was the tragic bombing in Oklahoma City. In November 1995, Yigal Amir, apparently linked with a fundamentalist group, killed the Israeli prime minister Yitzhak Rabin.

Events such as these have caused Christians and others to give attention to movements, which, if they had heard of them at all, they had probably regarded as irrelevant and 'lunatic fringe'. I have always regarded 'lunatic fringe' movements as important, and I believe we need to take very seriously some of the religious movements which have gathered strength in the pre-millennial period. One of these is Christian Identity. So far, it is only known, and then only slightly, in the USA – but it bursts incoherently upon the public on occasions when there is violence associated with such groups as The Order or the Aryan Nation. Yet its elaborate system of religious ideas often provides the driving force for the political agenda of one wing of the radical right.

The central belief of Christian Identity is that Jewish people are the result of Satan's seduction of Eve. The movement has three key beliefs: the belief that white Aryans constitute the lost tribes of Israel; the belief that Jews are the children of the Devil; and a commitment to apocalyptic violent struggle.

The first and the third are shared with other groups, such as the varieties of British Israelite and a range of survivalist and millenarian groups, not all of them influenced by Christian themes. The second is peculiar to, and crucial to, the Christian Identity movement.

The idea of the Jews as the offspring of Satan has a complex theological and political history. It was gradually pieced together out of strange fragments from religion, fringe scholarship and the occult, until a final synthesis was achieved after the Second World War. The notion of the satanic origin of the Jews was crucial to the way in which the movement developed. Jews, and in later thinking, Blacks, were the biological offspring of Satan – inhuman, demonic creatures, not simply contaminated humans. The Jews were in fact, in this theory, never human. These ideas, found in some ancient gnostic writings, were revived in the nineteenth century as a result of developments from the British Israel movement.

Many British people only know of British Israel through the fact that some key figures in UK Fascist groups belong to this movement. Its origins lie in the seventeenth century, but the first authentic figure who can be called a British Israelite was John Wilson in the nineteenth century. The origins of the theory and movement were related to the cult of the Great Pyramid. Though there has been an attempt to maintain a certain level of respectability and a distance from political demagogues, British Israelite history is full of strange and often sinister characters. There was the curious figure of Dominic McCausland who wrote *Adam and the Adamite* in 1864. McCausland believed that there was a group of people who were pre-Adamic and who were non-white, a theory which was taken up by later writers. In 1900 Charles Carroll introduced the idea of a humanoid serpent who was 'Negro', an idea shared by the Indiana Pentecostalist preacher William Branham, who died in 1965. The serpent, it was argued, was not a reptile but Satan himself. Because of Eve's sexual relationship with the serpent, there were two seeds of humankind: the descendants of Adam and Eve, and the descendants of Eve and the serpent, beginning with Cain. Adam was therefore not the first human being. There were also pre-Adamic people of an inferior status. The link between the 'two seeds' theory, well-known in American Baptist circles, and anti-Semitism was, of course, the figure of Cain. Michael Barkun has shown how:

Cain becomes the means by which the concept of the serpent seedline can be linked first to the Pre-Adamites and then to the Jews, and in the process the evolving British-Israel belief that Jewish blood had been corrupted by sexual contacts with forbidden peoples was incorporated.[22]

Barkun rightly stresses that the most distinctive doctrine of Christian Identity is the belief that Jews are the direct biological offspring of Satan.

British Israel peaked in the 1930s when it had 500 members in England, all middle class. By the 1940s Christian Identity's links with British Israel had been severed, and the movement took its own course. The key figure in the 1940s was the Massachusetts lawyer Howard Rand, who was responsible for opening up the movement to right-wing and anti-Semitic influences. Rand founded the Anglo-Saxon Federation of America in 1930. Another key figure was William Cameron who worked for Henry Ford. Gerald L. K. Smith was the leading anti-Semite in the USA until his death in 1976 – Smith brought coherence to the movement in the 1940s. One of his disciples, Conrad Gaard, was the first to express the idea of the Jews as the offspring of Satan to a wide audience. Another key figure was Wesley Swift, probably the most significant single figure in the emergence of the Identity movement. Many years later, The Order was founded in Idaho and was involved with counterfeiting and armed robbery. There are links between these groups and 'survivalism', a term coined by Kurt Saxon in 1976, in which believers anticipate the collapse of civilisation by concentrating on saving themselves and their loved ones. Although the links with British Israel need to be carefully assessed, there is one aspect which has aided the survival of the Identity movement. Unlike many millenarian movements, the British Israel type of eschatology was very flexible and capable of great adaptation, and had no commitment to any particular chronology – an approach adopted by Christian Identity.

It is wrong to see Christian Identity as merely one aspect of the wider Christian Right in the USA. The relationship of Identity to the wider Christian Right is perhaps similar to that of Ian Paisley to Billy Graham. Identity regards most of the Christian Right as their enemies, and differs from them fundamentally in both their attitudes to anti-Semitism and to eschatology. The dispensationalist millenarianism, involving the rapture of believers, is viewed with revulsion by Identity, committed as they are to the 'holy war'.

It is here that we see the dangerous potential of Identity, when it is allied to terrorist and paramilitary movements of the type that erupted in Idaho with the Aryan Nation and in the Michigan Militia, and which became notorious with the Oklahoma tragedy. Beliefs of this type may be dismissed as too absurd to be taken seriously. But the cost of ignoring such beliefs may be extremely high. Research in the USA has shown that, as the power of older movements such as the Ku Klux Klan wanes, so the militia groups have increased in importance.

The Church and the challenges of the future

As I suggested earlier, however bizarre and strange millenarian movements may be, they do represent a recognition that the earth is the site of the divine presence and activity. It is important for the Church to take seriously the future dimensions of the Christian Scriptures and to do so with intelligence and faithfulness. This will mean grappling with some neglected areas, but also it will mean discarding some preconceived assumptions.

So what should the Church be saying and doing about the future? The Church must learn from the millenarian movements. As long as we evade the challenges of the future and deny the earthly dimensions of our hope, millenarian groups will flourish. A number of areas seem to me to be important. For example, we constantly affirm that 'Christ will come again', but we rarely discuss what this might mean. My conviction – supported, I believe, by the Scriptures and by orthodox theology – is that this 'coming again' will be utterly different from Christ's first coming. The central point of the belief is that there is far more to be revealed, known and comprehended. We are not necessarily awaiting a literal return, but rather a further and fuller revelation. Christ's coming again, his apocalypse, will be a revealing of the mystery of God and of our true end. Our whole existence as a Christian community takes place within the framework of expectation of this future glory. Speculation about its precise form is idle and harmful.

It is the vision towards which Christians look and for which we long, it is 'the end of our exploring', 'the time of universal restoration' (Acts 3:21 NRSV). It seems to me, therefore, that it is of the greatest theological and pastoral importance that the Church repudiates biblical literalism. It has not only done great harm to individuals and communities, but it has also enabled us to miss the real meaning of the biblical vision. The repudiation of literalism is a necessity if true religion is to survive.

One of the signs of spiritual decay is the disappearance of prophecy. What is prophecy? What is a prophetic Church? Prophecy is not primarily about predicting the future, but about discerning the signs of the times, recognising and responding to the working of God in history, and this almost always involves seeking to warn the religious community of trouble ahead. Apocalyptic thinking begins at the point where the prophetic word is ignored, though the boundary between the two is blurred.

The prophetic role

Prophetic individuals stand within traditions: outside traditions they are incomprehensible, and it can be argued that their voices cannot be heard unless their hearers stand within a tradition which recognises their role. I am quite sure that prophets cannot arise from nowhere. On the other hand, unless we hold a doctrine of total depravity in such an extreme form that we say that people's ears have been utterly stopped and their eyes blinded, it seems likely that prophetic voices can spark off reactions and responses in people who do not fully, or at all, understand 'where the prophets are coming from'. Prophets may, and often do, ignite a flame which leads to a rediscovery of neglected truth.

Prophetic figures usually come from the margins, even from the wilderness. They do not seek status, they are often obscure and lonely voices, and their testimony and memory often survive beyond death after their more prominent contemporaries have been forgotten. William Stringfellow (1928–85) was such a figure. A lawyer in East Harlem, Stringfellow became a key figure in the Civil Rights Movement in the United States from the 1950s onwards, and a sign of contradiction and inspiration among American Christians for several decades. At the time of his death, Walter Wink predicted that there would be a series of academic studies of Stringfellow, but none has yet appeared – although we have seen, in the last few years, a revival of interest in this extraordinary man. He has been described as the most important American theologian of the twentieth century. Karl Barth, in a memorable encounter with Stringfellow in Chicago, said that he was the man to whom America should be listening. He had no formal theological training. His books have no footnotes or references, and they are all out of print. Yet for several decades he articulated the mood of the day, broke open the word of truth, sensed the moment of danger, discerned the signs of the times. What we saw in Stringfellow was a combination of three elements: a profound rootedness in the Scriptures; a close proximity to poor and displaced people; and a sense of outrage at oppression. Out of this threefold commitment to the word, the poor and the Kingdom of God, Stringfellow became one of the most prophetic figures in twentieth-century America. We will be hearing more of him in the future.[23]

The coming of the Kingdom

To return to the question of the Church's witness to the future, it seems to me that we need constantly to return to that old theme of 'the good news of the Kingdom of God'. Some modern writers (such as Beverly Harrison) have preferred (with older writers such as Conrad Noel) the expression 'Commonwealth of God', while others choose 'Reign of God'. What is essential is that we recognise that the central focus of the Christian hope is social, the hope of a new world. It is at the heart of the teaching of Jesus. The phrase 'Kingdom of God' occurs 122 times in the Gospels, 90 of them from the lips of Jesus. It is the controlling category of biblical theology, or, as Walter Brueggemann put it, 'the core metaphor for a new social imagination'.[24] It is a symbol, not a concept, and so can only be comprehended if we enter into it and shape our lives within it. It is the regulative principle of all our theology and all our work. Only the demands of the Kingdom of God are absolute, all else is relativised. The Church on earth is a community which prays daily and urgently, 'Your Kingdom come . . . on earth as in heaven'.

What does this mean in the context of the twenty-first century? The focal point for much of the speculation and reflection about the future is the actual year 2000, and it is seen by many as a Jubilee Year. But will this really be an 'epochal turning-point'? Pope John Paul, in his encyclical *Tertio Millennio Adveniente* of November 1994, called for a build-up to a Holy Year focused on the Year of Jubilee. It sounds very good, but is there any substance to it? There can be little doubt that the language and imagery of the Jubilee Year lie behind the proclamation of Jesus in Nazareth as recorded in Luke 4, and that the Jubilee symbol was central to his ministry. The original Jubilee was about the remission of debt, the release of prisoners, and the restoration of the land (Lev. 25:8–12). Jubilee is about justice. Is there any evidence that any contemporary Church has plans to cancel any debts, campaign to set any prisoners free, or urge a programme for the common ownership of land? I think not. Until there is evidence for these things, the idea of a Jubilee Year, like the millennium theme itself, will remain at the level of pious rhetoric without content.

Looking to the future can be a form of escapism and of fantasy. But it can be a dynamic and powerful way of liberating into present struggles the energy gained from yearning. Perhaps more than anything at the present time we need an eschatological way of praying and being, a way of prefiguring and embodying our future hope, seeking to express the future in the way we live, and to draw it into the present. Around the year 1140, Bernard of Cluny wrote a long prose-poem called *De Contemptu Mundi*. The best-known parts of it are the hymns '*Hora Novissima*' and '*Urbs Sion Aurea*'. In English they are 'The world is very evil', 'For thee, O dear, dear country' and 'Jerusalem the Golden'.[25] 'Jerusalem my happy home' is also a simple version based on '*Hora Novissima*'.

These hymns speak of the transitory nature of the world and the importance of conflict, the centrality of yearning for the world to come, and the social life of the City of God. Most people see them as otherworldly and heaven-focused, and certainly they long for 'another country'. But they are hymns which urge us to a sense of vigilance and urgency, which set our hopes on the future, and which commit us to 'the life of the world to come'. They are calls to struggle for:

the peace that is for heaven

and shall be too for earth.[26]

They challenge us to work with God for the coming of the new world into the present. They remind us that it is the world to come which should always set the agenda for the Church.

9

Tradition and Decay

The division of human life into the sacred and the secular is one that comes naturally to western thought. It is a division which at one and the same time bears the marks of its Christian origin and witnesses to the death of a properly religious culture. For when the sacred and the secular are divided, then religion becomes one more department of human life, one activity among others. This has in fact happened to bourgeois religion ... Only a religion which is a way of living in every sphere either deserves to or can hope to survive. For the task of religion is to help see the secular as the sacred, the world as under God. When the sacred and the secular are separated, then ritual becomes an end not to the hallowing of the world, but in itself. Likewise if our religion is fundamentally irrelevant to our politics, then we are recognising the political as a realm outside the reign of God. To divide the sacred from the secular is to recognise God's action only within the narrowest limits. A religion which recognises such a division, as does our own, is one on the point of dying.

ALASDAIR MACINTYRE

With these words Alasdair MacIntyre began his first book, *Marxism: an Interpretation*, published in 1953. At that time, fairly new to Christian faith in any serious way, and searching for a way of engaging faith with politics, I was deeply influenced by MacIntyre. For a time we belonged to the same parish on the edge of Manchester. These words have remained with me over the past 40 years, and they still articulate for me something which is of profound importance.

For me the understanding of tradition, and specifically of a tradition which seeks to unite sacred and secular, is inextricably bound up with my experience in the East End of London. In this part of London we can recognise a radical social tradition within the Church over the last hundred years. I will consider the meaning of the words 'traditional' and 'radical' in more detail a little later. For the moment I want to use the term 'tradition' to mean a body of thought and practice which is rooted in the past and is still developing, and the term 'radical' to mean a posture, critique and approach to social, political and other areas which is rooted in a distinctive tradition, and which is therefore more conflictual and prophetic than reformist and pragmatic. I shall also, in the course of this chapter, use the related word 'orthodox', a word associated in its usage more with tradition than with radicalism, yet in a deep sense akin to both.

Tradition, change and conflict

There is no point in debating whether there has been a tradition of social reform, based on Christian insights, in East London – or indeed throughout the country: such a tradition is perfectly clear. What is not so clear is the extent, if any, to which we can talk about a tradition which challenges the dominant order, and the extent, if any, to which we can speak of the Christian community as being a 'subversive' presence. If it has been subversive, to what extent, if at all, is this subversive character rooted in Christian orthodoxy? The answers to this are not simple. I certainly saw in the movements associated with Headlam, Groser, Evans and others, something of a rebel tradition which was concerned with more than reform or pragmatic patching. It moved beyond patching-up to resistance, testimony and the commitment to create a more just order. It was able to do this because it was grounded in a tradition which could challenge the prevailing models and assumptions. Indeed, the ability to challenge the dominant structures and models is central to the character of living tradition.

The whole notion of tradition has been raised in recent years from two quite different directions: a vulgar media-promoted populist one, and a more reflective one as philosophers, and cultural and social analysts, try to understand the nature of living traditions of enquiry and testimony. At the vulgar level the term 'traditionalist' is increasingly used as the opposite of 'liberal', with which it has no particular connection. The term often seems to refer to people with no particular grasp of the tradition in its richness and complexity, but who cling nervously to the conventions of several decades past. The media use 'traditionalist' as a way of describing someone, usually male and clerical, who resists various current developments. It is a negative concept, a synonym for conservative or conventional. Indeed, it would be better to use one of these words, for such a posture has little to do with tradition in its 'traditional' sense.

This trivialising and vulgarising of the whole notion of tradition has, curiously, occurred at exactly the time when philosophers such as MacIntyre have been drawing attention to the central place of tradition in the quest for rationality and the moral life. Much of MacIntyre's thought appears in embryonic form in his early writings of the 1950s. He has been described as an individual who embodies the fragmentations, changes and intellectual yearnings of the late twentieth century, an intellectual in search of a caring community for our age.[1] Certainly his thinking is crucial for any approach to ethical reflection or to thinking about tradition in our time.

MacIntyre makes two points strongly in all his recent work. The first is the need to root all movements for moral and spiritual change in a corporate tradition. He defines a tradition as an argument extended through time, and argues for what he calls tradition-constituted inquiry.[2] Only within some kind of tradition can serious discourse be productive. To exist outside of all traditions is, he argues, disastrous: 'To be outside all traditions is to be a stranger to enquiry: it is to be in a state of intellectual and moral destitution'.[3] Such people exist in a kind of limbo, speaking the languages of everywhere and of nowhere.

But MacIntyre's second point, and this is really important, is that traditions by their very nature embody continuities of conflict. Tradition is not static or free from conflict, ambiguity and development. Conflict and ambiguity are indeed of the very nature of developing traditions. The only traditions which are free from conflict are the dead ones.

MacIntyre's argument begins with the claim that the most striking feature of contemporary moral utterance is that so much of it is used to express disagreements, and that these debates seem interminable. They seem unable to find a terminus. There seems to be no way in our culture of securing agreement or common ground on moral issues. As a result of the collapse of moral coherence, all we have left is fragments of moral vocabularies. At the heart of his argument is his critique of the 'Enlightenment project'. The Enlightenment involved a rejection of tradition, and a notion of some kind of objective rationality, some universal knowledge. It is this which MacIntyre rejects, and he links his critique with an attack on the notion of the atomised self, the isolated individual with no social identity. The acids of individualism, he claims, have for 400 years eaten into our moral structures.

MacIntyre seems pessimistic. He claims that our state is so disastrous that there are no large remedies for it. His views have been criticised on various grounds: it is claimed that he exaggerates the coherence of the past as well as the incoherence of the present; that he opposes tradition to liberalism, though liberalism is (as he does recognise) itself a tradition, albeit one which he dislikes. Yet, in spite of reservations, I believe that MacIntyre's work is important for at least four reasons. First, he highlights the confusion and incoherence at the heart of our culture, including our inability to use a common vocabulary. Secondly, he stresses that 'morality' is inseparable from the story of life in a community and from the spiritual life of that community. Morality does not float freely, but is part and parcel of a lifestyle, rooted in a story, a narrative. Thirdly, he calls for a recovery of tradition, as a living rootedness. Fourthly, he sees the quest for community as the point to begin, and compares our present predicament with the role of the Benedictine monks in the Dark Ages. We are, he suggests, 'waiting . . . for a new St Benedict'.[4]

Today there is increased recognition of the place of tradition. Tradition is a complex of inherited and shared beliefs, practices and symbols which are capable of great flexibility, variety and development. Some would argue that late modernity is a post-traditional society, a society in which we are linked globally but have been uprooted from the sources of security.[5] My view is that, while many traditions are either fossilised or profoundly broken, the task of recovery and retrieval is not impossible. However, it involves hard work, and this is not helped by a simplistic view of the nature of tradition.

'Traditional', 'liberal', 'orthodox': the effects of trivialisation

One of the features of recent discussions on Church issues has been the highly polarised and extremely trivialised use of language. Thus, on the one hand, the terms 'traditional' and 'traditionalist' are used to describe people who hold conservative and conventional views on a fairly narrow range of subjects. On the other hand, the word 'liberal' is used as an umbrella-term to describe people of broadly 'progressive' views on a range of issues – or, equally commonly, as a term of abuse and an accusation. Yet 'traditionalists' owe more to 'liberalism' than they realise. An example of this occurred a few years ago when a prominent 'traditionalist' priest committed suicide after attacking the 'liberalism' of the Runcie era in Anglican affairs. His funeral was a solemn requiem Mass at which a number of 'traditionalist' bishops concelebrated. The irony of this tragic episode was the idea that a solemn requiem for someone who had committed suicide would have been inconceivable had it not been for the very 'liberal' tendencies of which the priest and his supporters complained.

The term 'liberal' as a political concept was closely allied to individualism and the defence of individual rights. It was used in a theological sense in the nineteenth and early twentieth centuries to describe a type of Christian thought which emphasised freedom in interpretation of the Bible, and an openness to modern thought, but which was often combined with a strong sense of tradition (as in its recovery of patristic studies), and of the Church and its sacramental life. Today it is often

211

assumed that theological liberals believe very little – a view which would have amazed Charles Gore or Conrad Noel. I have never been a liberal either in theology or in politics, but I deeply deplore and have consistently opposed the use of the term as an insult or accusation. As one who is rooted in Catholic tradition, I equally deplore the trivialising of the language and content of tradition. I am an unashamed traditionalist.

The process which leads to trivialising is connected with the collapse of a way of being 'orthodox' which is open, paradoxical and willing to change. For many, orthodoxy has come to mean conventionality and one-dimensional thought. We can see a parallel in the approach to scientific work in Oswald Spengler's book *The Decline of the West* (1918). Spengler argued that science goes through a romantic period of imaginative exploration, followed by a period of consolidation which can lead to ossification. As science becomes more arrogant and inflexible, society rebels and turns towards fundamentalisms and irrational belief-systems. Spengler predicted that this would occur at the end of this millennium. How right he was.

One of the consequences of an over-rigid and inflexible stance among orthodox Christians is that much creative and innovative activity is pushed to, and beyond, the margins, and may become more bizarre and unstable in the process. We see this happening today in the Roman communion. In a different way, the intellectual imprisonment of much mainstream theology and its inaccessibility to the mass of the people have led many to seek their spiritual nourishment elsewhere. So it seems that, as theologians believe less and less, ordinary people are prepared to believe more and more. A rigid centre produces a prolific and luxuriant periphery.

The true nature of tradition

But what is tradition? It is not simple. It is not the same as conservatism. Tradition is open to constant reinterpretation and critique. Newman, in spite of his opposition to liberalism, saw the place of complexity, uncertainty, diversity and darkness within the orthodox tradition. T. S. Eliot, in his memorable essay of 1919 on 'Tradition and individual talent', saw that tradition was not simply inherited but was obtained with great labour, interrogation, toil and struggle. Tradition is rooted in past events but it is a way of life, a form of practice, a framework which allows for tremendous expansion. Stravinsky saw this in relation to music, and said that a musical style which drew richly on tradition might at the end not look very traditional in a simple-minded sense. Tradition is rich and diverse – the opposite of conventionality.

Within the tradition one learns what Aristotle called practical wisdom, *phronesis*. To be formed within a tradition is more than the communication of cerebral knowledge. The difference was brought home to me several years ago by a man training for priesthood in an American seminary. He had previously been a plumber and he contrasted the two forms of 'training'. As a plumber, he was apprenticed to a master plumber whom he followed around, learning from his wisdom and accumulated practical skill (*phronesis*), being a disciple, and through companionship, picking up ways of working. In the seminary, by contrast, the training was largely theoretical, cerebral, and delivered to classes of students seated at desks. There was no sense of companionship or of learning a trade by practice. The young man said that he felt more of a disciple as a plumber's apprentice than he did as a seminary student. The experience of the plumber was closer to the classical Greek tradition of *paideia*, in which practical wisdom was taught, not simply through reasoned argument but through initiation into a culture, a community of practice as well as discourse.[6]

Tradition is dynamic, and it is essential to look forward, not backward. There are constant warnings in the Bible against looking back (Jer. 7:24). Lot's wife who looked back was turned into a pillar of salt (Gen. 19:26). Yet paradoxically to look back and to go back are important parts of the process of movement forward. To go forward we need first to go back in order to see how the present has emerged from the past, and to know where we are in order to move beyond it. A central element in Israelite tradition was a reflection, a looking back, to the rock from which they were hewn (Isa. 51:1). But the looking back was part of a commitment to the future and to a movement forward in confidence.

Angela West has written that:

    . . . tradition is the preservation of arguments about what is

213

true . . . It is the continuation of this same enquiry, together with evidence from our own times, that makes us members of a particular community of truth seeking.[7]

West compares tradition to a court in permanent session. This brings out the fact that tradition includes debate and conflict, and that these are essential parts of it. A religious movement which has everything neatly sown up and revealed has no need of tradition. Nevertheless the more rigid and closed the movement, the more it is likely to be shaped by cultural and social forces of which it is unconscious. The more debate and conflict are suppressed and excluded, the more these forces take over.

This raises the whole question of orthodoxy. Like 'liberal', 'orthodox' has become a term of abuse, albeit used by different people. Orthodoxy is always in danger of being corrupted and reduced to dreary conventionality, but in its deepest meaning it is quite different. Orthodoxy is a way of keeping debates open, not foreclosing them. Heresy, on the other hand, seeks to close debates by adopting one correct line to the exclusion of all others. Heresy is one-dimensional and cannot cope with paradox. Orthodoxy is an attempt to hold together truths which at first sight seem incompatible.[8] Orthodoxy is often seen as the enemy of radicalism, but I believe that this is to misunderstand the situation. What then do we mean by radicalism?

Radicalism, true and false

'Radical' is not one of my favourite words. In its general usage, I find it vague and unhelpful. It seems often to be used as an excuse for intellectual laziness, offering the rhetoric of 'going to the roots' as a means of avoiding any concrete commitments to any specific programme or strategy. Thus many Christians in the 1970s and 1980s called themselves 'radicals' as an alternative to calling themselves 'socialists'. Yet the nature of their radicalism, and the commitments involved, seemed so intensely varied that one wondered what meaning the word could have. Going to the roots seemed to produce a wide variety of plants – or maybe merely confirmed the wide variety that was already there. And with a definition so general, who could ever deny that they were radicals?

The word radical is often used as the opposite of fundamentalist, though the two words are etymologically almost synonyms – *radix*, root, and *fundamenta*, foundations, only differing in terms of application to organic and inorganic matter. The *radix* refers to vegetables, particularly radishes, while the *fundamenta* refer to the foundations of a building. Both are concerned with going down to the origins in order to be secure, and to grow and build. However, radical is used in contradictory ways – sometimes to mean returning to the roots, sometimes to mean laying an axe to the roots, needing to uproot and pluck away. I said at the beginning of this chapter that I use the term 'radical' to mean a posture, critique and approach to the social and political arena which is rooted in a distinctive tradition, and which is therefore more conflictual and prophetic than reformist and pragmatic. The radical is one who challenges the present and its values and practices in the name of an alternative vision, a tradition.

So this, like 'traditionalist', 'liberal' and 'orthodox', is a word which is used with many widely differing senses and shades of meaning, sometimes as a synonym for liberal or vaguely progressive (which is in fact its origin in political usage), sometimes – increasingly perhaps – in a right-wing sense. The idea of a 'radical right' has a long ancestry, preceding Margaret Thatcher by many years. 'Rootedness', *enracinement*, was a favourite concept of Maurice Barres and Charles Maurras who helped prepare the way for European Fascism. These thinkers, whose ideas are now flourishing in France and elsewhere, saw intellectuals and left-wing thinkers as *les déracines*, the uprooted, people without roots. And the idea of roots was seen in essentially national and racial terms. We can find echoes of this understanding of the need for roots in T. S. Eliot and other modernist thinkers. The notion of radicalism has never been the preserve of the left or of liberals. The word, like the idea, is a mixed blessing.

Within Christianity, the word radical has been used since the early 1960s to describe two rather different movements. One, identified by David Edwards as 'Christian radicalism' during the debate over *Honest to God* in 1963, was essentially a movement of renewal within the Church itself, a complement to the biblical, liturgical and ecumenical movements, concerned to reinterpret the foundations or roots of Christian faith for a new generation.[9] Robinson claimed to have originated the use of the term 'radical' in Christian theology,[10] and the 1960s saw books with such titles as *A Theology for Radical Politics* (written by that latter-day apologist for democratic capitalism, Michael Novak) and *Radical Theology and the Death of God.*[11] Over the years, much of this radical theology has been more critical of Christian doctrine than of secular society. The tendency for radical theologians to capitulate to the dominant secular ideology was central to E. L. Mascall's critique of it in 1965.[12] Indeed, many who call themselves 'radical theologians' occupy secure and privileged positions in universities and are extremely conservative culturally. They have been called 'tenured radicals'.

Robinson himself was an interesting figure. To read the debates about *Honest to God* today is to enter a strangely distant world, and it is difficult for many younger Christians to understand what all the fuss was about. *Honest to God* was a watershed in Robinson's thought. His early work was in New Testament and liturgy. As he grew older, his biblical scholarship became more conservative, while his ecclesiology and his liturgical and social consciousness became less so. But, as we look back on him, he seems very much a figure from the culture of academia, and particularly of Cambridge. More than this, he was an academic steeped in the Anglican ethos, striving to be a radical yet very much a child of the culture.

More recently we have seen the rise to fame of another representative of Cambridge radical theology in the shape of Don Cupitt, who has written a book called *Radicals and the Future of the Church.* Cupitt's book is mainly a critique of the power-structure of Churches and an argument for a new style of Christian presence based on smaller units. He argues that Christians in the future must be 'beliefless', that there is no fixed essence of Christianity, and that the Christian of the future will be vagrant and free. Cupitt seems to see himself and his disciples as an oppressed minority. He writes:

We are like dissidents in an East European country; journalists from the outside world may sometimes seek us out, authority affects to disregard us, and our books circulate like samizdat publications.[13]

As a description of Cambridge University in the 1990s, and of an author whose books are published by SCM Press and circulate through all the mainstream bookshops, this must strike readers as a little curious, and perhaps lead them to suspect a certain degree of self-delusion.

There is another type of radicalism which is very orthodox theologically. It also arose during the 1960s as evangelical Christians in particular were confronted by racism and the Vietnam War. It led to a new biblical radicalism of which Jim Wallis is the best-known representative. Although terms such as 'a new biblical radicalism' and 'radical discipleship' are used mainly by evangelicals, there are links with figures from other traditions – Roman Catholics such as the Berrigans, Thomas Merton, and Dorothy Day, or with Anglicans such as William Stringfellow. Anglicans will also look back to Headlam, Noel and so on. What do these movements have in common? I think there are at least five features.

First, they tend to find their home among oppressed, poor and marginal people. Secondly, they tend to be theologically orthodox but seek to bring their faith into dialogue and perhaps collision with current movements, and from this may develop shifts and changes. Thirdly, there is an anarchist strain. Dorothy Day was very explicitly anarchist, while Noel's socialism was of a libertarian kind. Fourthly, there is a stress on celebration and beauty. And, fifthly, there is a certain sectarian aspect. These radicals tend to be on the edge. Thus Anabaptists and those influenced by that radical Reformation stream see themselves as faithful witnesses, dissidents, resident aliens, a community of alternative vision, a minority movement of resistance. There may be a difference here between a radicalism of word and a radicalism of sacrament, and this would repay further study.

Here we encounter a problem. For while there is a consistent dimension in radical Christianity which is separatist and counter-cultural, sectarianism can lead to nothing or to the arrogance and elitism of the spiritually correct and the utterly pure. The Christian radical lives on a knife-edge. The dilemma of withdrawal versus communion is brought out in Angela West's critique of Mary Daly and her memorable act of 'exodus' from the Christian Church. West's words are worth quoting at length, for they embody the whole dilemma facing traditionalists who also claim to be radicals. She suggests that:

Perhaps the time has come to question this claim to radicalism – to suggest that her famous gesture of walking out
might just be a little old hat – decidedly old hat, in fact. For
members of the western intelligentsia have been doing it for
centuries – since the seventeenth, to be precise. And in
Western Europe large sections of the population have walked
out of the church ages ago, and have been existing in a
largely post-Christian society ever since. Daly, who lives in
a rather more churchgoing type of society than we do, might
not have noticed these things. She rests her claim to radicalism on the fact that she acknowledges no roots, no origins
in anything that would connect her to male values – for she
has been born again in her head . . . And here we encounter
the crux of the theological error that we are in danger of
perpetuating. We have believed that beautiful flowers grow
out of pure elements. In fact, as the lotus reminds us, their
roots go down into every sort of impurity and rottenness.
Thus our theological quest must proceed not by means of
separation, of walking out on ourselves, but rather by staying
on and going deeper.[14]

Movements in Anglican Catholicism

The need for a network within which there could be a dialectical encounter between the received tradition and the
demands of the present has been one of my central concerns
for many years. In 1974 a group of us formed the Jubilee
Group as a loose national network of Christians, mainly within
the Anglican Catholic tradition. One of our main tasks has
been to create a framework within which orthodox theology
can be related, through creative struggle and practice, with the
demands of the current political scene. We see ourselves as
part of a living, turbulent, and still evolving, tradition – a
tradition which I have called subversive orthodoxy because,
while being rooted in the tradition of Catholic orthodoxy, it
was deeply questioning of, and disturbing to, the established
conventions and structures.[14] We chose the name Jubilee
because of its origins in the Mosaic Law where it is a key symbol

of human liberation. The theme of Jubilee has been taken up by others recently, including Pope John Paul in his *Tertio Millennio Adveniente* (1995) which links the theme of the millennium with that of Jubilee. For us the symbol of Jubilee locates our hope within the context of debt, land and liberation of prisoners. It is a social hope, the hope of liberation and of the Kingdom of God. We have tried to create a supportive network and environment, a community of discourse, a fellowship of controversy, and a loving network of friends. We try to be faithful to the tradition, and to be open to the challenges and demands of God in the future.

The Jubilee Group grew out of the Anglican Catholic tradition, but most Anglican Catholics would disown us and be embarrassed by us. The use of the concept of traditionalism within the media has been associated in recent years particularly with Anglican Catholics. It is a term used proudly by those who oppose the ordination of women, resist what they see as 'liberal' trends in the Church, and often take up positions against a fairly limited range of issues – acceptance of gay and lesbian people, inclusive language in the liturgy, and so on.

But it is necessary to make some distinctions here, for the Anglican Catholic movement is not monochrome. Since the Oxford Movement, Anglican Catholicism has taken two broad directions. (I should add that my analysis here is over-simplified for the sake of space, and I take no account here of the broad area of 'liberal Anglicanism' with Catholic leanings, not because I do not consider it significant but because it does not seem to me to derive in any direct way from the Oxford Movement, while the two streams I refer to certainly do.)

The first stream is a Papalist one. To some extent I stand within this myself. I was brought up as a teenager within a parish which took the position that England formed two provinces of the Western Church which had been cut off from their main source of life by historical events for which they were not responsible.

Sadly the Papalists among Anglican Catholics attached themselves uncritically to Rome at one of its most decayed periods. Today, in the aftermath of the Second Vatican Council, many 'Anglo-Papalists' look to the more reactionary elements within the Roman communion, taking little account, and often knowing nothing, of the immense ferment which has taken place there, of the progressive forces which exist not only in

South and North America, but also in other parts of Europe. So Anglican Catholics cling to the more backward-looking elements within Rome, and those clergy who have left the Church of England for the Roman priesthood are usually among the more conservative elements within that Church.

The second stream, overlapping at certain points with the first, was more open, adventurous and flexible. It was the stream associated with Charles Gore and the 'sacramental socialists' who grew in numbers and influence after the 1870s. It is with this group that the Jubilee tendency is most sympathetic, and we have found close allies within the more radical wings of the Roman communion. Indeed, we find Roman Catholics more open to, and sympathetic with, our position than are many Anglicans.

In considering the present decayed state of the Anglican Catholic tradition, I found it depressing to re-read one of the first articles I ever wrote. Entitled 'Catholicism in decay', it was published in the journal of the Society for Promoting Catholic Unity in 1962.[15] Here I argued that Anglican Catholics had, on the one hand, become acceptable within the cultural climate of 'middle Anglicanism' and had ceased to challenge it, becoming a deviant enclave within the culture rather than a challenge to it. On the other hand, they had moved round and round within a world of increasing triviality and irrelevance, and had lost touch with the major issues of the world.

Today Anglican Catholics are more divided, fragmented and confused than they have been for a long time. The issue of the ordination of women is not the cause of this state, but it has opened up a whole Pandora's box of unresolved issues. My sense is that Anglican Catholicism is an ageing movement as well as a clerical one. While many young Christians have gained from, and value, the many aspects of sacramental life, they have not absorbed the theological basis of the faith. Anglican Catholic clergy have not been good at communicating with lay people or discussing with them what it is that matters in faith. Hence many debates around matters of faith and doctrine are exclusively clerical debates which lay people find incomprehensible or irrelevant. The issue of the ordination of women is a classic instance. I have ministered in a number of parishes whose clergy have either died, retired or defected over this issue. Once they have left, it has become perfectly clear that the lay people, while they did not wish to upset the clergy of whom they were fond, did not share their position, and in a number of cases called a woman to celebrate or to be their parish priest.

The tragedy of Anglican Catholicism lies in its inability to mature and develop, and in this it is a useful case-study of tradition in decay. I want to draw attention to four aspects of this phenomenon.

1. The movement has become dangerously negative. While I do believe strongly in the importance of resistance and opposition, it is impossible to build a movement purely on opposition, as many political factions have found. Yet many Anglican Catholic publications are full of negativity of the most bitter and unpleasant kind. A psychoanalyst would have a field-day with them. Almost 20 years ago Richard Holloway, now Bishop of Edinburgh, warned his hearers that this obsession with opposition could lead to a state of serious pathology.

> Negative movements, like negative theology, do not capture the hearts and minds of good men and women, only of the sick-minded, the marginal, the insecure ... We must not become a fanatical, self-righteous rump, a sort of ecclesiastical National Front.[16]

But his words were unheeded, and this is what, to a large extent, has happened.

2. The movement has become more precious and effete. The kitsch aspect goes back a long way. The fetish of correctness, the delight in fuss, the neurotic obsession with trivia – these are well-established phenomena in the Anglican Catholic world. But they have created a kind of world of unreality, a grotto, what Valerie Pitt has called a bubble world.

> It is difficult to fathom how a movement nourished on William Law, George Herbert, and the sober beauty of the Book of Common Prayer can have left this legacy of devotional bric-a-brac and the other debris cluttering Anglo-Catholic attics. But it is the most unfortunate of its legacies, for in fact the movement forced the great grace of its devotion, its revival of spirituality, into the matrices of this fantasy life which was often tawdry, and is, very often, psychologically dangerous. And it cannot be put down to the movement's

followers, for the twist and distortion which it represents comes out of the histrionics, the extravagant sensibilities of those extraordinary years in Oxford. Some indeed may be especially traced to the particular emotionalism of Dr Pusey's character. The real fault is that the Tractarians unconsciously made religion a life substitute rather than a life revealer, not a way into the splendours of the visible world but a way out. That habit of mind is fixed in us still and ultimately it is destructive of religion itself.[17]

3.   The movement has ceased to think. While the work of Gore helped to shape the progressive Catholicism of the future Roman Church, and Michael Ramsey's *The Gospel and the Catholic Church* (1936) anticipated much in the Second Vatican Council, it is difficult to call to mind serious thinkers today who belong to this tradition except in the most critical and marginal way.

4.   The movement is deeply affected by sexual confusion and dishonesty. The growth of Anglican Catholicism and the growth of a male homosexual subculture in Britain occurred at the same time. The closet and the sacristy were historically coincident. And for many years Anglican Catholicism provided a form in which gay people were able to be themselves in an oblique way. It was a therapeutic community in an age of secrecy. However, since the gay liberation movements of the 1970s and the spread of honesty about sexual identity, the Anglican Catholic movement, which had once been a place of safety, has become a zone of untruth and denial. So it is all too common to find Anglican Catholic priests and spokespersons in the forefront of hostility to homosexuality while following a closet homosexual lifestyle themselves. The contradictions of the closet have become endemic within the movement in a way which is really very serious.[18]

For these reasons I am not sure if Anglican Catholicism can survive as a discrete phenomenon within world Christianity or be a positive force within it. Certainly the features I identified above are serious obstacles to its future.

I have looked at Anglican Catholicism as an example of a tradition which seems to have fossilised. But traditions can be renewed and reinvigorated. I am not at all sure whether this particular tradition is open to such a process. The jury is still out.

10

Ministry and Marginality

We trained hard, but it seemed that every time we were
beginning to form up into teams we would be reorganised.
I was to learn later in life that we tend to meet any new
situations by reorganising: and a wonderful method it can
be for creating the illusion of progress while producing
confusion, inefficiency and demoralisation.

PETRONIUS ARBITER, 210 BC

A hungry, ill-fed sheep is ever on its feet, on the move,
searching for another scanty mouthful of forage to try and
satisfy its growing hunger. Such sheep are not contented,
they do not thrive, they are of no use to themselves or to
their owners. They languish and lack vigour and vitality.

W. PHILIP KELLER

Be a shepherd of a flock doomed to slaughter.

ZECHARIAH 11:4 (NRSV)

From my window in Whitechapel Road I can see the spot where the Salvation Army was founded in 1865, and the alley where Jack the Ripper committed his first murder in 1888, where the anarchist bookshop now stands. I live on the site of the original 'white chapel' of 1338 from which the district got its name, and where Altab Ali was murdered on 4 May 1978. If I stood on the roof, I would see the building where the Liberty Bell was made, the house where, in 1903, Lenin and Trotsky met to plan the Fifth Congress of the Russian SDLP and subsequent revolution, and the pub where my old parishioner Ronnie Kray shot George Cornell on 6 March 1966. A few hundred yards south is Cable Street where, on 4 October 1996, we celebrated the sixtieth anniversary of the famous anti-Fascist battle of 1936. A few miles north, in my first parish of Hoxton, Dickens wrote *Oliver Twist*, and the workhouse, which later became a geriatric hospital, has only recently been pulled down.

This part of the East End of London is full of complex, ambiguous and disturbing history. Its political history is unique. Part of the East End was the only constituency to elect a Communist MP in 1945 (Phil Piratin), while the Millwall Ward elected Derek Beackon of the British National Party in 1993, and the Teviot Ward of Poplar can claim the lowest vote for a Conservative ever recorded – 24 votes in a recent by-election.

The East End of London has been a place for explorers for almost 200 years. There were Henry Mayhew and Charles Booth in the nineteenth century. Booth, who began his work in the late 1880s, wrote of the East End in terms of scroungers, loafers, and 'the residuum', the antecedent of 'the underclass'. William Morris called the East End the 'city of dreadful night', while Judith Walkowitz has re-named it 'city of dreadful delight', highlighting the strange mixture of urban demonology and fascination with changing sexual practices and scandals at the approach to the *fin de siècle*.[1] A small pamphlet called *The Bitter Cry of Outcast London* was published in 1883, and alerted a wide section of Christianity to conditions here. Five years later Karanelli described Whitechapel as 'the resort of the residuum of the whole country and the refuse of the continent'.

More important in terms of its audience was Jack London's book *The People of the Abyss*, published in 1903. London's book was a best-seller, and certainly led to the reforms of Lloyd George and perhaps, very marginally, to the development of the welfare state. London summarised the East End in classic terms:

> No more dreary sector can be found on this earth than the whole of the awful East ... Everything is helpless, hopeless, unrelieved and dirty ... The very rain when it falls is more like grease than water from heaven ... Here lives a population as dull and unimaginative as its long grey miles of dingy brick.

In these words Jack London anticipated many later commentators who saw the East End as a place marked by depression, dreariness and despair.[2]

In the 1990s we are still being discovered. From Wilmott and Young's *Family and Kinship in East London* in the 1950s to the present day, we have been at the receiving end of constant research, experiment and media coverage. Poverty in the area is regularly being documented. Writing on racial attacks invariably focuses on this area. We attract attention because of health problems – TB notifications are seven times the national average. Week by week the local papers have headlines such as 'Whitechapel: the shame of London',[3] which reinforce the image of the area as a place of gloom, fear and desolation. Although many local people resent the demonising of the area, the East End in 1997 remains a place which is written about and its people are 'worked among'.

The East End is a microcosm, or a perspective or point of perception, from which to view trends in the wider culture, and particularly in other inner urban areas. I want in particular to look at the kind of demands on ministry which will ensue as a result of the spread of inequality and marginality. Ministry with marginalised people and communities will be a major crisis-area for the next century, but the forces working against it within the Church are formidable. Most Church strategy is aimed at maintaining established structures, particularly those which are 'successful'. But the Church is 'successful' in the main among the comfortable, conventional, affluent and secure. It could be that much innovative work, particularly if it does not bring in money, will be forced outside of the mainstream Church structures. But, whatever happens, and wherever such ministry occurs, the task will be an uphill one. For marginalisation and deprivation are certain to get worse in the coming years. This is true not only in Britain but throughout Europe, which some observers predict will become more and more a Third World continent.[4]

Whatever happens in the next few years, conditions in the deprived areas will not improve quickly, and they may not improve at all. Even if a really radical Labour government were to initiate a national campaign to attack the root causes of deprivation, so much damage has been done that it will take years to undo and repair it. And, while the Churches have a good record for ministry with marginal people and groups, I have a terrible fear that much creative work will come to an end, or be forced outside the official Church, technically through financial constraints, but in fact through a failure of imagination, courage and creativity, and a commitment to safety at all costs.

As I hope has become clear from the preceding pages, I am first and foremost a pastor. I hope that I am a thinking pastor. Indeed, I believe that a major part of the work of ministry is reflection. I am certainly a political pastor. I am a pastor with a specific commitment to marginalised people, people who are victims of urban deprivation and oppression. This book has reflected these features of my life. It is pastoral care – the giving and receiving of strength, support and guidance to and from actual people – which concerns me most deeply. It is because of these concerns that I look to the future with alarm, and see the sky as red and threatening.

In this final chapter, therefore, I want to raise some questions about ministry, pastoral care and priesthood in the coming years. The notion of a pastor arose within the Christian tradition. It has little importance, if it exists at all, in Judaism, Buddhism or Islam. The term 'pastoral care' has had a curious recent history, and is now often used in an entirely secular context without any reference to Christianity. There is nothing wrong with this, and I would be the last person to claim that 'caring' – whether it is the natural human kind of caring or the paid professional kind – is peculiarly Christian or even religious. But, curiously, this conceptual and practical shift has occurred also within the Christian Churches themselves, where pastoral counsellors abound but seem to have little contact with historic Christian thought. Much of what is called pastoral care has value within its secular framework of understanding, but my concern here is with pastoral ministry within, yet moving beyond, the Christian community, and this is a ministry which is inevitably rooted in reflective theology.

Yet here too it would seem that in many parts of Western Christianity, clergy and ministers interpret their role largely in terms derived from the pastoral counselling models of secular culture. This process has been most marked in the USA. Thus in a 1967 survey of clergy in the Episcopal Church, 36 per cent identified serving, helping and relating as the central motivations which brought them into ministry. Of course, these practices are commendable, yet they do mark a reduction and narrowing of the classical Christian understanding of the nature of pastoral care or, to use an old-fashioned term, the cure of souls.

The professionalisation of the clergy

In 1952 the late John A. T. Robinson predicted that the future clergy would be 'largely non-professional'.[5] Since then, ironically, there has been a shift towards increasing professionalisation, as many clergy have moved into such disciplines as social work, counselling and psychotherapy, not to mention accountancy, finance and commerce, and teaching. Again, there is no logical reason why priests and deacons should not function in these areas, though it would be nice to see more bus drivers, bakers and maybe carpenters. More important and more worrying has been the increased dominance of the idea of the clergy as professionals *per se*. So now we have diocesan departments concerned with 'professional ministry'. This process can be exaggerated, as in a recent American study where it is claimed that 'we have turned bishops into administrators and priests into therapists with the result that the building up of the People of God has been ignored'.[6] This is silly – and, since one of the authors is a bishop in an area where there are numerous examples to the contrary, ridiculously indefensible – but it contains some truth. However, the idea of a clergy separated by skill and function from the mass of the people is not of recent origin. The class-based, elitist, literate clergy developed, particularly in England, after the Reformation, in contrast to the medieval priests who were often poor. By about 1700 the Anglican clergy had lost any of the sense of identity with ordinary people which still pertained in Ireland, Poland, Italy and Greece.

What is a professional? In its origin it refers to someone who makes a profession or vow, but this early sense has long since disappeared. Indeed, it has almost come to mean the opposite. As opposed to the amateur (literally, the lover) who loves his or her work, the professional does what he or she is paid to do within the circumscribed hours. Harold Perkin sees the profession as a trade organised according to performance and function.[7] A list of characteristics of professionals would include the acquisition of skills, the need for credentials and accreditation, the acceptance of pay, and the recognition and observance of 'boundaries' (a very modern concept indeed). Most professionals keep their personal lives separate from their work, usually living apart from their job, their home addresses being unknown to their 'clients' and often to their colleagues. The word 'client' is important. Professionals have 'clients', an unpleasant word meaning one who clings or leans. It is a word which has been brought into the Christian vocabulary from elsewhere, and which is increasingly used.

Is this what Christian ministry is about? I fear that, for most parts of the Church, it is exactly this, and so I do see serious dangers in the spread, and general acceptance, of managerial and professional models of ministry. It reduces ministry to a secular model, and the Church, itself dominated by secular notions, has fallen in with this model. We see it, for example, in many of the responses to clergy sexual abuse where it is assumed that clergy are 'healing professionals'. There is no reference to God, and it is taken for granted that there is a financial transaction. I believe this whole approach to Christian ministry brings it into disrepute, and may well bring it to an end.

Many writers have criticised the professional model as theologically inadequate, but this seems to have had little effect on the institution.[8] The professional model is also rooted in gendered thought and in male notions of the self as strongly bounded – aspects which are likely to have had some effect on the institution.[9] It also seems that Churches have discovered the idea of the expert professional at the very point when more progressive voices in the secular world have called it into question. Thus Ivan Illich, as long ago as 1977, claimed that the age when people had problems and professionals had solutions was at an end. Illich warned of the dominance of the experts, a dominance which was:

> ... more deeply entrenched than a Byzantine bureaucracy, more international than a world church, more stable than any Labour union, endowed with wider competencies than any shaman, and equipped with a tighter hold over those they claim as victims than any mafia.[10]

Another common idea at the present time is that the Christian pastor is a 'leader'. The notion of leadership is one of many notions which seem to have been accepted without question throughout much of institutional Christianity. It is a concept with little biblical support. Indeed the word 'leader' only occurs three times in the Bible – once in a list from Paul (1 Cor. 12:28), and twice in relation to Moses and Aaron (Num. 33:1; Heb. 3:16).

The move towards remoteness

I find these developments towards professionalisation worrying, though not because I think that priests and ministers are the only agents of pastoral care. I do, however, believe that it is important that congregations and communities contain members who have a particular responsibility for pastoral ministry, in association with others in the community. This ministry should be shared, collaborative ministry (Rom. 16:1–23), but it does not rule out the fact that certain individuals may have a particular and crucial role. Yet this role is only of value if these persons are more easily accessible than most people. In many places, this seems now to be less so than ever before.

Thus a study of the Diocese of Birmingham in 1991 expressed concern that the bishop seemed overburdened and remote, and that diocesan administration was more and more bureaucratic and dysfunctional, marked by 'busy inertia'. The diocesan office conveyed a 'perception of remoteness'.[11] There is no evidence that the position has improved over the past six years, or that the position there is altogether untypical of other dioceses. This is bad enough, but it is only the beginning of the saga.

The fact is that in recent years, partly as a result of the spread of these ideas about professionalism and leadership, many clergy have become remote. There has been a widespread (often relieved) acceptance of managerial and bureaucratic notions, a collapse of intimacy (to some extent due to the surfacing of cases of sexual misconduct), and a concern with 'boundaries' which has in some places brought pastoral ministry of more than a superficial kind to an end. Many pastors are now inaccessible, hidden behind answerphones or secretaries, living apart from their work in places known only to friends. The somewhat anarchic but relaxed framework of parish and people has disappeared, as more walls and frontiers, more conditions and compartments, more distances and specialisations, have been erected.

One reason for this is that in recent years there has been great concern about attacks on clergy. And yet, and yet ... there is a way of responding to tragedy which is almost always wrong, and a way of giving advice which is both inappropriate and impractical. I am desperately concerned that the Church does not respond in the wrong way, as it so often does – the way of panic, the way of safety, the way of risk-avoidance, including yet again the way of taking over secular notions derived from non-theological sources. This is illustrated by a recent report from the Church in London.

Knocking at Heaven's Door, a report published by CARIS, the London Diocese's Board for Social Responsibility, is a disturbing document.[12] Strangely subtitled, 'Opportunities presented by the casual caller in the parish' – though in fact mainly about callers at vicarages – it seems, on the surface, to be a kindly, sensitive document. The Bishop of Willesden, commending it to London parishes, calls it an 'excellent report'. I find it worrying and depressing. Not surprisingly, sections of the media have made the report seem worse than it is. The *Evening Standard* of 8 May 1996 had a headline, 'Turn away the beggars, London vicars are told'. This was not quite fair to the report, which was not as bad as that. But the misrepresentation is entirely the report's fault. It is bad enough.

However, it is important to begin by saying that it does undoubtedly try to address some important questions, and it should be commended for doing so. Many parish clergy are exposed in a way that social workers and other 'professionals' are not. In most cases the addresses of these people are not known, indeed are carefully guarded by their organisations. Vicarages and clergy houses, on the other hand, are public buildings. Everybody knows – in theory – where a parish priest lives. Calls at 3 a.m. are not uncommon. And there have been some nasty incidents – rape, violent attack, threats to family, and so on. It would be irresponsible and cruel to ignore this history, and so it is not surprising that the Church should want to respond to it. Indeed, it is surprising that it has taken so long.

So why does it worry me? I am worried, first, because the report contains some appallingly bad advice. 'Do not engage with callers on the doorstep'. 'Do not invite the caller inside'. 'Do not undertake a pastoral relationship'. All this flies in the face of my own pastoral experience, and I am horrified that young clergy should be exposed to such stuff. There may well be people whom one should not invite inside, and the doorstep is not always the best place for pastoral encounters (though there does seem to be a rather elementary contradiction here, not unknown in Church reports). But to give such blanket advice to pastors is thoroughly irresponsible, and ignores the fact that pastoral ministry occurs in all kinds of odd places and at odd hours. Had I taken the advice in this report, much of my pastoral work would never have occurred.

Secondly, there is a specific problem about attitudes to the mentally ill. The report adopts conventional stereotypes and group clichés – 'con-men, the homeless, the mentally ill, beggars, the hungry, the thirsty . . .'. It does seem to collude with a current mood which regards mentally ill people as necessarily violent and dangerous. But this is not so. Research shows that most 'schizophrenics', for example, never commit an offence, violent or otherwise. This report may well encourage clergy to panic and withdraw in the face of mental distress.

But it is a third point which really concerns me. I am appalled at the way in which many priests and ministers are buying into secular (often outdated) managerial models, and are becoming increasingly difficult to contact (or should we now say 'access'?) after 5 p.m. I fear that this report will make the situation worse. Indeed, the report quotes one of the diocesan officials as admitting that clergy are more difficult to get hold of now than in the past. There is the inevitable language of 'boundaries'. Even Jesus set boundaries, we are told – no doubt, just as Jesus is a manager, according to Archbishop Carey. Oh dear! What did we do to deserve this?

What is really important is that priests, and other pastoral workers, in vulnerable situations – and not only in the inner city – are given proper support, care and solidarity, and this sadly often does not happen. At the end of the day, we cannot completely prevent attacks, including fatal ones. We can help to create networks of support, and, where necessary, protection. The worst response would be to withdraw and make the clergy more remote from people and from danger. Yes, there is a real danger that priests, and other grass-roots pastoral workers, will be victims of attack, and we need to be vigilant and aware. But there is a bigger problem at the moment of priests who are hardly ever available to people in crisis.

I once rang a well-known central London church and was given information (on a recorded message) about concerts, but nothing about pastoral care. I rang another, allegedly 'radical', parish and was told, on Thursday, that the parish priest would not be available until Monday. When I asked for his home number, I was informed that it was not to be released. I almost said that I was dying and needed the last rites – but assumed I would be told to delay the process.

I have been a priest for just over 30 years, and have spent the largest part of that time in the East End of London. I do not usually go in for nostalgia, but I have become extremely concerned of late at the way in which churches have closed their doors, and many clergy have become more remote and inaccessible. Today, worries about security often seem to take precedence over pastoral and spiritual need. Priests and ministers are, like so many other paid carers, in danger of retreating from the common life into safety and security.

Perhaps the real clue to this report lies in the words on the opening page which tell us that it was paid for by Ecclesiastical Insurance. When pastoral theology is determined, not by the gospel, but by the church insurance company, we are in deep trouble. The Church dies, as the Catholic anarchist Dorothy Day said, when security takes the place of the life and death of ordinary people. Let me stress that I am not advocating the 24-hour syndrome of pastors who are always on call. This cliché is a common type of response to my argument, but it does not deal with the problem. There are ways of dealing with this problem through co-operative work, and planning of times of rest, which do not lead to remoteness. There is a bigger problem at the moment of priests and ministers who are hardly ever available, and I fear that reports such as that from London may encourage this withdrawal. As for the door of heaven, if this report is any guide, it is clearly locked most of the time.

Locked doors raise the question of locked churches. Churches are meant to be places of prayer. The recent practice of closing of places of prayer has accelerated in direct relation to the increased hunger for prayer, silence and places of spiritual growth among many sections of the population. Of course, I am aware that there are real difficulties here, and I am not suggesting that it is an easy question. But it does seem to me that one of the major pastoral campaigns which we need to initiate is one which is committed to keeping churches open as far and for as long as is practically possible. However, church buildings need more than open doors. They need an atmosphere of prayerfulness. The obvious way to build such an atmosphere is for groups of people to pray in them in a regular and disciplined way, day in, day out. Prayerfulness is infectious, and there is no stronger witness to its reality locally than the existence of a committed group who make prayer a high priority.

We need also to consider other aspects of the church building. Is there a sensitivity to the fact that people are praying, and therefore to the need, as far as possible, to keep external noise to a minimum? Are there key focal-points of vision – altar, reredos, crucifix, icon, colourful banners, and so on – which help people to be attentive and directed? To reserve the Blessed Sacrament in a chapel set apart for concentrated prayer can be an immense strength to the active life of the local church. If priests and people meet daily to recite the divine office together, and groups meet for corporate prayer at other times, this can also act as a stimulus to others to join them. The creation, strengthening and sustaining of such prayer-centres will be of major importance as the next century progresses.

All this is very obvious, and one is almost ashamed to have to say it. But the shift to – it is no longer 'towards' – a secular, managerial model of the Church, with rectors as managers and the 'office' as somewhere to sit rather than something to pray, is so pervasive that these elementary points need to be emphasised. My view is that the Church is becoming more bureaucratic, more managerial, more remote, more caught into the structures of late capitalism. This is particularly alarming because, in the process, we seem to be moving away from many of the positive movements of the last 50 years. As I look back over more than 30 years of priestly ministry and look forward to the twenty-first century, I am disturbed by the dominance of bureaucracies, managers, consultants, counsellors and therapists in the Church, and by a corresponding lack of concern for intimate pastoral care, prayer, theological reflection, and struggle for righteousness. I am worried about the excessive concern with trends rather than with truth. Of course, I need to qualify this and stress, first, that I have no particular quarrel with the above disciplines as such, only with their dominance of the Christian community; and secondly, that I realise that there are many exceptions to what I say. Nevertheless the position is disturbing.

For example, in the 1950s the growth of the house-church movement stressed the cellular structure of the Church, and saw the local parish and neighbourhood community as the taproots of the vine. In recent years the house-church movement has been recovered, but much of it has been forced outside the main structures by the rigidity and centralisation of the ecclesiastical machine.[13] And while the Second Vatican Council emphasised the local church – the *ecclesia particularis* – many recent trends have been towards centralisation. This has been evident in the Church of England since the Turnbull Report.[14] Much of this emphasis on centralised bureaucracies has sapped the initiative and creative energy of the local church. Yet I believe that the future lies more and more with the local praying, thinking, acting community.

Church and state

My experience has mainly been within the Church of England, which is an established Church. I have never believed in established Churches, and have always found working within an established Church difficult to reconcile with my conscience. It has always seemed to me that the kind of relationship between

Church and state which prevails in England is not compatible with the gospel. But even if there were a case for an established Church, it would only apply where there was some sense of national identity reflected in a Church which could be seen as that of the majority of the people. This is clearly not the case – though the notion is deeply rooted in the thought of the Church of England, if nowhere else in the Anglican world. Indeed, the Church of England is unique within world Anglicanism in that it is the only Church which is established, and the only Church where the bulk of the membership is lapsed! (I suspect the two are not unconnected.)

The Anglican theologian Richard Hooker (1554–1600) stated the ideology of establishment clearly in his *Of the Laws of Ecclesiastical Polity*. Members of the Church of England, according to Hooker, were members of the commonwealth of England. Yet today Hooker's claim cannot be defended: the Church of England, with 1.8 million members, cannot claim to be a national Church. So the defence of establishment has become vaguer – references to 'public religion', to the 'values' of the state, and so on – and less convincing. The arguments for establishment have not changed essentially since Gladstone's *The State in its Relations with the Church* (1838). Gladstone argued for the establishment on the grounds that it gave the Church opportunity to influence education and public life. Since then there have been four reports on Church and state – Selbourne in 1917, Cecil in 1935, Moberley in 1952, and Chadwick in 1970. Today Archbishop Carey defends the establishment as an alternative to the 'privatisation of all religion'. None of the arguments are very impressive.[15] Their failure to impress and convince is one reason why, in recent years, disestablishment has become a live issue again in the national press.[16]

The struggle for a free Church involves a struggle to end the establishment. Establishment undoubtedly encourages the Church's acceptance of present structures of inequality, and its collusion with injustice. A good example of this is the collusion of the bishops with the 'public' school system. *Faith in the City* noted the excessive attention given by bishops to the public schools, which educate some 6 per cent of the population – but then ran away from the issue. It was what was expected. Nothing will improve in this respect until the Church is disestablished, and bishops are elected democratically by the

Christian community. As long as bishops hang out at the Athenaeum Club, toady to the monarchy, and constantly watch their backs in case their promotion by a secular (and most likely non-Christian) prime minister is jeopardised, we will never have a Church which can testify with integrity to liberation – nor indeed are we likely to have bishops who are chosen for reasons other than the fact that they are safe.[17]

The case against the establishment has been put well over the years by Valerie Pitt, Peter Cornwell, Colin Buchanan and others. Archbishop Trevor Huddleston, who has spent most of his life in other parts of the Anglican communion, has called the establishment a perpetual hindrance to mission.[18] I believe that the future of the Church of England is inextricably bound up with the issue of establishment. As long as we collude with this system, or regard it as an irrelevance and a time-wasting exercise, neither it nor we will change.

Church and community

This does not mean that until we have freed the national Church we are incapable of any effective action. The history of radical movements within Anglicanism in the last hundred years has been one of grass-roots action in spite of the hierarchy. This will continue, and must continue – but the struggle for the Church's freedom must be carried on at the same time. Today, as in the past, the strength of the Church is in the neighbourhoods, and we need to put a lot of energy into the renewal of the concept of parish. I am not advocating the perpetuation of the outdated concept of parish based on agrarian acreage, nor do I wish to deny the fact that in many places residence is no longer the basis of community life. Still less do I wish to defend a system of pastoral care based on the centrality, and dominance, of a clerical personage. Nevertheless, it is the small ecclesial community which is basic to the life of the Christian movement.

As always we can learn from past events, and in this area we can learn from the work of Alan Ecclestone in Sheffield. More than any Anglican priest this century, Ecclestone made the parish system work as a prayerful and political unit, a community dedicated to politics and to prayer.

The largest single part of Ecclestone's adult life was spent as parish priest of Darnall in Sheffield. Here he built up a committed Christian community around the two focal points: the parish Eucharist and the parish Meeting for worship and debate. The parish Meeting in Sheffield began on 13 May 1942 and remained a regular weekly feature of the community's life. It was a serious attempt to reconceive what it was to be a church, and it anticipated much later work in the base communities in Latin America. 'The whole world came through Darnall' was a central motto with a deliberate double sense: not only that large numbers of people from elsewhere visited the parish, but also that all world-issues were discussed from the initial perspective of this small area. Everything began with the local and ended with the global.

At the heart of Ecclestone's vision was the idea of a parish as a community of integrity – a community in which, through the practice of truth and love, contentious and painful issues could be debated and worked through. He wrote about this in a moving and profound way.

> Almost every parish is plagued by unresolved problems or hampered in its work by the necessity felt by some of keeping off certain dangerous questions. This reluctance is not seeking peace in the Christian sense at all. It is merely trying to have peace on the easiest possible terms, and devitalises the church ... The Parish Meeting becomes so much less than it ought to be if it cannot be the place where the personal problems of the church can be faced. Quickness to take offence, over-impulsive retorts, personal dislikes: it is in the wear and tear of such things over the years that the quality of life of church is tested.[19]

What was happening in the history of this parish was the gradual development of a community which, through many trials and failures, discovered a common life and plan of action, a community committed to its neighbourhood and to the wider world of action, a community rooted in prayer, thought and common action. In this rediscovery of what it was to be a local church, Ecclestone was a pioneer and prophet. Today most parishes are nowhere near the practice which he had begun to realise in the 1940s.

Ecclestone was strongly committed to the idea of an open church, a church open to the needs and demands of the world. Against this model, some Christians would see the local church as a separatist, highly disciplined community of faith. I do not believe that these two approaches are necessarily incompatible – indeed, I think that they need to be held together if we are to avoid the Scylla of isolation and the Charybdis of emptiness. The Church needs to love and challenge the world without losing itself. It is here that we can learn much from the Anabaptist tradition – about the need for corporate discipline in the Church; about the need for an authentic separation of the Church from the world's values; about the need for radical discipleship and not simply for faith; about the danger of ritual and interiority as substitutes for ethical praxis; and about the importance of life as the proof of faith.

The renewal of priestly ministry

The theme of the local church as a community, marked by commitment, discipline and prophetic witness, is an essential corrective to that of the 'servant Church' which has become very popular during the last 30 years. I certainly want to accept and affirm, but also to critique, the idea of the Church as servant. It has been with us for some time, and the revival of the diaconate in both Roman and Anglican Churches has led to a greater stress on 'servanthood'. Traditionally deacons are concerned with the poor and needy, and the American Book of Common Prayer refers to 'a special ministry of servanthood'. I do not want to question any of this (although I do think the biblical basis for much of the writing about *diakonia* is rather weak). The important issue is that there is much more to Christian pastoral care and to the identity of Church than the servant role. It is extremely important that the servant Church does not replace the prophetic Church, the Church as sign of contradiction, the Church as social critic and advocate.[20]

In the future Church I hope not only that we will recover the vocational diaconate, but also that we will come to see the diaconal character of all ministry. I hope too that we will see that the renewal of priesthood is not possible until we have deepened our sense of the priesthood of the whole body of Christ. The idea and the practice of priesthood are in deep trouble in both Roman and Anglican Churches. In the Roman communion, there has not really been any theology of ministry for hundreds of years, only a theology of priesthood, and that a very narrow one. Now the tide is turning among some Roman Catholics – but in a way which is potentially disastrous, resulting in a widespread lack of interest in liturgy and in sacramental theology in general. Yet I believe that it is in the rite, in the sacramental celebration, if you like, in the cult, that the character, the real meaning, of priesthood is most deeply and most dramatically revealed.

Much of the language we now use about priesthood is functional and instrumental rather than sacred. So I believe that we need to go back to the roots of the priestly role in the redemptive work of Christ. In his book *A Theology of Auschwitz*, Ulrich Simon said that priesthood is the office which ritually, inwardly and ascetically shares the dying and rising of Christ. In the context of the concentration camp, when the priest is without status and function, without bread and wine, the sacrificial heart of priesthood is laid bare, its essential character exposed.

> The priestly ideal uses and converts the nothingness which the world of Auschwitz offers. Here the priest's sacerdotal dedication encounters the vacuum with self-sacrifice . . . The priest at the camp counts because he has no desires of self-importance and gives life because he stands already beyond extermination. He is the exact opposite of the king rat. The hour of darkness cannot take him by surprise since he has practised silence in darkness.[21]

These seem strange words in an era of managerial and professional models of ministry, but they spoke more to me as a priest in Soho in 1967, when intravenous drug usage was at its height, than all the fashionable material that came from the Church bureaucracies. It was troublingly symbolic that it was on Wednesday 14 August 1996 – the feast of St Maximilian Kolbe, the Franciscan priest who gave his life at Auschwitz to save another prisoner from death – that we learned of the murder of a young priest, Christopher Gray, in Liverpool.

I did not know Christopher Gray, but I was impressed by his only published work, an essay in a collection called *The Fire and the Clay,* written with other priests who were all linked with the College of the Resurrection, Mirfield, where he trained. He wrote about the meaning of priesthood. Taking the image of the shepherd, he said that 'the supreme act of the shepherd is to lay down his life for the sheep', and went on to speak of priests who were called to 'grow to be like Christ in their faithful service of their flocks, even to the point of sacrificing their own lives'.[22]

How do we nurture and strengthen priesthood in the coming years? I believe a large part of the answer lies in the recovery and development of some very traditional themes – the spirit of sacrifice, the theme of priesthood as an interior life rather than a job, the emphasis on ascetical discipline and on the practice of the Christian life, and, most importantly, on the place of the priest within the larger priestly body.

The theme of the priesthood as an identity, an interior reality, was central to the thinking of R. C. Moberly, who wrote of the priestly spirit and the priestly heart.[23] To be a priest is to share in a new humanity, fashioned after God's likeness (Eph. 4:24). This new humanity is the fruit of baptism – but it does not simply happen, as it were, magically. The new humanity is in fundamental conflict with the dominant value-system. There must be therefore a disciplined, supportive, corrective and critical community which enables the virtues to be nourished. Two writers who have contributed to my own thinking are Martin Thornton and Urban T. Holmes. I want here to refer to their thinking, along with the neglected study by Kenneth Mason on *Priesthood and Society.*

Martin Thornton and remnant theology

Thornton came to popular notice in 1956 with his book *Pastoral Theology: a Reorientation.* His work is a fierce attack on what he termed 'multitudinism' – the view of the parish priest as an omnicompetent, multi-dimensional activist, for ever engaged in visiting, administering, preaching, evangelising, and the sundry paraphernalia of the 'successful' parish. In his book *Spiritual Proficiency* (1959), Thornton devoted most of his reflections to the character of the corporate discipline of 'the remnant', a discipline focused on the office and the Eucharist. Thornton returned to the attack on multitudinism in *Essays in Pastoral*

Reconstruction (1960) where he argued that the pastoral system of the multitudinists had completely broken down. According to Thornton, the emphasis of the conventional Church was numerical, membership was nominal, and this meant convention, respectability, Pelagianism, apathy and spiritual sterility. All of Thornton's early work was a protest against, and a rejection of, the conventional notion of parish ministry, involving large-scale and diverse organisations, emphasis on numerical growth, evangelism, and the parish priest as a kind of chief executive. In place of this, Thornton argued for a remnant theology, based on a disciplined local unit.

When I first read Thornton, I found myself temperamentally, socially, culturally and theologically outraged. I was opposed to virtually everything he said. It seemed elitist, sectarian, precious and escapist. Later, in the context of inner London, some of his insights came to life, and I realised how important was his emphasis on the ascetical base of priesthood and pastoral ministry.[24]

Urban T. Holmes and the risks of the priesthood

Urban T. Holmes is hardly known in Britain, and most of his works are out of print in the United States where his influence was considerable. At the heart of Holmes's thought was a refusal to accept reductionist models of priesthood. According to Holmes, the priest is one who raises and expands the consciousness of those to whom she or he ministers. She is an agent for the illumination of consciousness of the community at all levels. This places the priest firmly in the context of theological discernment and prophetic vision. Priests are called to be more than pastors, more than managers, more than liturgical celebrants. There is a core aspect of priesthood which is concerned with the raising of consciousness, with discernment of the signs of the times, with helping to point people beyond the trivial and temporal to the transcendent and the eternal. Holmes speaks of the priest as shaman. Central to Holmes's theology of priesthood is his view that the roots of priestly function 'lie squarely within the wilderness of the antistructure'.[25]

What are the implications of Holmes's thought for our approach to priestly ministry? The most important is that we need to approach our ministry with fear and trembling, with a sense that we are on holy ground, that we are exposed to the possibility of being consumed. We are entering a lifestyle and a ministry which is fraught with great danger, both to ourselves and to others. The priestly task involves an engagement with human life at its most profound, most vulnerable, most explosive and most terrible levels. We should not be surprised that priests stand on the borders of madness, depravity, violence and abuse. The realm of the sacred is open to the strong probability of the demonic.

Priesthood, then, is not an easy and tidy job – not in fact a job at all. We are not in control of our material. We are playing with fire, capable of doing great harm. Hence the spiritual preparation and spiritual resources for such ministry are literally matters of life and death. I believe, therefore, that spiritual warfare is more than a troublesome phase, a temporary visitation of the evil one, in an otherwise tranquil journey to holiness. It is of the very essence of the holy, of the priestly task. One could say that priesthood – including the priesthood of all the baptised – is an entry into that conflict with the powers which is the paschal mystery. Spiritual warfare is what priesthood is about, and it calls for prayer and fasting, and a real solidarity with Christ in his conquest over evil. Only by that solidarity, that sense of being *en Christo*, can we hope to stand firm in the evil day.

Certain features of priesthood are strongly emphasised in Holmes: the close link between priesthood and sexuality, between priesthood and the potentially destructive forces of human life, between priesthood and the reality of death. At the time he was one of the few writers on pastoral theology to address these areas. By the very nature of their role, priests are called to enter into the areas of the erotic and of human passion, as well as into the realms of dark and destructive forces. To share priesthood is to expose oneself to risk. According to Holmes, to be a priest is to share deeply the antistructural dimensions of people's lives, to face the erotic realities in their demonic and angelic forms, and to discern what makes whole and what destroys. The choice for the priest is to be an ineffective 'cold fish' or to risk being consumed.

It is essential to choose the risk, but to do so prayerfully in the grace of God. 'Angel' and 'demon' are terms which Holmes uses throughout his writing to interpret the priestly role. Many priests avoid risks, and, as a result, become less than fully human, and therefore ineffective. Yet to take the alternative route is to risk being consumed and destroyed – and destroying others. Holmes devotes over 20 pages of *The Priest in Community* to the theme of 'the priest as demon', in an attempt to convey something of the power which priests are called to invoke in people – a power which can be destructive and disintegrating, as well as saving and healing. As a result of this emphasis, I believe that Holmes is one of the most important writers on priesthood in the twentieth century. He helps us to see that we need to approach priestly ministry with fear and trembling, with a sense that we are on holy ground.[26]

Kenneth Mason and the priest as interpreter

It is valuable to read Mason's study with these perceptions in mind. Mason points out that priests work at those points in human life where a specific tradition meets the varied circumstances of human life, and it is at these points that they work as interpreters, trying to express the relevance of the one to the other, and offering people a fresh perception of both. Like Holmes, Mason stresses the role of the priest as interpreter, one who offers insight and illumination, a task she can only perform if she has herself practised reflection, silence and prayerful attention. The marginal position of the priest is central in Mason, for she is not a purely cultic figure – though Mason sees the priest as essentially a symbolic figure, and the liturgy as central to her life – but plays a social role. Central to Mason's argument is the recognition that a Church which has turned its back on society and become simply a voluntary religious organisation has no need of priests at all, though it will want pastors, teachers and other officials to service the organisation. But priesthood only has a place, and only makes sense, at the point of interplay of the sacred and the secular. Once it is cut loose from this, it ceases to have significance. This seems to be something which many priests do not understand.[27]

Not surprisingly, Mason emphasises the centrality of *ascesis*, of interior spiritual discipline, in the formation of priestly life. The concept of 'training' has often been interpreted in terms of the acquisition of skills, techniques and methods, almost all of them derived from secular and untheologically motivated models of thought. I want to point rather to the formation of the inner core of priesthood, a formation which involves the practice of certain key disciplines, such as silence, solitude, the discipline of the divine office, the offering of the Mass, and the cultivation of the receptive spirit – that openness to God and to people which helps to create communion.

The future of ministry in Anglican Catholicism

I want to end this book by looking at two areas: the future of the idea of ministry within the Anglican Catholic tradition, not least in the context of the ordination of women as priests; and the pastoral consequences of the fact that areas of marginal ministry are certain to increase.

I was brought to Christian faith within the framework of an Anglican Catholicism of 'advanced' type – 'full Catholic privileges', as it used to be known. When I arrived in London almost 40 years ago, it was the pastoral ministries of people such as St John Beverley Groser, Stanley Evans, Father Neville, SSF, and Joe Williamson who shaped my whole understanding of priesthood. While I do not think that the past can be recaptured – and indeed, I believe that I was, in those years, involved in the end of an era – it would be an appalling tragedy if we were to lose some of the strengths of that tradition. For example, take the figure of Father Joe Williamson, the most flamboyant, sensationalist, even exhibitionist, priest of the post-war period. I was both influenced and infuriated by Williamson: influenced by lack of respectability, his courage and willingness to take risks, his insistence that priests do not have to be gentlemen, his refusal to be intimidated by bureaucrats, bishops, lawyers, pimps or slum landlords, his combination of public prophetic fire and personal pastoral gentleness; yet infuriated by his determination to see everything in terms of his work, his single vision, his contempt for factual accuracy, and his extreme individualism and clericalism. Yet Williamson left a permanent mark on me, and had it not been for him, my ministry would have been much more cautious, much more timid, much too bothered about what bishops and Church leaders might think of me. I am particularly grateful to

Williamson for his total lack of interest in 'promotion' – whatever that might mean in gospel terms – and for his utter dedication to the poorest and most neglected of God's people.

A central feature of the radical Anglican Catholic approach to ministry was its closeness to people, its strong commitment to the local area, its refusal to separate personal from political issues, and its rootedness in prayer and sacrament. This approach has inspired and nurtured many thousands of people, including many women, some of whom are now themselves priests. The question therefore needs to be asked: what will be the impact of the ordination of women on the Anglican Catholic tradition?

It is repeatedly claimed that Anglican Catholicism is in terminal decline since the ordination of women. It is certainly true that one stream of the movement has effectively become extinct – apparently as a result of the decision to ordain women, but in fact as a result of factors which go back much further. (This stream only continues to exist as the final manifestation of a tradition which has in fact fulfilled its historic role.) I want to put a rather deviant alternative view: that, far from representing the end of the Oxford Movement, the ordination of women is itself a result of the Oxford Movement, albeit not quite what the Oxford fathers had in mind. For without that revival of Catholic consciousness, linked with a strong emphasis on women's ministry in areas other than priesthood, why would women have even thought of being Catholic priests at all? It is no accident that, in all parts of Anglicanism, many – and in some cases most – of the ordained women come from the Catholic tradition, and so it is not unreasonable to suggest that the renewal of Catholic sacramental and social theology may to some extent lie in the hands of women.

Pastoral ministry on the margins

Whether that is true or not will become clear in the coming years. What is already clear is that there is a massive problem in Britain and elsewhere of marginalisation – of people and communities who are pushed to the edge of society – and a corresponding problem of how pastoral ministry in this context is to be defended and extended. In the last few years it has been a privilege for me to have been involved in creating a national network in Britain called Mission on the Margins. This network grew from the work of a remarkable woman, Mary Beasley, in Birmingham. Mary, a disabled woman and former social worker, had been working with homeless and alcoholic people, as well as with other marginal groups, for some years. Through writing a university thesis on her work, she came into contact with a wide range of people doing similar work in other towns and cities, and the network was born. It has brought together a diverse group of people from all the Churches, including many who themselves are marginal to the institution, who share a common commitment to service and to advocacy on behalf of those who have been cast off or rejected by the system.[28]

The work of Mission on the Margins brings out some important features of the Christianity of the twenty-first century. One is the inextricable link between the response to poor people and the humanity of the whole community. The old socialist slogan, 'An injury to one is an injury to all', comes home to us with a new ferocity and intensity in the context of our throw-away culture. Jon Sobrino has pointed out that to stand before poor people with honesty is a first step toward the humanisation of all human beings.[29] Yet much ministry seems to be directed towards the respectable, secure and well-behaved, among whom success and financial stability are more likely. This is not to deny that there is a good deal of work 'among' poor and despised people and groups, but much of it is very patronising and dehumanising. The fact that pastoral ministry can, and often does, dehumanise was recognised by William Booth in the nineteenth century.[30] It remains a serious danger for us in the twentieth and twenty-first centuries.

In the coming years, there are many people in all sections of society who will find themselves in hard times. The position of Black youth in the inner-city areas is, and will continue to be, marked by fragmentation and deprivation. Cornel West, writing out of the North American experience, has claimed that the Black churches and the mosques are the chief institutional bulwarks against ghetto meaninglessness.[31] The position in Britain is less clear, and there is considerable evidence that both the Black-led churches and the mosques are losing teenagers to a massive extent. The whole issue of how Muslim and Christian traditions can work together in the face of serious oppression and despair will become more urgent in the coming years. Equally urgent is the problem of physical and mental isolation and ill-health among the elderly. The 'demographic time-bomb' may have been exaggerated, but it seems clear that we are likely to become a society with very large numbers of old people and with increasingly inadequate provision for their welfare. There will be an increase in loneliness, mental illness and dementia which will present enormous pastoral demands on Churches and voluntary projects.

Again, it seems certain that the coming years will see the persistence, and probably the increase, of the high numbers of homeless people on the streets, many of them with serious mental health problems. The presence of mentally ill people on the streets is not new. It has been noted since the 1959 Mental Health Act.[32] But the position has worsened recently in a number of ways. The policy called Care in the Community – a term which is well-known among 'street people' as a euphemism for neglect – is not working well. In London in particular, the mental health services are at breaking-point and will not be sustained in the next decade.[33] Violence, both structural and personal, against homeless, mentally ill people – as well as against other minorities – seems likely to continue and increase. Violence against gay and lesbian people is also likely to increase, and, while in other areas the Church has been a voice urging compassion, I am afraid that the high level of anti-homosexual emotion and rhetoric in parts of the Church has made the position of gay and lesbian people worse than it needed to be. The debate in the General Synod in 1987, for example, helped to fuel the torrent of hatred, malice and violence against this section of the population. The refusal to accept responsibility – as far as I know, no official of the Church of England has ever publicly expressed penitence for their role – is comparable to the rhetoric on race in the 1960s, when politicians distanced themselves from the consequences of the atmosphere which they had helped to create.

All these represent areas where pastoral, and indeed prophetic, ministry will be needed in the coming years. None of them are free from danger; all of them will be extremely stressful and demanding. All of them directly affect our work at St Botolph's, Aldgate, and hundreds of inner urban parishes.

But I want to look at one area which, in terms of the sheer dimensions of the problem, and in the speed of its growth, stands out. It stands out also in the extraordinary character of the response from some sections of the Church. I refer to the spread of HIV and AIDS.

HIV/AIDS: a changing world

From the beginning of the identification of the HIV virus, the rhetoric used in the dominant media was drawn from military jargon – the language of battle, invasion, and so on. The responses to AIDS had ample precedents in history. As the Black Death was blamed on the Jews, the plagues on sinners, the cholera on the 'great unwashed', and syphilis on prostitutes, so – although the HIV virus affects a wide range of persons – the perception that it did not affect people within 'mainstream' society, but only those who were in some sense 'marginal', seems to have been a major factor in the delay in policy development in the United States[34] and probably here.

Subsequent events have changed things dramatically. At the opening of the Seventh International Conference of the Global Network of People Living with HIV and AIDS, held in Cape Town in March 1995, the vice-president of South Africa, Thabo Mbeki, compared the challenge of HIV and AIDS with the struggle against apartheid. In each case there has been a need for a profound, symbolic re-ordering of life. Some have spoken about the communities living with AIDS as eschatological communities – communities marked by the closeness of death, the realities of heaven and hell – but marked also by joyful anticipation, by celebration, warmth and solidarity.

It is important not to sentimentalise the experience around HIV and AIDS. Nevertheless, the way in which not only gay people but whole sections of the population, especially young people, have responded to the tragedy has helped to form real communities characterised by compassion and by a serious commitment to life together. It has been a real *kairos* moment, a moment of renewal and sanctification. The Churches have not been unaffected by this movement, and many churches have been renewed in their corporate life and witness by AIDS. It has led to a deeper sense of solidarity and interdependence, a deeper sense of what it is to live – and die – within the body of Christ, the body of the resurrection.[35]

On the other hand, many churches have been unaffected by this vast movement of love, either because they have averted their eyes and hearts, or because their barriers of resistance have been too powerful. The vast reservoir of love and care has passed them by. The warmth and intensity of compassion has not melted them. They remain cold, immovable, erect, frozen. What could have been a source of renewal has not been allowed to touch them. Indeed, they have feared its touch, feared contamination and defilement. It is particularly sad that the Church has often been so incapable of dealing sensitively and spiritually with the two critical areas of sex and death. Yet, of course, this is not new. The quest for purity has been a recurring theme throughout this book, as throughout the Church's history. Many commentators have drawn attention to the similarity between attitudes to people with AIDS and the attitudes to lepers in the ancient world. In the case of AIDS, the attention has not been simply on the disfigurement of the skin but specifically on the sexual organs. Just as in the early Church, the penis was at the centre of the debate over circumcision, so now the penis figures again in the debate over homosexuality. Just as lepers were cast out beyond the gate, beyond the pale, so today there is a danger of stereotyped, stigmatised thinking and feeling which writes off, even casts off, a whole section of the population.

In biblical terms we are faced with what is called 'abhorrence'. To abhor means to shrink from, to loathe, to abominate. It is the responsibility of a compassionate and faithful Church to preach the gospel that God does not abhor the affliction of the afflicted ones (Ps. 22:24). For many, the experience has been confusing and troubling. AIDS has 'opened a Pandora's box of unfinished spiritual business'.[36] The experience has emphasised and focused the real hopelessness and helplessness which pastoral workers encounter, and that experience extends well beyond the specific area of incurable illness. All over the country and the world, pastoral care takes place in environments where there seems little or no hope, no future, no jobs, no likelihood that things will improve. How do we sustain hope in such places?

The struggle to hope

The whole issue of hope and hopelessness is one which continues to trouble and disturb me – and it is troubling and yet right that this book should end on this note. For I cannot, we cannot, leave things neat and tidy. The struggle against nihilism, hopelessness and the dominion of death goes on after the last word has been typed. The future must lie in a movement for hope beyond the recognition and confrontation of danger. The sky is red and threatening, but we will continue to look up in expectation of our liberation, even though much of the time, like King Jehoshaphat we can only cry, 'Because we do not know what to do, we look to you' (2 Chr. 20:12).

It is important to remember that 'hope is a piece of work, not a state of mind'.[37] Much of our ministry in the future, as in the past, will consist in the nurturing and sustaining of hope in the midst of unutterable pain and anguish. It has been said that real ministry occurs when the skin of the soul is rubbed raw.[38] Yet it is here, at the heart of pain and apparent emptiness, that the community of the resurrection often emerges. In the apostolic age, the most powerful element in evangelism seems to have been the quality and witness of the Church's own life as a community of the resurrection. The power of God, which created the Christian movement as a resurrection force, has to be experienced in the hope of a new order and a new humanity which stands beyond extermination. The truth about the risen Christ must be proclaimed and lived with confidence and humility. When confronted by the horror of death and destruction, of despair and desolation, we need to hold one another firm in the faith that, in the words of the Orthodox liturgy of Easter, 'Christ is risen from the dead, trampling down death by death, and upon those in the tombs bestowing life'.

References

Introduction

1.   This is a phrase which I owe to Dr Judith Pinnington.

Chapter 1:   Solitude and Solidarity

Chapter epigraph: Thomas Merton, 'Christianity and mass movements', *Cross Currents* 9:3 (1969), p. 211.

 1.   Thomas Merton, *New Seeds of Contemplation*, New York, New Direc-
       tions 1966, pp. 112ff; Karl Barth, cited in Jim Garrison, *The
       Darkness of God: Theology after Hiroshima*, SCM Press 1982, p. 1.
       On Merton's approach to peace and nuclear weapons, see Jim
       Forest, *Thomas Merton's Struggle with Peacemaking*, Erie, Pa, Benet
       Press 1983.
 2.   See Robert J. Lifton, 'The sense of immortality: on death and
       the continuity of life', *American Journal of Psychoanalysis* 33 (1973),
       pp. 3–15.
 3.   On developmental psychology, see Erica Burman, *Deconstructing
       Developmental Psychology*, Routledge 1994.
 4.   On Myers-Briggs see Kenneth Leech (ed.), *Myers Briggs: Some
       Critical Reflections*, Jubilee Group 1996; and 'Myers-Briggs and
       other modern astrologies', editorial in *Theology Today* 49:3
       (October 1992), pp. 291–5.
 5.   See Andrew Greeley, 'Pop psychology and the gospel', *Theology
       Today* 33:3 (October 1976), pp. 224–5. We can see the influence
       of pop psychology in the work of Scott Peck, whose book *The
       Road Less Travelled* (1978) was still at the top of the USA paper-
       back list in 1993. The book is individualistic, elitist, and gnostic.
 6.   Paul Hoggett, *Partisans in an Uncertain World: the Psychoanalysis
       of Engagement*, Free Association Books 1992, p. 3.
 7.   On social dimensions of psychotherapy, see Joel Kovel, 'On
       being a Marxist psychoanalyst', *Radical Science* 15 (1984),
       pp. 149–54; Barry Richards, 'Psychotherapy and the public

REFERENCES

domain', *British Journal of Psychotherapy* 3:1 (1986), pp. 42–51; Renata Saleci, *The Spoils of Freedom: Psychoanalysis and Feminism after the Fall of Socialism*, Routledge 1995; and Andrew Samuels, 'Therapists with attitude', *Red Pepper*, July 1996, pp. 28–9.

8. See Stanislav Grof and Christina Grof (eds.), *Spiritual Emergency*, New York, G. P. Putnams 1989.

9. See R. D. Laing, 'Religious experience and the role of organised religion' in *The Role of Religion in Mental Health*, National Association for Mental Health 1967, pp. 51–8; and *The Politics of Experience and The Bird of Paradise*, Penguin 1968.

10. Theodore Roszak, *Unfinished Animal*, Faber 1975.

11. Philip Rieff, *The Triumph of the Therapeutic*, New York, Harper and Row 1963.

12. On the post-Gilligan debate, see Mary Jeanne Larrabee (ed.), *An Ethic of Care*, Routledge 1993.

13. Perry Anderson, in Perry Anderson and Robin Blackburn (eds.), *Towards Socialism*, Fontana 1965, p. 12.

14. At the same time, we need to hear John Milbank's warnings on the uncritical acceptance of sociological theories. See his *Theology and Social Theory*, Blackwell 1993.

15. David Nicholls, *Deity and Domination*, Routledge 1989.

16. Michael Polanyi, *Personal Knowledge: Towards a Post-Critical Philosophy*, University of Chicago Press 1958.

17. Richard J. Bernstein, *Beyond Objectivism and Relativism; Science, Hermeneutics and Praxis*, Philadelphia, University of Pennsylvania Press 1983.

18. Bruce Mazlish, *The Fourth Discontinuity*, Yale University Press 1994; Hans Rheingold, *The Virtual Community*, Secker and Warburg 1994.

19. On psychopharmacology, see James B. Ashbrook, 'Psychopharmacology and pastoral counselling', *Journal of Pastoral Care* 49 (Spring 1995), pp. 5–17. On the 'prehistory' of the mind, see Steven Mithen, *The Prehistory of the Mind*, Thames and Hudson 1996.

20. On the new physics, see Paul Davies, *God and the New Physics*, New York, Touchstone 1983; and James Gleick, *Chaos: making a New Science*, New York, Viking 1987.

21. R. A. Lambourne, in *Contact*, Spring 1974, p. 38.

22. Thomas S. Kuhn, *The Structure of Scientific Revolutions*, University of Chicago Press 1962. See also Paul Hoyningen-Huene, *Reconstructing Scientific Revolutions: Thomas S. Kuhn's Philosophy of Nature*, University of Chicago Press 1993; and Barry Barnes, *T. S. Kuhn and Social Science*, Columbia University Press 1982.

23. E. L. Mascall, *Theology and the Future*, Darton, Longman and Todd 1968, p. 26.

24. Grace Jantzen, *Power, Gender and Christian Mysticism*, Cambridge

University Press 1995. Margaret Miles speaks of the 'threadbare inadequacy of the Christian tradition on these issues' (*The Image and Practice of Holiness*, SCM Press 1988, p. 160).

25. Angela West, *Matthew Fox: Blessing for Whom?*, Jubilee Group 1994.

26. James Baldwin, *The Fire Next Time*, cited in bell hooks and Cornel West, *Breaking Bread*, Boston, South End Press 1991, p. 1.

27. See Wolfhart Pannenberg, 'Homosexuality and Scripture', *Church Times*, 21 June 1996.

Reform were quoted as comparing the Lesbian and Gay Christian Movement service at Southwark Cathedral to the use of the cathedral by neo-Nazi or pro-apartheid groups (*The Guardian*, 13 November 1996). This must represent an all-time low even for the most bigoted of evangelicals. Yet the LGCM is a group of responsible Christian people whose experience, theology and viewpoint differ from that of Reform. To compare them with Fascist and racist groups, at whose hands many of them have suffered – often at times when other Christian people, Catholic and evangelical, have strongly supported such groups – is deplorable. Gay and lesbian people have as much to fear as Blacks from the activities of the Christian Right groups. They are more likely to have received swastikas and death-threats than Reform will ever be.

At a similarly low level of 'argument' are statements from the Archdeacon of York, George Austin. Austin's reported comments on a suggestion by the Bishop of Bath and Wells that same-sex unions should be recognised was: 'The traditional pattern of the Church has been that these people should keep it in their trousers. The Bishop of Bath and Wells appears to believe they should keep it in each others' (*The Independent*, 16 December 1996). There are many other examples where attempts at serious debate are reduced to gutter-level polemic.

28. *Church Times*, 17 March 1995.

29. On the history and work of St Botolph's, see Malcom Johnson, *Outside the Gate; St Botolph's and Aldgate 950–1994*, Stepney Books 1994, obtainable from St Botolph's Church, Aldgate, London EC3 N 1AB.

30. In a talk given to the Jubilee Group at St Matthew's, Bethnal Green, on 30 June 1977, Ramsey said that the assumption that sex only legitimately took place within monogamous marriage needed serious questioning by Christian social thinkers. For the text of the talk, see Kenneth Leech, *The Gospel, the Catholic Church and the World: the Social Theology of Michael Ramsey*, Jubilee Group 1990, pp. 20–4.

31. On friendship, see Janice G. Raymond, *A Passion for Friends: Towards a Philosophy of Female Affection*, Women's Press 1986; and

Elizabeth Stuart, *Just Good Friends: Towards a Lesbian and Gay Theology of Relationships*, Mowbray 1995.

32. Anders Nygren, *Agape and Eros* [1930], ET, Philadelphia, Westminster Press 1953, p. 684.

33. Herbert Marcuse. *Eros and Civilisation*, Boston, Beacon Press 1955, and *An Essay in Human Liberation*, Penguin 1972; Audre Lorde, *Sister Outsider*, Trumansburg, NY, Crossings Press 1984, pp. 53–9. It should be noted that the Anglican writer Charles Williams also saw the importance of *eros*. See his *Religion and Love in Dante*, Dacre Press, no date, p. 40. Also on the erotic in theological context, see Philip Sherrard, *Christianity and Eros*, SPCK 1976. Rita Nakashima Brock, *Journeys by Heart: a Christology of Erotic Power*, New York, Crossroad 1988, Alexander C. Irwin, *Eros Towards the World: Paul Tillich and the Theology of the Erotic*, Minneapolis, Fortress Press 1991. Kate Soper has called for a new eroticism as an integral element in politics. See her *Troubled Pleasures*, Verso 1990, pp. 33–4.

34. *Issues in Human Sexuality*, Church House Publishing 1991.

35. Sam Keen, *To A Dancing God*, Fontana 1970, Chapter 5, 'The importance of being carnal: notes for a visceral theology', pp. 141–60, especially p. 142.

36. See Ross Terrill, *R. H. Tawney and his Times: Socialism as Fellowship*, Harvard University Press 1973; John Macmurray, *The Philosophy of Communism*, Faber 1933, p. 46.

37. See Elizabeth Fox-Genovese, *Feminism Without Illusions: a Critique of Individualism*, Chapel Hill, University of North Carolina Press 1991; and Sandra Harding, *The Science Question in Feminism*, Ithaca, New York, Cornell University Press 1986.

38. Sara Maitland, *A Big Enough God*, Cassell 1994, p. 91.

39. Henri de Lubac, *Catholicism*, ET, Burns Oates 1950.

40. V. A. Demant, *Theology and Society*, Faber 1938, Chapter 1, 'The Christian doctrine of human solidarity'.

41. A. M. Ramsey, *The Gospel and the Catholic Church* [1936], Longmans 1956 edn, p. 54.

42. George Florovsky, 'Sobornost: the catholicity of the church' in *The Church of God: an Anglo-Russian Symposium*, Fellowship of St Alban and St Sergius 1934, pp. 53–74; and John D. Zizioulas, *Being as Communion*, Darton, Longman and Todd 1985.

43. Clifford Stevens in *American Benedictine Review*, March 1969, p. 7; David Tracy, cited in Gerald Twomey, *Thomas Merton: Prophet in the Belly of a Paradox*, New York, Paulist Press 1978, p. 1.

Chapter 2:   Theology and the Future

Chapter epigraph: Charles Gore, preface to *Lux Mundi*, 1889.
1. Alasdair MacIntyre, *The Guardian*, 3 March 1965.
2. Alasdair MacIntyre in *Journal of Theological Studies*, New Series 7 (1956), p. 340.
3. For simplistic views of the 1960s, see Chapter 5, note 4.
4. Richard Holloway, *Let God Arise*, Mowbray 1972, pp. 47–8.
5. Stanley Evans, *The Faith We Teach*, delivered posthumously in 1965, reissued by the Church Literature Association for the Jubilee Group, 1975.
6. Langdon Gilkey, 'Dissolution and reconstruction in theology', *Christian Century*, 3 February 1965, reprinted in Dean Pearman (ed.), *Frontline Theology*, Richmond, Va, John Knox Press 1967, p. 29.
7. Laurie Taylor, *New Society*, 4 October 1973.
8. Andrew Greeley, *The Persistence of Religion*, SCM Press 1973.
9. E. L. Mascall, *Theology and the Gospel of Christ*, SPCK 1982.
10. On early approaches to theology, see George Dragas, *The Meaning of Theology: An Essay in Greek Patristics*, Darlington 1980; Daniel M. Rogick, 'The development of a theologian according to St Gregory the Theologian', *Greek Orthodox Theological Review* 39: 1–2 (Spring/Summer 1994), pp. 63–81; Steven Peter Tsichlis, 'The nature of theology in the theological orations of St Gregory Nazianzen', *Diakonia* 16:3 (1981); Frank Whaling, 'The development of the word "theology"', *Scottish Journal of Theology* 34:4 (1981), pp. 289–312.
11. Henry Clark, *The Church Under Thatcher*, SPCK 1993.
12. Daniel Bell, *The End of Ideology*, Glencoe, Ill, The Free Press 1960.
13. There are numerous examples of such use of the word 'theology' in political discourse from the time of Hugh Gaitskell onwards. The late John Smith, for example, called the debate on Clause Four a 'theological distraction' (Peter Kellner, *Sunday Times*, 6 February 1994), while Ian Taylor described the commitment to the free market as a 'theological belief' (*New Statesman*, 8 October 1993, p. 18). *The Economist* wrote of 'the theology of European union' (3 July 1993, p. 5). J. K. Galbraith warned of the 'escape from thought into theology' (*The Guardian*, 25 November 1992). A list of such uses since the 1960s would be enormous.
14. Vladimir Lossky, *The Mystical Theology of the Eastern Church*, James Clarke 1957.
15. Justin Martyr, Apol. 61.
16. John Reader, *Local Theology*, SPCK 1994.

17. Rosemary Ruether, *Liberation Theology*, New York, Paulist Press 1972.

18. He has been called 'postmodern' by Rocco Butiglione in *New Perspectives Quarterly* 5:3 (1988), p. 62. Rocco has been an important influence on John Paul's thought, and more will be said on him in Chapter 3.

19. Pope John Paul II, *Agenda for the Third Millennium*, HarperCollins 1996.

20. Demetrios Koutroubis, cited in A. M. Allchin, preface to E. C. Miller, *Towards a Fuller Vision: Orthodoxy and the Anglican Experience*, Wilton, CT, Morehouse Barlow 1984, p. xii. For the concept of 'Western orthodoxy', see C. B. Moss, *The Orthodox Revival 1833–1933*, Mowbrays 1933, and H. A. Hodges.

21. A. M. Ramsey, 'What is Anglican theology?' *Theology* 48 (January 1945), pp. 2–6.

22. See Aidan Nicholls, *The Panther and the Hind: a Theological History of Anglicanism*, Edinburgh, T. and T. Clark 1993.

23. Elie Halevy, *A History of the English People in 1815*, Book 3, Penguin 1938 edn, p. 13.

24. See Ephraim Radner and George R. Sumner (eds.), *Reclaiming Faith: Essays on Orthodoxy in the Episcopal Church, and the Baltimore Declaration*, Grand Rapids, Eerdmans 1993; George Egerton (ed.), *Anglican Essentials: Reclaiming Faith within the Anglican Church of Canada*, Toronto, Anglican Book Centre 1995.

25. See Richard Kew and Roger J. White, *New Millennium, New Church*, Cambridge, MA, Cowley Press 1992, Chapter 4, 'A groundswell towards credal orthodoxy'.

26. Mamphela Ramphele, 'On being Anglican: the pain and the privilege' in Frank England and Torquil Paterson (eds.), *Bounty in Bondage: The Anglican Church in South Africa*, Johannesburg, Ravan Press 1989, pp. 177–90.

27. John R. Kevern, 'A future for Anglican Catholic theology?' *Anglican Theological Review* 76: 2 (Spring 1994), pp. 246–61.

Chapter 3:   Fear and Fascism

Chapter epigraph: Michael Binyon, *The Times*, 27 November 1991.

1. Sir Oswald Mosley, speech on 15 November 1946. See 'The birth of a new idea: Europe a nation', *Action* 80 (1 August 1961), p. 6.

2. Jean Monnet, cited in John Habgood, 'Finding a moral heart for Europe', lecture at St George's House, Windsor, 5 June 1992.

3. Habgood, ibid.

4. Jacques Delors, cited in Peter Hebblethwaite, 'Missing the European bus,' *The Tablet*, 29 April 1989, pp. 478–9.

5. Cited by Peter Hebblethwaite in *National Catholic Reporter*, 13

December 1991. I owe much of this section to discussions with the late Peter Hebblethwaite.

6. Nigel Harris, *The New Untouchables: Immigration and the New World Order,* Tauris 1996.

7. Thomas Merton, *Raids on the Unspeakable,* Burns Oates 1977 edn, pp. 44–54.

8. Susan J. Smith, *The Politics of Race and Residence,* Polity Press 1989.

9. See *The Passing Winter,* Church House Publishing 1996.

10. Peter Berry, letter in *The Times,* 2 January 1992.

11. Pope John Paul II, *Centesimus Annus* (1991), para 56.

12. Christopher Dawson, *Religion and the Modern State,* New York 1936, pp. 135–6.

13. Kenneth Leech, *The Social God,* Sheldon Press 1980, pp. 97–115.

14. John Austin, *Fairacres Chronicle* 14:2 (Summer 1981), pp. 41–3; Andrew Kirk, *Crucible,* July–September 1982, p. 139.

15. On the Christian Right, see Steve Bruce, *The Rise and Fall of the New Christian Right,* Oxford, Clarendon Press 1988; and Sara Diamond, *Spiritual Warfare: the Politics of the Christian Right,* Pluto 1989, *Roads to Dominion: Right Wing Movements and Political Power in the United States,* New York, Guilford Press 1995, and *Facing the Wrath: Confronting the Right in Dangerous Times,* Monroe, Maine, Common Courage Press 1996. On anti-WCC groups, see Derrick Knight, *Beyond the Pale: the Christian Political Fringe,* Leigh, CARAF Publications 1982. On Christian Identity and racist groups, see Michael Barkun, *Religion and the Racist Right: the Origin of the Christian Identity Movement,* Chapel Hill, University of North Carolina Press 1995, and Douglas Rose (ed.), *The Emergence of David Duke and the Politics of Race,* Chapel Hill, University of North Carolina Press 1992.

16. See R. J. Neuhaus, 'The Pope affirms the "New Capitalism" ', *Wall Street Journal,* 2 May 1991; Pat Windsor, 'Neoconservatives capitalise on papal encyclical', *National Catholic Reporter,* 17 May 1991; Robert A. Sirico, 'Encyclical swings church deep into capitalist camp', *National Catholic Reporter,* 24 May 1991.

17. Mary Jo Weaver, *Being Right: Conservative Catholics in America,* Indiana University Press 1996.

18. Andrew Greeley, 'Who are the Catholic Conservatives?', *America,* 21 September 1991.

19. The word was coined by Curtis Lee Laws, editor of *The Watchman Examiner,* who suggested that those who cling to the fundamentals should be called fundamentalists. See C. L. Laws, 'Convention sidelight', *Watchman Examiner,* July 1920, pp. 834–5. *The Fundamentals* had been published in ten volumes from 1910. In 1919 a World Congress of the Fundamentals of the Faith was held, and the word 'fundamentalist' was first used here. Since

1916 a British journal *The Fundamentals* had been published by the Wesley Bible Union.

20. Richard Pierard, *The Unequal Yoke: Evangelical Christianity and Political Conservatism*, Philadelphia, J. B. Lippincott 1970, pp. 18–19.

21. James Barr, *Fundamentalism*, SCM Press 1977, p. 5. See also his *Beyond Fundamentalism*, Philadelphia, Westminster Press 1984, p. x.

22. John S. Spong, *Resurrection: Myth or Reality?*, San Francisco, Harper 1994, pp. 19, xii, 99.

Chapter 4: Despair and Desolation

Chapter epigraph: Sir Michael Howard, cited in *The Times*, 29 November 1984.

1. 'Miners' children in the pit of heroin', *The Observer*, 6 October 1996. See also the maiden speech by Jeff Ennis, MP for Barnsley East, in the House of Commons, 14 January 1997. The 1996 film *Brassed Off*, based on Grimethorpe, should be compulsory viewing for everyone who is concerned about the future of British communities.

2. See Manuel Castells, *The Rise of the Network Society*, Blackwell 1996.

3. Alasdair MacIntyre, 'A society without a metaphysics', *The Listener*, 13 September 1956, pp. 375–6; Sean Desmond Healy, *Boredom, Self and Culture*, Rutherford, NJ, Farleigh Dickinson University Press 1984.

4. Philip Slater, *The Pursuit of Loneliness: American Culture at Breaking Point*, Penguin 1975.

5. Elaine Showalter, *Sexual Anarchy: Gender and Culture at the fin de siècle*, Virago 1992.

6. Michiko Kakutam, 'Designer nihilism', *New York Times Magazine*, 24 March 1996, pp. 30–1.

7. See *The Times*, 2 December 1965, 25 July 1966, 9 November 1966, 4 March 1967, 27 June 1967, 28 July 1967, 16 and 28 July 1968.

8. *The Times*, 3 August 1966.

9. Ministry of Health to K. Leech, 19 August 1966.

10. Kenneth Leech, 'The junkies' doctors and the London drug scene in the 1960s: some remembered fragments', in D. K. Whynes and P. T. Bean (eds.), *Policing and Prescribing: the British System of Drug Control*, Macmillan 1991, pp. 35–59.

11. Report to the United Nations by HM Government . . . on the Working of the International Treaties on Narcotic Drugs, 1965, para 37.

12. E. M. Schur, *Narcotic Addiction in Britain and America*, Tavistock

1963, pp. 144–6; David M. Downes, *The Delinquent Solution*, Routledge 1966, p. 135. For further material on drug use, see my forthcoming *Pastoral Care and Drug Use* (Darton, Longman and Todd 1998).

13. R. H. Tawney, *Poverty as an Industrial Problem*, William Morris Press 1913, cited in Hilary Russell, *Poverty Close to Home*, Mowbray 1995, p. 13.

14. Vandana Shiva, *Monocultures of the Mind*, Zed 1994.

15. For the research on poverty, the following texts are useful: Kay Andrews and John Jacobs, *Punishing the Poor: Poverty under Thatcher*, Macmillan 1990; P. Johnson and S. Webb, *UK Poverty Statistics: a Comparative Study*, Institute for Fiscal Studies, Commentary 27, 1991; Ruth Lister, *Citizenship and the Poor*, Child Poverty Action Group 1990; *The Rising Tide of Poverty*, Child Poverty Action Group 1983; Peter Townsend, *Meaningful Statistics on Poverty 1991*, University of Bristol, Statistical Monitoring Unit, 1991; Peter Townsend, *The Poor Are Poorer: a Statistical Report on Changes in Living Standards of Rich and Poor in the UK 1979–1989*, University of Bristol, Statistical Monitoring Unit, 1991. There are numerous reports also in *Social Trends* and in the data from the Inland Revenue.

　　While unemployment is a major factor in poverty, it is important not to underestimate the role of low pay. The report *Life on Low Income* (Joseph Rowntree Foundation, June 1996) shows that around 14 million adults in Britain are on incomes at or below half the national average.

16. *The Cohesion Report*, Brussels, European Commission, November 1996.

17. Richard G. Wilkinson, *Unhealthy Societies: the Afflictions of Inequality*, Routledge 1996.

18. Carey Oppenheim and Lisa Harker (eds.), *Poverty: the Facts*, 3rd edition, Child Poverty Action Group 1996, especially Chapter 7, 'The geography of poverty', pp. 136ff; *Profiling Poverty in Tower Hamlets*, Tower Hamlets Corporate Policy and Equality, November 1996.

19. See John H. Westergaard, *Who Gets What? The Hardening of Class Inequality in the Late Twentieth Century*, Cambridge, Polity Press 1995.

20. Ian Angell, 'The signs are clear: the future is inequality', *The Independent*, 25 September 1996.

21. John Rex and Sally Tomlinson, *Colonial Immigrants in a British City*, Routledge and Kegan Paul 1979; and John Rex, *The Ghetto and the Underclass*, Aldershot, Avebury 1988.

22. Robert Moore, 'The idea of an underclass', Inaugural Lecture, University of Liverpool, 5 November 1990.

23. On the underclass debate, see Ken Auletta, *The Underclass*, New

York, Vintage Books 1983; Michael B. Katz (ed.), *The Underclass Debate*, Princeton University Press 1993; Bill E. Lawson (ed.), *The Underclass Question*, Philadelphia, Temple University Press 1992; N. Lemann, 'The origins of the underclass', *Atlantic Monthly*, June 1986. For the views of Murray and Wilson, see Charles Murray, *Losing Ground*, New York, Basic Books 1984, and 'How I would tackle the new rabble', *The Independent*, 9 March 1995; Charles Murray *et al*, *The Emerging British Underclass*, London, Institute of Economic Affairs 1990, and *Underclass: the Crisis Deepens*, Institute of Economic Affairs 1994; Ruth Lister (ed.), *Charles Murray and the Underclass*, Institute of Economic Affairs 1997; W. J. Wilson, *The Truly Disadvantaged: the Inner City, the Underclass and Public Policy*, University of Chicago Press 1987, and *When Work Disappears: the World of the New Urban Poor*, New York, Knopf 1996. On the British situation, see Ralf Dahrendorf, 'The erosion of citizenship and its consequences for us all', *New Statesman*, 12 June 1987, pp. 12–15; Frank Field, *Losing Out: the Emergence of Britain's Underclass*, Blackwell 1989; Kirk Mann, *The Making of an English 'Underclass'?*, Milton Keynes, Open University Press 1992. For the critique of the concept, see Herbert J. Gans, 'Deconstructing the underclass; the term's dangers as a planning concept', *Journal of the American Planning Association* 56: 3 (1990), pp. 271–7, and his recent study, *The War Against the Poor: the Underclass and Anti-poverty Policy*, New York, Basic Books 1995.

24. See Alice S. Baum and Donald W. Burnes, *A Nation in Denial: the Truth about Homelessness*, Boulder, Col, Westview Press 1993.

25. Sue Mayo in a talk to clergy and community workers in Bethnal Green, May 1996.

Chapter 5: Spirituality and Narcissism

Chapter epigraphs: Both statements were made in Christmas Day sermons in 1996, in Canterbury Cathedral and York Minister respectively.

1. Kenneth Leech, *Youthquake: a Counter-Culture through Two Decades*, Sheldon Press 1973; revised edition, Abacus 1976. See also Kenneth Leech, 'The hippies and beyond', *The Modern Churchman* (New Series) 16:1 (October 1972), pp. 82–92.

2. See Robert S. Ellwood, *The Sixties Spiritual Awakening*, New Brunswick, NJ, Rutgers University Press 1994.

3. There are so many depressing examples of such trivialisation, not least from politicians such as Margaret Thatcher and Norman Tebbit. But journalists also frequently write in similar terms. Peregrine Worsthorne has written of the 'hedonistic frivolity of the 60s' (*Sunday Telegraph*, 15 November 1987). A

particularly bad recent example of such writing was Virginia
Ironside, 'The Sixties? Those weren't the days', *The Independent*,
5 December 1994. The decade, she claimed, was 'absolute hell'.
'Everyone mumbled in the Sixties, probably because they were
too stoned to articulate properly'. She used the standard excuse
for inaccuracy and exaggeration – 'I *do* remember the Sixties,
and I *was* there'. Sweeping generalisations about the 1960s often
occur in the writings of otherwise highly intelligent people,
such as the journalist Melanie Phillips. Even the well-respected
theologian Martin Marty talks of 'the chaos of the mid-sixties'
(foreword to Parker J. Palmer, *The Company of Strangers*, New
York, Crossroad 1989, p. 11). Such generalisations have also
been passed on to many younger people as part of the mythology. Thus a Manchester University undergraduate said that
'the whole sixties' ethic was based on selfishness' (*The Independent*, 8 October 1987). There seems to be something about this
decade which encourages people to lose their bearings when
discussing it. So it was refreshing to read Carter Heyward's words:
'I am disappointed in my generational peers who look back
upon "the 60s" with patronising scorn as if we ought to be a
little embarrassed for having dreamed those dreams' (*Staying
Power*, Cleveland, Ohio, Pilgrim Press 1995, p. 17). So am I!

4. Grace Davie, *Religion in Britain Since 1945: Believing without
    Belonging*, Oxford, Blackwell 1994. For a different view in relation
    to East London see Greg Smith, 'The unsecular city: the revival
    of religion in East London' in Tim Butler and Michael Rustin
    (eds.), *Rising in the East: the Regeneration of East London*, Lawrence
    and Wishart 1996, pp. 123–45.

5. I have gathered these data from various sources. See H. E.
    Manning, *England and Christendom*, Longmans 1867, p. xcvii;
    Leslie Paul, *The Deployment and Payment of the Clergy*, Church
    Information Office 1964, Chapter 1. For more recent material
    see '*Christian*' *England*, Marc Europe 1991, and the regular
    editions of *The UK Christian Handbook*, and *Social Trends*, pub-
    lished by HMSO. For more general background on religion in
    Britain, see Grace Davie, op. cit., and Steve Bruce, *Religion
    in Modern Britain*, Oxford University Press 1995.

6. *Youth A Part: Young People and the Church*, General Synod Board
    of Education 1996.

7. Timothy Leary, *The Politics of Ecstasy*, Paladin 1970; Timothy
    Leary, *Psychedelic Prayers after the Tao Te Ching*, New York, Poets
    Press 1966; Timothy Leary, Ralph Metzner and Richard Alpert
    (eds.), *The Psychedelic Experience*, New York, University Books
    1965; G. M. Weil, Ralph Metzner and Timothy Leary (eds.), *The
    Psychedelic Reader*, New York, University Books 1965.

8. Charles Reich, *The Greening of America*, New York, Random

House, 1970. On Haight-Ashbury, see David E. Smith, John Luce and Ernest A. Dernberg, 'Love needs care: Haight-Ashbury dies', *New Society*, 16 July 1970, pp. 98–100. Interestingly Donald Nugent called the hippies 'the first mystery cult of the post-modern world' ('The City of God revisited', *Cross Currents* 19: 3 (Summer 1969), pp. 241–55.

9. Michael Hollingshead, *The Man Who Turned On The World*, Blond Briggs 1973; William Braden, *The Private Sea: LSD and the Search for God*, New York, Bantam, 1968 edn.

10. Theodore Roszak, *The Making of a Counter Culture*, Faber 1968, p. 177.

11. William Sargent, 'The psychology of faith', *New Society*, 17 July 1969, p. 92.

12. Allan Y. Cohen, 'The journey beyond trips', *ARE Journal* 3: 4 (1968), p. 31; 'Youth, mysticism and the search for God', *Crucible*, May 1970, pp. 72–83; and *LSD and the Search for God*, talk given at St Anne's, Soho, in 1969, and published in the early 1970s by the Church Literature Association.

13. See Phyllis A. Tickle, *Rediscovering the Sacred: Spirituality in America*, New York, Crossroad 1995.

It is interesting here to look at the career of Harvey Cox as a leading example of a theologian who has changed his position on this area. After writing *The Secular City* (1965), with its naïve and fairly uncritical praise of secularisation and urbanism, Cox went on in subsequent writings to argue that there was a resurgence of religion. In *The Seduction of the Spirit* (Wildwood House 1974), he discussed popular religion. In *Turning East: the Promise and Peril of the New Orientalism* (New York, Simon and Schuster 1977) and *Religion in the Secular City: Towards a Post-modern Theology* (New York, Simon and Schuster 1984), Cox examined further the reappearance of religion in the West. In his most recent work he sees Pentecostalism as a new great awakening. See his *Fire from Heaven: the Rise of Pentecostal Spirituality and the Reshaping of Religion in the 21st Century*, Reading, MA, Addison-Wesley 1995.

14. James Bjornstad and Shildes Johnson, *Stars, Signs and Salvation in the Age of Aquarius*, Minneapolis, Dimension Books 1971.

15. Andrew Brown, *The Independent*, 10 September 1996.

16. *The Sunday Times*, 5 May 1996.

17. *The Independent on Sunday*, 14 July 1996.

18. Billy Graham, 29 November 1971, cited in Roger C. Palms, *The Occult: a Christian View*, Oliphants 1972, p. 9; Billy Graham, *The Jesus Generation*, Hodder and Stoughton 1972, p. 161.

19. Frank Peretti, *This Present Darkness*, Monarch 1986. At one recent count, this book had sold 76,000 copies in the UK.

REFERENCES

20. Theodore Roszak, *Unfinished Animal*, Faber 1975, pp. 12, 31, 57, 68, 69.

21. Christopher Lasch, *The Culture of Narcissism*, New York, W. W. Norton 1978. See also his earlier aricle 'Narcissist America', *New York Review of Books*, 30 September 1976, p. 8, and his la'er work *The Minimal Self: Psychic Survival in Troubled Times*, New York 1984.

22. Christopher Lasch, 'Probing gnosticism and its modern derivatives', *New Oxford Review*, December 1990, pp. 4–10.

23. Ann Loades, *Searching for Lost Coins*, SPCK 1987, Chapter 3, 'Christ Also Suffered: why certain forms of holiness are bad for you', pp. 39–60.

24. Simon Tugwell, *Ways of Imperfection*, Darton, Longman and Todd 1984.

25. Grace Jantzen, *Power, Gender and Christian Mysticism*, Cambridge University Press 1995, p. 20.

26. H. P. van Dusen, 'The Third Force in Christendom', *Life*, 9 June 1958, p. 13.

27. Leo Parrott and Robin D. Perrin, 'The new denominations', *Christianity Today*, 11 March 1991, p. 29. On the Assemblies of God, see Margaret M. Poloma, *The Assemblies of God at the Crossroads: Charisma and Institutional Dilemmas*, Knoxville, University of Tennessee Press 1989.

28. An exception is Peter Hocken, *The Glory and the Shame: Reflections on the 20th Century Outpouring of the Holy Spirit*, Eagle Press 1996. On Pentecostal theology, see Donald W. Dayton, *Theological Roots of Pentecostalism*, Peabody, MA, Hendrickson 1987.

29. *National Catholic Reporter*, 11 October 1996.

30. On the political dimensions of Pentecostalism, see Karla Poewe (ed.), *Charismatic Christianity as a Global Culture*, Columbia, University of South Carolina Press 1994; and Eldin Villafane, *The Liberating Spirit*, Grand Rapids, Eerdmans 1993.

31. See Ian Cotton, *The Hallelujah Revolution: the Rise of the New Christians*, Little Brown 1996.

32. See Dave Tomlinson, *The Post-Evangelical*, SPCK Triangle 1995. The well-known radical evangelical journal *Sojourners* was originally called *The Post-American*.

33. See Andrew Walker, *Restoring the Kingdom; the Radical Christianity of the House Church Movement*, Hodder and Stoughton 1985.

34. James A. Beverley, 'Toronto's mixed blessing', *Christianity Today*, 11 September 1995, pp. 22–7.

35. R. S. Thomas, 'Emerging', *Long Poems 1972–1982*, Macmillan 1983; Alan Ecclestone, *The Scaffolding of Spirit*, Darton, Longman and Todd 1987.

36. Urban T. Holmes, *The Future Shape of Ministry*, New York, Seabury Press 1971, p. 142.

37. Mission Theological Advisory Group, *The Search for Faith and the Witness of the Church*, Church House Publishing 1996. For the use of the 'pick-and-mix' cliché, see Richard Harries, Bishop of Oxford, *The Guardian*, 1 January 1997, and the Christmas Day 1996 sermons by the Archbishops. It has also been increasingly used by politicians.

38. Christopher Lasch, *The Culture of Narcissism*, op. cit., pp. 245–7. On New Age spirituality, see Richard Woods, 'New Age spiritualities: how are we to talk of God?', *New Blackfriars*, April 1993, pp. 176–91, and 'What is New Age spirituality?', *The Way* 33:2 (July 1993), pp. 176–88; Michael Northcott, *The New Age and Pastoral Theology: Towards the Resurgence of the Sacred*, Contact Monograph No 2, 1992; and David Toolan, *Facing West from California's Shores: a Jesuit's Journey into New Age Consciousness*, New York, Crossroad 1987.

39. J. V. Langmead Casserley, *The Retreat from Christianity in the Modern World*, Longmans 1952, p. 5.

40. Denys Turner, *The Darkness of God: Negativity in Christian Mysticism*, Cambridge University Press 1995, p. 7.

41. Walter Wink, *Sojourners*, October 1990, pp. 10–14.

Chapter 6: Society and Sanctity

Chapter epigraphs: John Wesley, in *The Poetical Works of John and Charles Wesley*, Volume 1, Wesleyan Methodist Conference Office 1868, p. xxii; Theodore Roszak, *Where the Wasteland Ends*, Faber 1972, p. xxii; Enoch Powell, *Wrestling with the Angel*, Sheldon Press 1977, p. 28. (However, Powell has never been the most consistent of thinkers: compare his later comment, 'Man . . . is born as an individual, he dies as an individual, and if there is forgiveness and redemption, he is forgiven and redeemed as an individual. It is to Man the individual that the Gospel speaks' – *Theology* 85, 1985, p. 476, cited in Duncan Forester, *Christianity and the Future of Welfare*, 1985, p. 96.)

1. Conrad Noel, *Jesus the Heretic*, Religions Book Club 1939.

2. Tom Thomas, talk to History Workshop, 1974.

3. A recent example was Archbishop Carey's speech to the Bishops' Advisory Group on Urban Priority Areas at High Leigh in November 1996. The *Daily Mail* headline on 15 November 1996 was, 'Carey admits: the Church was wrong to play at politics', and the article went on to say that he had 'admitted yesterday that the Church was wrong to meddle in politics'. While this was not at all what Dr Carey said, there was, in the speech, a misleading distinction between general moral comment on the one hand, and political detail on the other. Yet churches contain an enormous body of expertise on political detail and could contribute

greatly here. This seems to be a restatement of the old 'general principles' argument.

4. *Faith in the City*, Report of the Archbishops' Commission on Urban Priority Areas, Church House Publishing 1985, p. 55.
5. Karl Polanyi, *The Great Transformation*, Boston, Beacon Press 1957 edn.
6. See, for example, Zygmunt Bauman, 'Age of extremes', *New Statesman and Society*, 3 February 1995, pp. 18–20; R. N. Bellah *et al.*, *Habits of the Heart*, Los Angeles, University of California Press 1985, p. 281; 'Culture of separation': Sarah Dunant and Roy Porter (eds.), *The Age of Anxiety*, Virago 1996 (the phrase was coined by W. H. Auden but the editors seem unaware of this); J. K. Galbraith, *The Culture of Contentment*, Sinclair Stevenson 1992, and *The Good Society*, Sinclair Stevenson 1996; Robert Hughes, *The Culture of Complaint: the Fraying of America*, Oxford University Press 1993; John McKnight, *The Careless Society*, New York, Basic Books 1995; and Avishai Margalit, *The Decent Society*, Harvard University Press 1996.
7. See, for example, Reginald Tribe, *The Christian Social Tradition*, SPCK 1935, p. 13.
8. *Faith in the City*, op. cit., p. 48.
9. See Kenneth Leech, 'Liberating theology: the thought of Juan Luis Segundo', *Theology* 84 (July 1981), pp. 258–65.
10. Tony Blair, 'War on the streets', *The Guardian*, 8 January 1997.
11. Alasdair MacIntyre in *The Christian Newsletter* 3: 3 (July 1955), p. 152.
12. Chris Wigglesworth in *Third Way*, 9 February 1978, p. 5.
13. George Hillery, 'Definitions of community: areas of agreement', *Rural Sociology* 20 (1955).
14. For a North American version of this view, see Hillary Rodham Clinton, *It Takes A Village*, New York, Simon and Schuster 1996.
15. For example, Anna Coote, writing in *The Independent* on 3 July 1995, described Alasdair MacIntyre, Charles Taylor and Michael Sandel as 'the high priests of communitarianism', and linked them, in the same article, with Amitai Etzioni to whom they never refer and with whom they have little in common. MacIntyre and Taylor rarely even use the word 'communitarian'. However, MacIntyre has recently used it in a response to his critics where he speaks of 'contemporary communitarians, *from whom I have strongly dissociated myself whenever I have had an opportunity to do so*' (in John Horton and Susan Mendus (eds.) *After MacIntyre*, Polity Press 1994, p. 302, italics mine). Some high priest! His words underline the need for intellectual rigour and accuracy, and the extent of journalistic confusion.

    For further material on communitarianism, see Dick Atkinson, *The Common Sense of Community*, Demos 1994; Jonathan Boswell,

REFERENCES

Community and the Economy: the Theory of Public Cooperation, Routledge 1994; Amitai Etzioni, *The Spirit of Community*, Simon and Schuster 1994; Elizabeth Frazer and Nicola Lacey. *The Politics of Community*, Harvester 1993; Derek L. Phillips, *Looking Backward: a Critical Appraisal of Communitarian Thought*, Princeton University Press 1994; Iris Marion Young, 'The ideal of community and the politics of difference' in Linda J. Nicholson (ed.), *Feminism/Postmodernism*, Routledge 1990, pp. 300-21. Among shorter pieces, see Bea Campbell, 'Praise the community, blame the mothers', *The Independent*, 29 November 1994; Amitai Etzioni, 'Common Values', *New Statesman and Society*, 12 May 1995, pp. 24–5.

16. Madeleine Bunting, *The Guardian*, 25 January 1996.

17. *Encyclopaedia Britannica*, Vol. 10, 1977. For a critique, see Robert P. Wolff, *The Poverty of Liberalism*, Boston, Beacon 1968. For a defence of liberalism, see Stephen Holmes, *The Anatomy of Antiliberalism*, Harvard University Press 1991, and Martha Nussbaum, 'The sleep of reason', *Times Higher Educational Supplement*, 2 February 1996, pp. 17–18. Nussbaum argues that the weaknesses of liberalism are due not to defects but to inconsistencies.

18. Francis Fukuyama, *The End of History and the Last Man*, Penguin 1992. The original article was 'The end of history', *The National Interest 16* (Summer 1989), pp. 3–18. See also Ulrich Duchrow, *Alternatives to Global Capitalism*, Utrecht, International Books/Heidelberg, Kairos Europa 1995.

19. Robert J. Ross and Kent C. Trachte, *Global Capitalism: the New Leviathan*, Albany, NY, SUNY Press 1990; Susan George and Fabrizio Sabelli, *Faith and Credit: the World Bank's Secular Empire*, Penguin 1994.

20. Robert Reich, *The Work of Nations*, New York, Vintage 1992; Paul Hirst and Grahame Thompson, *Globalisation in Question*, Polity 1996.

21. Simon Jenkins, *Accountable to None: the Tory Nationalisation of Britain*, Hamish Hamilton 1995. On East London and the Docklands developments, see Sue Brownill, *Developing London's Docklands*, Paul Chapman 1990.

22. The issues around the election of Derek Beackon and the struggle against neo-Nazism on the Isle of Dogs will be the subject of a forthcoming Jubilee Group pamphlet by Nicholas Holtam and Sue Mayo.

23. Leonardo Boff, *Church, Charism and Power: Liberation Theology and the Institutional Church*, SCM Press 1985, p. 54.

24. Will Hutton, 'Shock that threatens downtown America', *The Guardian*, 24 January 1996.

25. Alasdair MacIntyre, *Marxism and Christianity*, second edn, Duckworth 1995, pp. xiii–xiv.

26. See John H. Westergaard, *Who Gets What? The Hardening of Class Inequality in the Late Twentieth Century*, Cambridge, Polity Press 1995. Also on class, see Ellen Meiksins Wood, *The Retreat from Class: a New 'True' Socialism*, Verso 1986.

27. Terry Eagleton, in *London Review of Books*, 20 June 1996, p. 9.

28. Tony Benn, Address at Alliance for Socialism Weekend, cited in *Socialist Action*, 22 November 1985.

29. Cornel West, *Prophesy Deliverance: an Afro-American Revolutionary Christianity*, Philadelphia, Westminster Press 1982, p. 95.

30. Louis Althusser, *For Marx*, Allen Lane, The Penguin Press 1969, p. 14.

31. Paul VI, *Populorum Progressio* (1967), para 26.

32. Michael J. Schultheis *et al.*, *Our Best Kept Secret: the Rich Heritage of Catholic Social Teaching*, Catholic Fund for Overseas Development, 1988.

33. Anthony Eden, foreword to Conservative Manifesto 1955, cited in *New Reasoner*, Spring 1959, p. 4; John Atherton, *Faith in the Nation*, SPCK 1988, p. 79.

34. 'It is difficult to overestimate the importance of the Fifth Report' – Bruce Wollenberg, *Christian Social Thought in Great Britain Between the Wars*, University Press of America 1996, p. 7.

35. Valerie Pitt, *Old Bottles and New Wine: Valedictory Thoughts on Mervyn Stockwood*, Jubilee Group Discussion Paper 102, 1996.

36. Charles Gore, preface to *Lux Mundi*, 1890 edn, p. ix.

37. Bishop Richard Holloway, *Church Times* and *The Guardian*, 10 January 1997; Archbishop of York, Sunday, BBC Radio 4, 12 January 1997. Dr Hope's unscripted interview seemed to be moving away from the stress on specifics as outlined, for example, in the Roman Catholic bishops' document *The Common Good* and in the comments of Bishop Holloway, and to be returning to the allegedly neutral notion, of 'general principles'.

38. This disastrous episode illustrates how Christian social ethics can go astray when areas of morality are taken out of their context, and when the basic morality of the social, economic and political structures is taken for granted. Dr Coggan was alarmed by the prospect of a 'drift to chaos', but his response was a string of clichés. See *The Guardian*, 16 October 1976, and Kenneth Leech, 'Some thoughts on hearing the voice of non-prophecy', *The Times*, 25 October 1976.

Recent utterances by Archbishop Carey fall into the same trap, and seem to be formed more by cliché than by deep thought and reflection. There is the familiar rhetoric about the collapse of civilisation, the 'loss of a shared sense of values that used to bind us together', the need for 'common values', and so on.

(Andrew Marr, interview with George Carey, *The Independent*, 24 June 1996).

I suspect we will see more of this kind of stuff.

39. William Stringfellow, *Dissenter in a Great Society* (1966).

40. This is articulated in the thought of Stanley Hauerwas. While I am very wary indeed of the way in which Hauerwas's thought has been used by his many devotees, and while I am ignorant of how it works out in his own political praxis, his writing about the Church as itself a social ethic needs to be taken extremely seriously. Here we see the working out of the Anabaptist vision in terms of social ethics. Hauerwas sees the Church as a contrast model to that of worldly politics. He argues – and I believe this is a fallacious argument – that the Church should not be involved in worldly politics but in what he calls 'the polity of the Church' (*A Community of Character: Towards a Constructive Christian Social Ethic*, South Bend, University of Notre Dame Press 1981, p. 74).

Chapter 7: Liturgy and Liberation

Chapter epigraphs: William Temple, *The Hope of a New World*, New York, Macmillan Co. 1941, p. 27; Virgil Michel, 'The liturgy the basis of social regeneration', *Orate Fratres* 9 (1935), pp. 536–45; Romano Guardini, cited in Carl A. Last (ed.), *Remembering the Future: Vatican Two and Tomorrow's Liturgical Agenda*, New York, Paulist Press 1983, p. 45.

1. Aidan Kavanagh, *On Liturgical Theology*, New York, Pueblo 1984.

2. Eugene Masure, *The Christian Sacrifice*, ET, Burns Oates and Washbourne 1943, pp. 17, 24.

3. Seamus Heaney, *The Government of the Tongue*, Faber 1988, p. 107.

4. Otto A. Piper, 'The Apocalypse of John and the liturgy of the ancient church', *Church History* 20 (1951), pp. 10–22; Massey H. Shepherd, *The Paschal Liturgy and the Apocalypse*, Lutterworth Press 1960.

5. Irenaeus, *Adv Haer* 5:2.

6. Christopher Dawson, *Religion and the Rise of Western Culture*, New York, Image 1958 edn.

7. Eamon Duffy, *The Stripping of the Altars: Traditional Religion in England c. 1400–c. 1580*, New Haven, Yale University Press 1992, p. 11.

8. Ibid., p. 92.

9. Donald Gray, *Earth and Altar*, Alcuin Club Collections 68, 1986.

10. *The Philokalia*, transl. G. E. H. Palmer, P. Sherrard and K. Ware, Vol. 2, Faber 1981, p. 324.

11. Donald Maxwell, 'A trip to the Middle Ages', *Church Times*, 29

May 1931; 'Conrad Noel and Thaxted: a village revolution', *Church Times*, 22 July 1938.

12. Sidney Dark, 'Conrad Noel', *New Statesman*, 1 August 1942.

13. Conrad Noel, *Memories*, MS, Chapter 14, p. 6. In the Noel archives at the University of Hull.

14. *The New World* 8 (November 1928). Further on Noel, see Reg Groves, *Conrad Noel and the Thaxted Movement*, Merlin 1967.

15. *The Church Militant* 14 (December 1937), p. 3. For more on Sneyd, see Tim Gorringe, *Alan Ecclestone: Priest as Revolutionary*, Sheffield, Cairns 1994, Chapter 2, 'Burslem and the Catholic Crusade', pp. 17–29.

16. Stanley Evans, from a BBC broadcast of about 1962. The tape is in the possession of the author.

17. On Stewart Headlam, see John R. Orens, *The Mass, the Masses and the Music Hall*, Jubilee Group 1977.

18. R. W. Franklin, 'The 19th Century liturgical movement', *Worship* 53 (1979), pp. 25ff; Paul B. Marx, *Virgil Michel and the Liturgical Movement*, Collegeville, Liturgical Press 1957.

19. Wolfhart Pannenberg, *Christian Spirituality*, Philadelphia, Westminster Press 1983, pp. 31–49.

20. Annibale Bugnini, *The Reform of the Liturgy* 1948–1975, Collegeville, MN, Liturgical Press 1990.

21. I owe much of what I have written about St Paul's, Bow Common, to the invaluable MS by William McCrossan, *Customary of the Church of St Paul, Bow Common*, November 1994, and to discussions with him on the matter over several years.

22. Salman Rushdie, 'Is nothing sacred?', *The Guardian*, 7 February 1990.

23. See Liz Ellis, 'Communities of interest: sites of significance', *Feminist Arts News* 3:9 (1991), pp. 2–5.

24. Paul Evdokimov, *L'art de l'icone: theologie de la beauté*, Paris, Desclées de Brouwer, 1970; John Baggley, *Doors of Perception: Icons and their Spiritual Significance*, Mowbrays 1987.

25. Mary Douglas, *Natural Symbols: Explorations in Cosmology*, Pelican 1973; Victor Turner, *The Ritual Process*, Chicago, Aldine 1969.

26. See Marghanita Laski, *The Times*, 20 November 1980; David Martin, *Church Times*, 8 September 1978.

27. Annie Dillard, *Holy the Firm*, New York, Harper and Row 1984, p. 4.

28. David Martin, '1662 and all that', *Church Times*, 8 September 1978 and 'Profane habit and sacred usage', *Theology* 82 (March 1979), pp. 83–95. Cf. Anthony Archer, *The Two Catholic Churches: a Study in Oppression*. SCM Press 1986, p. 140.

29. Ulrich Simon, *Theology* 74 (May 1971), p. 201; Gail Ramshaw in Michael W. Merriman (ed.), *The Baptismal Mystery and the*

Catechumenate, San Francisco, National Liturgical Conference 1983, p. 73.

30. Anthony Archer, *The Two Catholic Churches: a Study in Oppression*, SCM Press 1986, pp. 140–2. For more reflection on current liturgy, see Eamon Duffy, 'The stripping of the liturgy', *The Tablet*, 6 July 1996. Cf. his 'Rewriting the liturgy: the theological implications of translation', *New Blackfriars*, January 1997, pp. 4–27.
31. Herbert McCabe, *God Matters*, Geoffrey Chapman 1987, p. 103.
32. Kieran Flanagan, *Sociology and Liturgy*, Macmillan 1991, pp. 38, 47. See particularly Chapter 9, 'Apophatic Liturgy: representing the absent in rite', pp. 288–320.
33. Nathan Mitchell, 'The spirituality of Christian worship', *Spirituality Today* 34:1 (March 1982), pp. 5–17.
34. Stanley G. Evans, *The Social Hope of the Christian Church*, Hodder and Stoughton 1965.
35. J. A. T. Robinson, *On Being the Church in the World*, SCM Press 1964 edn, Chapter 3, 'Matter, power and liturgy'.
36. Walter Brueggemann, *Israel's Praise: Doxology against Idolatry and Ideology*, Minneapolis, Fortress Press 1988.

Chapter 8: Prophecy and the Millennium

Chapter epigraphs: Ronald Reagan, cited in W. Rose, 'The Reagans and their Pastor', *Christian Life*, May 1968. For Reagan's views on Armageddon, see *People*, 26 December 1983; *Jerusalem Post*, 28 December 1983; *Weekly Compilation of Presidential Documents*, Washington DC 1983, pp. 1708–13; Caspar Weinberger, 'Washington Talk', *New York Times*, 23 August 1982.

1. Nicholas Berdyaev, *The End of Our Time*, Sheed and Ward 1935, p. 12.
2. *Financial Times*, 14 October 1993.
3. John Naisbitt, *Megatrends: Ten New Directions Transforming our Lives*, New York, Warner Books 1984, p. 279.
4. Norman Cohn, *The Pursuit of the Millennium*, New York, Oxford University Press, 1970 edn. For the reference to paranoia, see the 1961 edition, p. 309. Significantly Cohn omits the passage in the second edition. See also Cohn's recent study *Cosmos, Chaos and the World to Come: the Ancient Roots of Apocalyptic Faith*, New Haven, Yale University Press 1994; Tonina Talmon, 'Pursuit of the Millennium: the relation between religious and social change', *European Journal of Sociology* 3 (1962), pp. 125–48; David A. Aberle, 'A note on relative deprivation theory as applied to millenarian and other cult movements' in Sylvia Thrupp (ed.),

Millennial Dreams in Action: Studies in Revolutionary Religious Movements, New York, Schocken Books 1970.

5. Michael Barkun, *Disaster and the Millennium*, Yale University Press 1974.

6. The Prince of Wales, 'Make it a matter of the spirit', *The Guardian*, 25 January 1996.

7. Tertullian, Apol. 39.

8. Stanley G. Evans, *The Social Hope of the Christian Church*, Hodder and Stoughton 1965, pp. 78–9. For a helpful reflection on the book, see Allan Boesak, *Comfort and Protest: Reflections on the Apocalypse of John of Patmos*, Edinburgh, St Andrew Press 1987.

9. Adela Yarbro Collins, *Crisis and Catharsis: the Power of the Apocalypse*, Philadelphia, Westminster Press 1984, p. 124. See also her 'The political perspective of the Revelation to John', *Journal of Biblical Literature* 96 (1977), pp. 253ff.

10. Adolf Deissmann, *Light from the Ancient East*, Harper and Row 1927, p. 341.

11. On the Antichrist, see Robert C. Fuller, *Naming the Antichrist: the History of an American Obsession*, New York, Oxford University Press 1995.

12. On dispensationalism, see C. Norman Kraus, *Dispensationalism in America*, Richmond, Va, John Knox Press 1958.

13. On Jehovah's Witnesses, see Heather and Gary Botting, *The Orwellian World of Jehovah's Witnesses*, University of Toronto Press 1984, and M. James Penton, *Apocalypse Delayed*, University of Toronto Press 1985.

14. On the appeal of millenarianism, see Steven D. O'Leary, *Arguing the Apocalypse: a Theory of Millenarian Rhetoric*, Oxford University Press 1994.

15. *Nature*, 25 April 1996.

16. See 'Armageddon and Mr Reagan', *America*, 10 November 1984; David Edwin Harrell, Jr, 'Dispensational millenarianism and the religious Right' in Joseph Bettes and S. K. Johannesen (eds.), *The Return of the Millennium*, Barrytown, NY, International Religious Foundation 1984; Pat Robertson, *The End of the Age*, Waco, Texas, Word Books 1995. On modern American 'prophetic' movements, see Paul Boyer, *When Time Shall Be No More: Prophecy Belief in Modern American Culture*, Harvard University Press 1992.

17. Pope John Paul II, cited *Sunday Times*, 22 December 1996. See Sandra L. Zimdars-Swartz, *Encountering Mary: from La Salette to Medjugorje*, Princeton University Press 1991.

18. See Rosemary Ruether, 'Apocalyptic breeds the Oklahoma City syndrome', *National Catholic Reporter*, 25 August 1995, p. 15.

19. Pat Robertson, cited in Martin Gardner, 'Giving God a hand', *New York Review of Books*, 13 August 1987, pp. 17–23.

REFERENCES

20. David O. Beale, *In Pursuit of Purity: American Fundamentalism since 1850*, Greenville, SC, Unusual Publications 1986, p. 8.
21. Gresham Kirkby, 'Kingdom Come: the Catholic faith and millennial hopes', in Kenneth Leech and Rowan Williams (eds.), *Essays Catholic and Radical*, Bowerdean Press 1983, pp. 52–69.
22. Michael Barkun, *Religion and the Racist Right: the Origin of the Christian Identity Movement*, Chapel Hill, University of North Carolina Press 1995, p. 162.
23. On Stringfellow, see Andrew McThenia (ed.), *Radical Christian and Exemplary Lawyer*, Grand Rapids, Eerdmans 1995.
24. Walter Brueggemann, *Hope Within History*, Atlanta, John Knox Press 1987, p. 22.
25. *English Hymnal*, numbers 495, 392 and 412. Number 371, 'Brief life is here our portion', is also from the same source.
26. *English Hymnal*, number 495, verse 4.

Chapter 9:   Tradition and Decay

Chapter epigraph: Alasdair MacIntyre, *Marxism: an Interpretation*, SCM Press 1953,
1. Robin Gill, *Moral Communities*, University of Essex 1992.
   On MacIntyre's recent thinking, see his *After Virtue, Whose Justice, Which Rationality?* and *Three Rival Versions of Moral Inquiry*, all published by University of Notre Dame Press and Duckworth, 1981, 1988, and 1990; Peter McMylor, *Alasdair MacIntyre: Critic of Modernity*, Routledge 1994; Stephen Holmes, *The Anatomy of Antiliberalism*, Harvard University Press, Chapter 4, 'MacIntyre: the anti-liberal catechism', pp. 88–121; John Horton and Susan Mendus (eds.), *After MacIntyre*, Polity Press 1994.
2. Alasdair MacIntyre, *Whose Justice, Which Rationality?* op. cit., pp. 12, 389.
3. Ibid., p. 367.
4. Alasdair MacIntyre, *After Virtue*, op. cit., p. 245.
5. See, for example, Anthony Giddens, *Modernity and Self Identity: Self and Society in the Late Modern Age*, Polity Press 1991.
6. Werner Jaeger, *Paideia: the Ideals of Greek Culture*, ET, Oxford, 1939.
7. Angela West, *Deadly Innocence: Feminism and the Mythology of Sin*, Cassell 1995, p. 92.
8. E. L. Mascall, *Via Media: an Essay in Theological Synthesis*, Longmans Green 1956.
9. D. L. Edwards, 'Radicalism for Christians', *New Society*, 30 May 1963.
10. J. A. T. Robinson, 'The theological excavator', *New Christian*, 28 May 1970, pp. 5–6.

11. Michael Novak, *A Theology for Radical Politics*, New York, Herder 1969.

12. E. L. Mascall, *The Secularisation of Christianity*, Darton, Longman and Todd 1965.

13. Don Cupitt, *Radicals and the Future of the Church*, SCM Press 1989, p. 8.

14. Angela West, op. cit., pp. 84, 86.

15. Kenneth Leech, 'Catholicism in decay', *The Pilot* 10: 7 (Autumn 1961), pp. 150–3.

16. Richard Holloway in Loughborough Conference Report, Church Literature Association, September 1979, p. 33. Cf. Richard Holloway, 'An Open Letter', *Affirming Catholicism* 12 (Summer 1993), pp. 3–6. Here he argues that the traditional Anglo-Catholic structures will never again be a dynamic force within Anglicanism but rather 'an exotic anachronism destined only to die'. If anything good is left in the Catholic tradition, he claims, it will either die or be carried forward through the Affirming Catholicism movement.

17. Valerie Pitt in Kenneth Leech and Rowan Williams (eds.), *Essays Catholic and Radical*, Bowerdean Press 1983, p. 223.

18. See Kenneth Leech, 'Beyond gin and lace: homosexuality and the Anglo-Catholic subculture' in Ashley Beck and Ros Hunt (eds.), *Speaking Love's Name*, Jubilee Group 1988, pp. 16–27.

Chapter 10: Ministry and Marginality

Chapter epigraphs: Petronius Arbiter, cited in Gordon Jeff, *Spiritual Direction for Every Christian*, SPCK 1987, pp. 94–5; W. Philip Keller, *A Shepherd Looks at Psalm 23*, Grand Rapids, Zondervan Publishing House 1970, p. 46.

1. Judith Walkowitz, *City of Dreadful Delight*, Virago 1994.

2. On the East End in the late nineteenth century, see W. J. Fishman, *East End 1888*, Duckworth 1988.

3. *East London Advertiser*, 19 September 1996.

4. Wim Wenders, cited in *Financial Times*, 14 October 1993.

5. John A. T. Robinson, 'The theological college in a changing world', *Theology*, June 1952, cited in Eric James, *A Life of Bishop John A. T. Robinson*, Collins 1987, p. 43.

6. Richard Kew and Roger White, *New Millennium, New Church*, Cambridge, MA, Cowley 1992, p. 79.

7. Harold Perkin, *The Rise of Professional Society*, Routledge 1989.

8. See Urban T. Holmes, *The Future Shape of Ministry*, New York, Seabury Press 1971, Chapter 10, 'The problem of professionalism', pp. 195–200; Regis A. Duffy, 'A theological critique of the professional model in ministry', *St Luke's Journal of Theology* 25

(1982), pp. 86–105; A. V. Campbell, *Paid to Care? The Limits of Professionalism in Pastoral Care*, SPCK 1985.

9. Celia Davies, 'Cloaked in a battered illusion', *Nursing Times*, 6 November 1996, and *Gender and the Professional Predicament in Nursing*, Buckingham, Open University Press 1995.

10. Ivan Illich, *Disabling Professions*, Marion Boyars 1977, p. 15.

11. *A Fresh Start: a Report by the Birmingham Diocesan Structures Review Commission*, Bishop of Birmingham 1991.

12. *Knocking at Heaven's Door*, CARIS, 1996. Curiously, unlike most publications, although the booklet's copyright belongs to the Diocese of London, no address is given. So people on the 'inside' will presumably know the address of London Diocesan House, but the rest of us will not. It does rather reinforce my point! I have gone into this whole area in greater detail in my book *Care and Conflict: Leaves from a Pastoral Notebook*, Darton, Longman and Todd, 1990.

   For a valuable warning against 'liability driven guidelines – that is, pastoral theology determined by the church insurance company – see Jacqueline Schmitt, Editorial in *Plumbline* 22:4 (March 1995).

13. John A. T. Robinson, 'The house church and the parish church' in *On Being the Church in the World*, SCM Press 1964 edn, pp. 83–95; Nigel G. Wright, 'Restorationism in the house church movement', *Themelios* 16:2 (1991), pp. 4–8.

14. *Working As One Body: the Report of the Archbishops' Commission on the Organisation of the Church of England*, Church House Publishing 1995. The report claims to be a 'radical' document (p. xi). On Turnbull see William Paley, *Visions at Regular Intervals*, Jubilee Group Discussion Paper 108, 1996.

15. George Carey cited in *The Observer*, 4 April 1993.

16. See *The Economist*, 26 December 1992–8 January 1993, p. 30; Cal McCrystal, *Observer Life*, 24 September 1995.

17. *Faith in the City*, op. cit., p. 313.

18. See Colin Buchanan, *Cut the Connection*, Darton, Longman and Todd 1994; Peter Cornwell, *The Church and the Nation: the Case for Disestablishment*, Blackwell 1983; Valerie Pitt, 'Memorandum of Dissent', Appendix to the Chadwick Commission report, *Church and State*, Church Information Office 1970, pp. 68–79; Trevor Huddleston, CR, MS in the author's possession, 4 January 1988.

19. Alan Ecclestone, cited in Tim Gorringe, *Alan Ecclestone: Priest as Revolutionary*, Sheffield, Cairns Publications 1994, p. 103.

20. On the idea of 'the Church as servant', see Stanley G. Evans, *The Church in the Back Streets*, Mowbrays 1962.

21. Ulrich Simon, *A Theology of Auschwitz*, Gollancz 1967, p. 124.

22. Peter Allen *et al.*, *The Fire and the Clay: the Priest in Today's Church*,

REFERENCES

SPCK 1993. Christopher Gray was the author of Chapter 3, 'Who is the priest?', pp. 41–66.

23. R. C. Moberly, *Ministerial Priesthood*, John Murray 1910, p. 261.

24. See Martin Thornton, *Pastoral Theology: a Reorientation*, SPCK 1956, *Essays in Pastoral Reconstruction*, SPCK 1960, and other works.

25. Urban T. Holmes, *The Priest in Community*, New York, Seabury Press 1978, p. 26.

26. On Holmes, see *The Priest in Community*, op. cit.; *The Future Shape of Ministry*, op. cit.; *Ministry and Imagination*, Seabury 1976; *Spirituality for Ministry*, Harper and Row 1982.

27. Kenneth Mason, *Priesthood and Society*, Norwich, Canterbury Press 1992.

28. Mary Beasley, *Mission on the Margins*, Lutterworth Press 1997.

29. Jon Sobrino, *Spirituality of Liberation*, Orbis 1988, p. 109.

30. William Booth, *In Darkest England*, 1890, p. 72.

31. Cornel West, *Prophetic Fragments*, Grand Rapids, Eerdmans 1988, p. 62.

32. See Henry Rollin, 'From patients to vagrants', *New Society*, 15 January 1970.

33. *London's Mental Health*, King's Fund, January 1997.

34. See Randy Shilts, *And the Band Played On: Politics, People and the AIDS Epidemic*, Viking Penguin 1988.

35. On the experience of the Church in relation to AIDs, see Kittredge Cherry and James Mitulski, 'We are the church alive, the church with AIDS', *Christian Century*, 27 January 1988, pp. 85–8; Letty M. Russell (ed.), *Renewal in the Midst of Crisis: the Church with AIDS*, Louisville, Westminister / John Knox Press 1990; Earl E. Shelp and Ronald H. Sunderland, 'The challenge of AIDS to the church', *St Luke's Journal of Theology* 30:4 (September 1987), pp. 273–9.

36. John E. Fortunato, *AIDS: the Spiritual Dilemma*, San Francisco, Harper and Row 1987, p. 35.

37. Sue Mayo in a talk to clergy and community workers in Bethnal Green in May 1996.

38. Mary Pellauer, *Sexual Assault and Abuse: a Handbook for Clergy and Religious Professionals*, HarperCollins 1991.

Short Index